Public Administration
Steel or Plastic Frame

PUBLIC ADMINISTRATION STEEL OR PLASTIC FRAME

V. Bhaskara Rao

KALPAZ PUBLICATIONS
DELHI-110052

Public Administration: Steel or Plastic Frame

Rs. 750

ISBN: 81-7835-561-2

Published in 2008 in India by
Kalpaz Publications
C-30, Satyawati Nagar,
Delhi-110052
E-mail: kalpaz@hotmail.com
Phone : 9212729499

Lasser Type Setting by: Quick Media, Delhi
Printed at : Vishal Kaushik Printers Delhi

Dedicated To

Professor Krishna K. Tummala

Contents

Foreword

I have great pleasure in placing this volume in the hands of the readers dealing with the select areas of public administration in India. This book is an outcome of research by a well known academician, Prof. V. Bhaskara Rao. He poses a serious and interesting question to all, whether public administration in India in 60 years of independence still remained a steel frame or has been transformed into a plastic one. The word plastic is a new word brought into the literature of public administration denoting its adoptability to environmental changes undergoing plastic surgery for its reconstruction, repair of its body structure. Whether the treatment is for the injury or for cosmetic reasons the readers have to find out. The papers focus on the nature of bureaucracy in India as a part of Indian political and economic system.

This book makes an attempt to analyze the changing nature of public administration in India over the years. In many of the papers the author expressed what he could perceive in the development of the discipline of Public Administration in the Indian Universities and the policies and their implementation by the governmental machinery.

About half of the book contains papers on trade unionism and civil service staff relations in India in the early eighties which is a part of history of Indian administration.

A part of the book is on the analysis of the recent policies of the government of India. One paper is on public administration in 21st century. The author argues against the present state of India and pleads for a more democratic state which contributes to the good of common man as per the ideals of the constitution of India.

I am confident that the research papers in the book will be found useful by the academic community, the administrators and the general readers as citizens.

NEW DELHI **S.P. Verma**

October 1, 2007

Preface and Acknowledgements

The bureaucracy of British India acted in the word of Lord Morley as a "caste-iron bureaucracy" believing in "nothing but the virtue of will and arbitrary powers". The "steel frame" civil service that was transferred to India could not translate the ideals of freedom movement and the objectives of the constitution of India. India is celebrating 60th year of its independence this year. By this time, the Indian political system could have created a "human frame" of civil service, but in its place to-day it delivered a 'plastic frame' of civil service. This book has no deliberate design to stŭdy the evolution of bureaucracy in independent India but in essence many papers of the book expressed deep concern about the plight of the ongoing situation over the last two decades. It has become very clear by now the present plastic frame cannot achieve any of the goals of the nation benefiting the masses at large. Above all the plastic bureaucracy cannot protect the values of "substantive democracy".

The people in India have started loosing their faith in the government for the government has become "matter of invisible negotiations conducted in public offices by experts and private interests". The Indian politics - administrative order is fast moving "towards authoritarian semi-fascist model".

If not all these aspects, many papers highlighted the issues involved in the Indian polity and the directions that it is taking. Finally, whatever may be going on, it is the responsibility of all to see that "democracy is on the march" and the "common good" is protected through public administration in the 21st Century is the core message of this volume. How to achieve these goals, the future citizens of India have to take care in their own interest.

As a serious and sincere student and teacher of public administration for more than four decades the author has been very keenly observing the ongoing history of the Indian polity and expressing deep concern on the unhappy events and happenings.

The papers in the book were contributed at different times as per the requirements of the occasions, therefore, there may not be a continuum or one may find that the issues are not discussed with a particular methodology. However the papers throw some light on certain aspects of administration in a critical manner. I wish it will be useful to the students, teachers and the practitioners of public administration in India.

Some of these papers are already published in some journals and seminar volumes, therefore, I thank the editors of the journals and the editors of the seminar volumes for their kind consent to reproduce the same here. The sole idea is only to bring all my papers published and unpublished in to one volume for the benefit of the entire readers.

I thank my teacher late Professor P.A. James with whom four papers were published in early 70s. I thank my students and colleagues who co-authored some papers, particularly Professor M. Kistaiah, Dr. R. Ram Reddy and Dr. T. Narsimha Rao. I thank all my former colleagues in the department of Public Administration and Human Resources Management, Kakatiya University for their kind co-operation in writing all these papers.

But for the kind invitations from the distinguished colleagues and friends from different universities to participate in the seminars and conferences, I might not have attempted to write the papers and my thoughts could not have come in print. Therefore, I am deeply indebted to all my friends and well wishers who encouraged me to write papers, they include particularly, Prof. S.R. Maheshwari, Prof. R.B. Jain, Prof. Noorjahan Bava, Prof. T.R. Sharma, Prof. Krishna, K.Tummala, Prof. Ravindra Sharma, Prof. C.P. Barthwal, Prof. Hoshiar Singh, Prof. Pardeep Sahni and his Colleagues, Prof. Pai Panan Diker, Dr. P.L. Sanjeeva Reddy, Prof. V.S. Prasad, Prof. G. Haragopal, Prof. K. Madhusudan Reddy, Prof. Ramesh, K. Arora, the Editors of Indian Journal of Public Administration, Indian Journal Political Science, Journal of Higher Education, Journal of Administrative Change, Journal of National Academy of Administration, Journal of Labour Economics.

I express my gratitude to Prof. S.P. Verma, the Director of Indian Institute of Public Administration for readily responding to contribute a 'Foreword' to the book. Prof. S.P. Verma has been a constant source of inspiration for over three decades, I sincerely thank him.

Finally, it is pleasure to thank Kalpaz Publications, for publishing the book in a very short time and in such a good form.

Warangal

22/5/2007 V. BHASKARA RAO

1

Administrative Personnel in India

The primary purpose of this survey of research is to examine afresh certain fundamental issues concerning the role, relevance and performance of administrative personnel in particular and public services in general in the context of democracy and development where the administrators share power with their political masters in the governance of the country. The higher civil servants make an impact on public policy-making and its implementation. The timely achievement of socio-economic goals and resolution of basic public problems are dependent on the competent and resourceful administrative personnel and their general ability to sustain the essential presence of government. However, the public in India has been highly sceptical of the capability of the Indian bureaucracy.[1] The role and performance of bureaucracy has been a controversial subject of considerable concern in the post-independent India, particularly during and after the emergency period. Almost every study on the role and performance of the buraucracy in India is highly critical about the problem of bureaucratic non-performance. No one seems to be sympathetic to the bureaucratic non-performance and its causes. They blamed primarily the bureaucracy as the cause and consequence of its inefficiency and non-performance. The problem of bureaucratic non-performance acquired widespread dimensions having far-reaching implications in the realm of planning and development.

This survey examines whether the research studies conducted during 1979-88 cover the major problems of capability of the administrative personnel and whether the suggestions made for changes in the direction of administrative personnel policy are adequate and suitable. For this purpose, while briefly tracing the history of bureaucracy, the literature on administrative personnel during the last decade is reviewed. The study in its analysis endeavoured to identify the existing situation, recommend remedial measures and take steps in the following aspects:

> Recritment, Training, Politico-Administrative Relations, Administrative Reforms and Problems of Central, State and Local Governments administration. Any critical analysis of the role and performance of the bureaucracy in India in the context of planning, development, democracy and the governance of the country needs to look into some of its historical legacies, its profile in general and the political context in which the bureaucracy functions.

Imperial Legacy

One of the most lasting legacies left behind by the British colonial power in India was a system of administration which had been designed to meet the demands of the times. The administrative network established a system of bureaucracy with two outstanding features of "elitism" and "loyalty" to its masters. Its purpose was to serve the regime and rule a vast sub-continent through the device of a unified district administration informed by common principles of government and disciplined by a structure of authority invested in an "all-India" civil service.[2]

India, even after the transfer of power, retained the structure and functions of the colonial model of bureaucracy that was designed for the imperial purposes during the British India.[3] For, the Indian National Congress or the leaders of the Indian National Independence Movement were more interested in the transfer of political power rather than the administrative change.[4] Perhaps, they might have thought that issues of administrative change would evolve automatically once India attained independence.[5] But the "Steel Man of India", Sardar Vallabhbhai Patel, had certified "the steel frame" as "patriotic, loyal, sincere and able" that cannot be "substituted". Therefore, the civil service was given all the constitutional guarantees of privileges and rights. Thus, not only a sense of security was assured to it, in that its position in the new government would remain the same as in the out-going government but the politicians were told not to interfere with its functioning.[6] Thus, the powers of the bureaucracy not only remained intact but further increased, particularly those of the all-India services after Independence with extended functions of a welfare state, specially when they were asked to take charge of the public sector undertakings.

Bureaucracy is after all an instrument of a government and a creation of a political philosophy. Vallabhbhai Patel believed in an efficient, impartial and free from political influence and non-committed civil service.[7] The creation of the Indian Administrative Service, much against the will of some provincial governments, was guided by the desire to build up an elitist administrative cadre. It was required to function like its predecessor, separate and distinct from the apparatus of the government, and to maintain the standard of administration in the entire country.[8] It was argued that due to the pressure of emerging conditions, independent India was compelled to adopt the British administrative system without any change. The British bureaucratic approach in India was "typically" rule bound, juridical and its whole emphasis was on administrative efficiency. It hardly took notice of socio-economic and political developments. The administration treated socio-economic movements as a problem of law and order and resorted to repression as the only possible remedy, joining hands with feudal and aristocratic sections in the society.[9]

The advent of Independence and the concomitant change in the role of the government, the administrative system was called upon to undergo an attitudinal change. But it was not easy to accomplish such a transformation. For, under the British regime it was "aloof, distant, domineering and haughty" in its relationship with the people.[10] But the tasks of the popularly elected governments at the Centre and the States required an administrative system able to manage social, economic, political and scientific problems. The new tasks, developmental and promotional activities, were of a quite different nature demanding knowledge of new disciplines and possession of new skills. Therefore, if the inherited system of administration was to be adopted, it had to undergo a change to respond to the combined challenges of "democracy, development, state-building and nation-building". Though they reached in inadequacies of the inherited administrative system the framers of the constitution of India did not give much thought to the system of administration needed for free India. They might have thought that the administration being an instrument would automatically undergo the required transformation under the political impact.[11]

If the Indian government wanted a change in the administrative system it inherited, it would have been easier immediately after Independence and at the time of drafting of the constitution of India, but it did not happen, giving the impression that the nature of transfer of power and the context of that occasion prevented a change. However, it was very soon realised that the bureaucratic system, though lacking in intrinsic qualities, succeeded in perpetuating its existence and stranglehold on administration.

During the Nehru era, though bureaucracy could not be reformed, it was kept in its place due to Nehru's "supra official" position of a great national leader.[12] In the later years due to weak leadership, bureaucracy arrogated more powes to itself.[13]

O.P. Dwivedi and R.B. Jain concluded that "a careful examination of India's historical experience, both during the British Raj and since Independence, reveals an image of bureaucracy as the instrument of political purpose."[14] The "Leviathan" growth of Indian bureaucracy should be realised that the future democracy in India depends upon its ability to maintain and control a fully organied bureaucracy.[15] It is also important to realise that the thrust of the bureaucratic power in India is irresistible and Indian politics is too weak to fight against the power of bureaucracy and its entrenched culture.[16]

Thus, bureaucracy in India could not fully subscribe to the ideals of the state as enshrined in the constitution on account of "deep seated atttachment to feudalistic-cum-bureaucratic-cum-capitalistic values of contemporary Indian society" and could not change as it lacked "initiative, innovative and enterprising spirit". [17]

The Profile of Indian Bureaucracy—1979-88

L.K. Jha identified the factors responsible for the decline of Indian bureaucracy.[18] He felt the very virtues of the bureaucracy which Max

Weber had praised have turned to be a source of weakness due to the changes in the nature of responsibilities of the administration and environment in which it functions. The selection of the best on the basis of competitive examination had established only the general intellectual ability without providing any test of the ability to perform different tasks of administration over a period of years. He emphasised that the administrators as a class and economic administrators in particular must be properly equipped in terms of education, training and experience to discharge their responsibilities.[19]

Jha pleaded for the revision of rules, regulations and laws to re-adapt them to the changing goals and objectives. Referring to the promotions, he observed that officers get promoted to any senior posts which fall vacant whether or not their past experience has equipped them for it.[20]

Jha further pointed out that within the administrative framework itself, "there are weaknesses which needed to be remedied if the bureaucracy is to perform its role in a dynamic democracy creditably and efficiently". He suggested decentralisation of decision-making process, redefinition and re-establishment of the role of bureaucracy in democracy, radical chages in working methods, and administrative procedures and also the basic assumptions about the ways in which the conduct and performance of the people can be influenced.

P.C. Alexander incisively commented on some distressing trends in the present civil services:[21]

(i) Lack of involvement in what they are doing.

(ii) hyper-critical and cynical attitude about everything.

(iii) dilution of the responsibility for decision-making.

(iv) reluctance to meet the members of the public and

(v) keep every file secret or confidential.

T.N. Chaturvedi said "deveopmental planning has become the milch-cow of the few with unhealthy nexus between the politicians, officers, businessmen, contrators and industrialists."[22] Reviewing the studies on administration evaluation he listed out[23] the reasons for inadequate performance of administration—"lack of clarity of objectives, lack of appropriate locus and focus on the planning functions, leading to unsound resource planning and budgeting and financial management, lack of coordination, paucity of trained and competent technical and managerial staff, centralisation of administrative authority, poor institutionalised arrangements for reporting, monitoring and feedback, lack of morale, motivation and commitment among the staff, lack of political perception about the nature and limits of control and accountability."[24]

Summing up the proceedings of a seminar, S.C. Dube listed out the weaknesses of the public services in India.

Bureaucracy, especially its higher echlons, has acquired a class character...it emerges as an end in itself, insensitive to the needs of the citizen. It has become a slow-moving and dull-witted giant; [there are] contradictions and incompatibilities at different levels of bureaucracy; [bureaucrats have become] prisoners of their own procedures and precedents, proving increasingly inadequate to meet the new tasks and challenges. The generalist tradition still prevails. The public services act only by hunches, and intuition, not by trained insights.[25]

The Seminar also Suggested Remedial Measures

Enlargement of the catchment area for recruitment to ensure better representation of the society; innovative desocialisation and re-socialisation of the new recruits; task and performance-oriented training programme; performance audit for promotions; setting-up brains trusts and high level planning groups; re-examination of procedures to simplify and rationalise; setting up new organisational structures to meet new demands and situations, and fostering of new operating cultures within administration.

Satya Deva[26] considers bureaucracy as an instrument of class rule which maintains exploitation of masses and impedes basic structural change. In support of his Marxian analysis, he quotes the Report of the National Commission on Agriculture, "the official machinery has been trained and conditioned to function as the guardian of status-quo and the defender of existing property relations". The Report of the Task Force on Agrarian Relations has squarely blamed the administrative organisation for the failure of the implementation of land reforms. The Report notes that the bureucracy was generally "lukewarm and apathetic" because those in the higher echelons of the administration are also substantial landowners themselves or they have close links with the big landowners.[27] Thus, the ruler and the bureaucracy act as complementaries to each other. In this situation, Satya Deva felt, it is futile to expect any administrative reform which would lead to the reduction of the power of the bureaucracy. Hence, administrative reform must wait until power has been more evenly dispersed.

Pradeep Saxena[28] attempted to analyse the personnel policies for reform and orientation in public bureaucracy for development. He felt that Max Weberian model of bureaucracy based on the colonial recruitment policy failed to generate an ideology of Indian administration.[29] But the interests based administrative system emerged to demolish the ideology of liberal democracy. The civil service can remain relevant only if it has its own philosophy whose basic core will have to be uprightness in behaviour and magnanimity in outlook.[30]

K.K. Khanna[31] found both Weberian and contemporary models as inadequate and formulated a generic behavioural model based on interaction approach. In another research,[32] Khanna recommended a creativity approach to make the human resource development more relevant and meaningful and to make the Indian bureaucracy switch to the concepts of Theory "Y" from Theory "X". Mrs Indira Gandhi in a confidential memo said:

> A major cause of deterioration (in administration) is the tendency of higher officers to shirk responsibility. The feeling has grown that taking decisions is risky and invites criticism. A file-pusher feels safe because he commits no mistakes. Officers should be judged on the basis of the results they show and the contribution they make to the fulfilment of the objectives of the organisation they serve. They should be assured that the Government will draw a distinction between

genuine errors of judgement and those based on fraudulent motives. It is essential that full protection is given to officers in all cases where their action is bonafide even though they may have committed mistakes.[33]

Describing the causes and consquences of the decline, demoralisation and decay of bureaucracy in India, B.S. Appu is of the firm view that several key positions in administration are occupied by sycophants and incompetent civil servants and the result is rampant corruption, growing incidence of violence and frequent breakdown of law and order machinery and lack of enthusiasm in the formulation and implementation of development projects and programmes. Appu suggested that the committed administrators to the constitution should be encouraged to render free, frank and fearless views. Efforts should be made to upgrade their professional conpetence by imparting relevant training.[34]

The bureaucracy in India, with its class background and regulatory and financial power, assumes the role of "giver" against the vast mass of poor "receivers". The political leadership is not strong enough to compel the bureaucracy to help the poor.[35]

If the bureaucracy wants to be an "agent of change" and "committed", it has, according to Krishna K. Tummala,[36] three possible options: *(i)* Manipulation of the composition and structure of bureaucracy hoping for consequent behavioural changes, *(ii)* to alter attitudes imparting rigorous training, and *(iii)* use of coercion to obtain compliance. He observed that with the latest round of reforms, manipulation of composition and structure remained intact; it has become clear that overt coercion is not possible and also no changes can be introduced, only subtle pressure over the higher civil servants has been applied by transferring them to have compliance or at least get rid of those who were perceived to be not sympathetic to government policies.[37]

Since January 1980, there has been a large-scale transfers of higher civil servants based on considerations other than administrative. Some welcomed the transfers. But they, it is observed,[38] have affected not only public administration, but public undertakings and finacial institutions also.

To secure a committed bureaucracy, it is suggested, [39] the attitude of a bureaucrat must be taken into account. Two kinds of other "structural additions" have also been suggested: *(a)* to appoint experts and *(b)* to adopt the French "ministerial cabinet" model.

For a thorough modernisation of the bureaucratic structure, a flexible, innovative, controlled and representative bureaucracy in place of the steel frame and an open structure to bring rapid social change and development is suggested.[40]

Mohit Bhattacharya[41] points out that administrative growth in India is generally incremental and rarely radical. The organisational design subsumed in Weberianism does not always suit the conditions in developing countries. He therefore calls for innovation in public organisation in the changed circumstances. Bureaucracy must be, he suggests, change-oriented, result-oriented and people-oriented. To the extent popular participation in administration will become a reality, this is bound to bring in a good deal of pressure on the bureaucracy to change.

K.K. Khanna[42] in a series of writings on Indian bureaucracy and its behavioural patterns pointed out that due to diversity in view and basic ideologies of the people and the government, there is a wide gap between abilities required of and abilities actually available with the developing bureaucracy results in common maladies of rampant inefficiency and corruption.

In another study by Umapathy,[43] the inadequate response of the bureaucracy is attributed partly to structure and partly to the bureaucratic behaviour enmeshing itself in rules, regulations and procedures.

B.R. Sharma in his research studies on the behavioural aspects of Indian administrators examined the motivational crisis,[44] frustration[45] and administrative stress.[46] They discussed the problems of frustration and administrative stress in the context of new challenges that have emerged due to role erosion in administration. Sharma finds some gap between the administrators's thinking and actual doing. Consequently, he opines, the administrators have developed some sort of "cognitive dissonance, egocentricity, and

Machiavallianism in their personality". The administrative system is the root cause of the frustrational stress, leading to hostility, psychophysical impairment due to dissatisfaction with the job, poor mental ability, intolerance to authoritarian and incompetent behaviour, low self-esteem created by lack of timely promotion.[47] Therefore, administrative system need to be overhauled and renovated to adapt the confidence in its people.[48]

David C. Potter identified three broad features of Government in India.[49] "Lower-level administrators in India tended to be excessively deferential to their superiors and excessively rule-bound; feelings of mistrust and distrust between the politician and the civil servant; bureaucracy found it easier to cope with problems of unity, stability and order, than with problems requiring innovation, specialist expertise and responsiveness for local demands. Thus, the bureaucratic structures of state power continued to be good at maintaining unity and order, dealing with any serious internal opposition to their rule, while making development programmes less successful in the districts".

Development Bureaucracy

An attempt is made in this part to review the literature in Raj Singh's terms, viz., "how India's dysfunctional administrative system has acted, in ways more than one, as a decelerating force which has slowed, its pace of development".[50]

Jain and Chaudhuri in their comparative study of bureaucratic values and orientation in development and non-development fuctions of the government in Punjab and Madhya Pradesh, find that the bureaucracy in India whether engaged in developmental or non-developmental tasks share the same role perceptions and values.[51] Though the officials possessed the necessary skills and capabilities for development work, they were not adequately utilised due to structural components. Therefore, the study suggested certain changes like reduction in the levels of the decision-making process, requisite authority and power to field staff, encouraging team work, and continuous process of socialisation and training to inculcate in the officials values of concern for community welfare and achievement of development.

Pai Panandiker, Bishnoi and Sharma in their empirical study of two districts in Gorakhpur (U.P.) and Karnal (Haryana) found that there is no deliberate and conscious development of administrative strategy or administrative policy—a dimension which is commonly absent in the culture of the Indian administrative system. The general practice everywhere is to graft the development functions on the old regulatory system.[52] However, the study admittedly did not answer the basic question whether the bureaucracy is the best instrumentality for development, as it is partly ideological and partly one of "available options."[53]

Ram Reddy and Hargopal in their essay[54] analysed the characteristics of rural bureaucracy with special reference to Andhra Pradesh based on empirical data. They concluded:

> The characteristics in the working style of the bureaucratic organisations in the rural sector do not fit into any existing conceptual paradigms. The slow, lethargic and indifferent bureaucratic organisational style neither fits into economy and efficiency model developed in the West nor Weberian legal-rational model. Even the Riggsion prismatic model also does not help us to understand it. This calls for a more dynamic and comprehensive conceptual framework which is capable of embracing the totality of the development phenomenon. The administrative theory developed in response to the needs and demands of western societies cannot explain the nuances of organisational experience of a developing country like India.

Ram Reddy and Hargopal in their study conclude that the administrative structures responsible for implementing the anti-poverty programmes are "modelled on traditional administrative arrangements known for their complexity, cumbersomeness, elitism, centralisation, legalism, red tape, and inertia".[55] The existing administrative structures are based on the colonial approach—that the higher levels are honest and efficient and the lower levels are not trustworthy. This colonial postulate continues to condition the administrative culture in India.[56]

Hargopal also points out that the efforts of development personnel in rural develoment are neutralised by the regulatory personnel. He indicated the instances where the "revenue culture" in rural administration did not allow the development personnel to function.[57]

Hargopal's another research[58] reveals that the group of developmental personnel and its leaders lacked commitment and proper orientation towards the goals and the group pulled in different directions dissipating its energies.

Mishra in his study on panchayati raj bureaucracy and rural development observed, "The existing literature does not provide adequate guidelines for evaluating the functioning of bureaucracy in the development context...because of a peculiar slant given to the study of bureaucracy, by perspective use to observe and evaluate its functioning".[59] This perspective is derived from Max Weber and it is assumed that any study which ignores the Weberian model is not sociological. He suggests that "study of bureaucracy in the context of developing societies like India will have to depart from the Weberian model and develop a framework which can enable to observe its performance under rapidly changing conditions".[60] He felt that in the past the main reason for the gap between the goal desired and the goal achieved is due to the dismal performance of the local-level bureaucracy which worked in complete isolation and did not motivate the panchayati raj representatives to participate effetively in the rural developmental programmes.[61]

Balaramulu[62] observed that rural development and anti-poverty programmes suffered due to the bureaucratic rigmarole, lack of coordination between different departments, political pressures on bureaucracy over-burdened staff, negative and corrupt bureaucracy Low morale in the field staff, lack of promotional opportunuities to the lower level officials,[63] steep hierarchy which prohibits frank discussion, linkages with middlemen. *pyravikars,* irresponsibility towards the problems of the poor, etc.

Some of the failures of public services in reaching the targetted poor groups arise from the way the bureaucracies are organised and operate[64] and the approaches of administrative strategy and planning.[65]

The characteristic features of bureaucracy such as, lack of accountability, absence of incentives, long decision-making processes, overstaffing, hierarchy, rigidity, maintenance of status quo, conservatism and lack of innovative approaches[66] adversely affect the objectives in view.

However, Kuldip Mathur in his study in Karnal district of Haryana concludes that "the role of the bureaucracy is tied to the groups that propel a particular type of development and that its functioning is not dependent in its internal competence alone but is determined to a great extent by the policies, their logic and intentions."[67]

Seven case studies[68] of different states in India have been made to understand the dynamics of implementation of poverty alleviation programmes by officials engaged in executing those programmes. Based on field experiences, they suggested:

1. There is a dysfunctional diffusion of responsibility in the implementation of Integrated Rural Development Programme (IRDP). Strengthened organisational set-up at the block, district and state level will only ensure a sharp reduction in the misutilisation and misappropriation of allocated resources through widespread dilatory, wasteful and corrupt practices.

2. The present policy of frequent transfers of the key personnel of DRDA is dysfunctional. Selected senior field officers should be made responsible for results.

3. Strengthening the understanding and motivation of field workers at the village level through training, incentives and promotional opportunities is necessary.

4. Improvement in the knowledge and skills of the rural welfare officers is inescapable.

5. Bottom-up planning should play an important role in the process of socio-economic development.

6. The performance evaluation of the functionaries should be based on the actual gains made by the clients.

7. Through an integral sub-system of the strengthened organisation system, the delivery system should be radically redirected to play a strong proactive, driving role in support of the backward classes and weaker sections.

8. Involvement of beneficiaries in the development decision-making process and activising panchayati raj institutions, mobilisation of rural poor along with strengthening the network of other pro-poor programmes like land reforms enforcement of minimum wages, effective public distribution system, etc., should be ensured.

In sum, "Lack of unity of command, inadequate co-ordination, paucity of financial resources, dual operational control over the functioning of extension personnel, overlapping of functional responsibilities and under political interference in day to day routine matters seriously undermine the effectiveness of these agencies both as institutions of local self-government and as instruments of social and economic development planning."[69]

A micro-level empirical study also concluded that the inadequacy of powers and resources, lack of trained and competent staff, concentration of powers, improper supervision, insensitive bureaucracy were the maladies of the entire panchayat raj system.[70]

State Administration

Aleem discussed the issues and problems of personnel management in the state administration of Andhra Pradesh. He suggested more "fresh blood" in the services, clear-cut and imaginative policy on training, pay policy on principles of minimum wage, streamlining the disciplinary procedure and rules, joint consultation, and steps to contatin corruption in the civil services.[71]

Aleem and Shamim observed lack of systematic effort on the part of the state government to make comprehensive research-based studies on administration. Due to the absence of the ideological commitment, administrative reforms did not achieve desired results.

They recommended the establishment of a separate department of administrative reforms at the state level on the line of the Department of Personnel and Administrative Reforms of the Government of India.[72]

Srivastava, in his research work[73] on the system of recruitment and training of civil servants in India with special reference to the Bihar State Services, evaluated the role of Bihar Public Service Commission. The work emphasised the need for a sound system of recruitment and training in order to attract the best persons towards the public services.

The Institute of Management in Government, Trivandrum, Kerala, published the lectures delivered by twelve senior administrators in Kerala during June 1984 to May 1985. Some common threads discussed through all the papers are:

> In many departments and levels of government, the temptation generally has been to sacrifice sound administrative judgement and decision at the altar of populism, expediency of vested interest; that if one must make the system productive, greater attention must be paid to human resource development (HRD) in all spheres of government activity, i.e., qualitative management must improve; that leaders are not born but made, and so training to cope with one's job and to adapt to change is a necessary and vital part of the package of HRD. It is increasingly being realised that only by a policy of concern and desire to make people realise their potential can human being be motivated to contribute their maximum.[74]

Meena Sogani and Khandelwal while studying Rajasthan State Administration highlighted that “the civil servants, especially the higher level bureaucracy, are still blamed for irresponsiveness to “public” in general and attitude towards “service” in particular”.[75]

G.C. Singhvi examined the problems of district and state administration and to solve them he suggested enhancement of powers of district officers and scrapping the system of independent Heads of Departments for greater effectiveness. He recommended[76] against the existing several all-India services, only one all-India administrative service strengthened with proper training in a suitably designed structure, and pleaded for the strengthening of the state-level services.

B.C. Das and K. Das in their empirical study[77] analysed the social background of Orissa Secretariat Service.The study finds that rural representation in the service is more than the urban one, with no remarkable educational or intellectual attainments and that the service remains a bastion of the people of the coastal districts and of caste Hindus.

R.K. Sapru in his work[78] on the civil service administration in the state of Haryana is critical of the prevalence of class consciousness and inadequate incentives under the existing hierarchy of civil service system. He suggested a career development plan and reorganisation of various training programmes.

Rajni Goyal while studying the structure, content, methods and evaluation of the training of the Rajasthan Administrative Service officers observed that the need was to develop in the senior officers of the state government "a spirit of inquiry and a love for learning. In-service training should be based on this crucial premise of continuing education".[79]

The "Teleguidance" of State Administration

Balveer Arora in his paper[80] referred to the extension of Central political control over the state administration as "teleguidance". The visits of the Prime Minister and senior Central officials to state capitals in order to review and assess the performance falls this category. This practice was instituted during the emergency and the visits were renewed in July 1981. The Central government officially defined the purpose of these visits as to identify the problems hampering faster development.[81] The Prime Minister's Secretariat and Cabinet Secretary resorted to keep a "check on the bureaucratic machinery of the states".[82] Rajiv Gandhi as Prime Minister also convened five meetings of the district collectors and addressed them during 1986-88. This kind of "teleguidance" supplemented by more direct forms of political control, resulted in further weakening of state's administrative capabilities. The Chief Minister and sometimes the chief secretary have been bypassed due to the existence of the network of the all-India services.[83]

The existence of an all-India service, like the IAS, "controlled from the Centre, restricted the States' right, as they saw it, to recruit and control their own Civil Servants needed to plan out the tasks allocated to them under the federal Constitution".[84]

In a letter[85] to the Chief Ministers in August 1980, the Prime Minister had written to exercise self-restraint and withstand all the pressures for transfer from political and other public figures in the interest of efficient and impartial functioning of administration.

Therefore, some state governments of opposition political parties like the CPI (M) and CPM in West Bengal and Kerala, the TDP in Andhra Pradesh and the DMK in Tamil Nadu demanded more powers to the states over all-India services.

District Administration

Goyal in his study attempted to explore the orientations of the bureaucrats towards norms of bureaucracy, i.e., professionalism, hierarchy of authority, impersonality, and formalism and rules and initiative. According to his findings:

> Public bureaucrarcy, even at the district level, is dominated by the people belonging to high castes and well-to-do sections of the society. However, in its hierarchical arrangement of different layers, it continues to exemplify the characteristics of almost a class-based social stratification.[86]

The study further finds unconsistency between the 'belief-in' and the 'practice-of' the norms of bureaucracy, display of non-rational bureaucratic values, resulting in dysfunctional consequences. The author views that the present bureaucratic structure cannot keep pace with new social structures. The rational model of bureaucracy "demands modification of the alien pattern in view of the changed historical circumstances and indigenous culture".[87]

In a field survey[88] conducted in three districts of Maharashtra, it was found that the inter-relationship between political leadership and bureaucracy was tension-ridden, resulting from the differing perceptions of roles of two divergent cultures—bureaucratic and political. The study recommended better relationship; statutory precision regarding the mutual area operation; exhaustive and well-defined specific rules in all administrative spheres; full protection of subordinate officials by the higher officials; re-orientation of political leaders and administrators with respect to their mutual relationship in the context of development.

Dayal observed[89] that the institution of district officer has not served to advance the pace of rural development, for he has not been selected, trained and retained according to the requirements of his new tasks. He is likely to function as a co-ordinator rather than a controller, only if his selection, training and tenure are re-oriented in accordance with the requirements of his role as a leader, and an agent of change.

Field studies on "the past, present and future role of District Officer in India" with special reference to Bihar found that deterioration had taken place in the role of the district officer, not because of the nature of the personnel recruited but due to structural changes.[90] In most cases the district officers recognised development as a major goal, but they failed to carry it out effectively because of their preoccupation with the maintenance of law and order, lack of commitment, short tenure in a district, political interference, the ad hoc nature of the officer, and individual differences in ability and motivation.[91] They suggested relieving the district officer completely of his law and order responsibility to enable him to serve as a catalyst of change. The law and order responsibility should be given entirely to the police head of the district.[92] The study revealed that the scope of the district officer's function had been expanding, combined with contraction of power. To meet the demands of all levels of politicians, to listen to them and handle them as diplomatically as possible, he must be good at public relations and create an image of a sympathetic listener.[93]

The present arrangement of having district collectors with only four or five years of services has ruined district administration due to their lack of maturity and experience. Therefore, to eanble him to work more fearlessly and to act as the captain of the district administration or to meet the "trade blows or wits of the politicians", the district officer must be a "senior, mature and powerful officer, not a tiny lot, as is happening today".[94] The district officer cannot offer his best if he is under threat of transfer all the time. This vulnerability of the office cripples the initiative of the district officer.[95]

Recruitment

The internal system of bureaucracy comprises mainly recritment and training. The capabilities of administrative personnel and the morale in the civil service would mainly depend upon the fair policy of recruitment, placement and the type of training imparted to achieve the goals assigned and tasks allocated.

Discussing the recent trends in the public personnel organisations in the USA, the UK and India, it was opined[96] that "constitutional agencies, i.e., the Public Service Commissions, should continue till India becomes more mature and political environment assumes a higher moral and ethical level". In India, the powers of the Commissions have been curtailed by presidential regulations and by making a number of ad hoc appointments by the governments without consulting Commissions.

The Commissions' autonomy has also been threatened by appointing the members of the Commissions on political patronage. As the Commissions neutrality and competence is suspected[97] it is suggested that the composition and functioning of the Public Service Commissions should be critically evaluated and their fuctioning[98] streamlined.

R.K. Sapru[99] with special reference to Haryana suggested that the recruitment system needed to be streamlined and the government should take steps to protect the Public Service Commission against political pulls and pressures.

It is charged[100] that the Union Public Service Commission has yet to acquire a set of guidelines that may help in recruiting civil servants who identify themselves with the common people. The method of testing the ability and competence of the candidates has still remained the hang-over of the British Raj.

The Union Public Service Commission, it is observed, [101] is still functioning the same way as it did forty years ago. The written examination needs overhauling and so does the interview process. At the interview stage, there is no conscious assessment of the candidates' mental calibre. But much weightage is given to the interview for all-India and Central services. The interview is called a "personality test" although none of the known tools, such as psychological tests, for testing the personality is used. The present system of examination and selection is biased in favour of the powerful.[102]

Many studies indicated that the all-India services are not attracting the best talent coming out of universities. The IAS officials occupying senior positions in government departments have been challenged by specialists and technocrats. Therefore, they suggested close re-examination of the relevance of IAS and its restructuring.[103] Some felt that to foster objectivity and freedom from bias, no IAS should be allocated to his home state, particularly to the border states.[104] It is suggested that the IAS recruitment from the State civil services should be more rigorous and their training needs should not be overlooked. Some writers lamented[105] that the quality of civil services was deteriorating with the increasing reservations for Backward Classes, Scheduled Castes and Scheduled Tribes.

The analysis of recruitment methods and training to the all-India services indicates that no attempt is made to find out social beliefs and attitude which can be contrary to the general national goals of secularism. No mechanism has been evolved to find out the depth of caste prejudice in the young entrants to the IAS.[106]

Training

In a country like India, the changing social situation demands restructuring training programme for administrative personnel. But such restructuring has not been planned or undertaken, for want of clear-cut social goals. Therefore, a mismatch between theoretically evolved training programme and actual practice emerges because the premises of training are not in conformity with the expected practice of public administrators. "The mismatch has emerged because our expectations from training programmes are based on wrong premises and expectations."[107]

It has been roughly estimated that about 70 per cent of the Class III and 90 per cent of the Class IV personnel are at present untrained. The grassroot level functionaries include patwaris, agricultural assistants, foresters, and all other categories of employees working interface with citizens at lowest levels and training of such personnel alone can bring effective change in the administrative system.[108]

It is observed that there is a general fallacy widely prevalent in the senior circles of bureaucracy that the top level administration does not really need any kind of traning and there is very little for them to learn.[109]

It is felt that in India there has been no organised effort to provide specialised training and those officers who have undergone such kind of training are often entrusted posts which have no relation whatever to the course of study to which they had been exposed.[110]

Writing on the shaping process of IAS successfuls David Potter remarks[111] that "much remained essentially the same at the National Academy of Administration in 1983". "The visitors to Academy in Mussoorie have never had much difficulty in recognising the general ambience—Typical public school with a distinct Western bias"[112] though the Academy has been engaged in a deliberate shaping exercise of the IAS, even attempting to weed out those who do not fit.[113]

To inculcate development orientation, mid-career training was advocated[114] providing professional knowledge base, basic management skills imparted by professionals working as trainers. K.S. Bhat's suggestion of "action research approach" as a strategy for training needs to be introduced, to look into the realities of the problems.[115] Through a sustained scientific policy of training, the bureaucracy must be made to respond to the people and acquire self-confidence and does not become a plaything of party of factional politics.[116] They should be trained to recognise their role in policy-making and encouraged to practise it.[117]

A three-day conference[118] on "Issues in In-service Training", organised by the training division of the Department of Personnel, Government of India in 1981, was well attended by experienced administrators. Inaugurating the conference, the Minister of State for Personnel & Training referred to the need for research in training and setting up research cells in all training institutions. He also referred to the need for constantly evaluating training programmes periodically and linking them with the realities and changing conditions. The in-service training aimed at reorienting the concepts of the job and their relationship to the process of development. It was emphasised that it should aim at improving the technical skills at lower levels, human and managerial skills at the middle level and conceptual skills at higher levels. As there is no provision for conceptual training to the top management in civil administration, it was felt worthwhile to structure suitable course for senior civil servants towards imparting conceptual training. It was realised that the prestige of the training institutions should be enhanced by attracting suitable trainers to the faculty.

Training in government has emerged out of close linkages with the government. There has been a marked quantitative expansion in training activities during the last decade. In certain instances, training institutions have been built up and grown as regular government departments.[119] Saxena stressed more on the changing role of the trainers, as they have to seize the opportunities to initiate and sustain innovation in the stream of training. At present, instances of innovations are few and far between and the bulk of the training reflects initiative and a reiterative character. In spite of all-round expansion of training activities in government, its qualitative and professional base has yet to be strengthened.[120]

The administration of police training in India on the basis of empirical data is analysed by Krishna Mohan Mathur,[121] an IPS officer. In the concluding remarks of the study he emphasised that although the Sardar Vallabhbhai Patel National Police Academy, Hyderabad, has been doing a commendable job in imparting useful training to the senior police officers of the country, still the police has to be humanised through education and training in the democratic values of the society to cope with the changing needs and to ensure secularism, socialism and social justice.

S.N. Sadasivan[122] finds that the civil servant is "contemptuous of formulated or organised knowledge", which he inclines to dub as "academic" or "abstract" or of "no practical utility". This resistance to theory from the bureaucratic quarters, even "as input of knowledge", remains a major hindrance yet to be overcome "for scientific organisation of training courses at various levels of administration". Sadasivan with his long experience of training institutions observes that "an average probationer of IAS has hardly exhibited an abiding interest in acquisition of knowledge as a pre-condition for serving society" and the bureaucrat in India has easily rebutted the proposition that knowledge is power. He refers to the interaction between the government and the intellectual, after Independence, which has been virtually brought to a halt by "bureaucratic cynicism and vagaries, and political inaptitude" but it should actively be revived to maintain interest of training in public administration.

Politico-Administrative Relations

The administrative set-up in India has been under crisis. Much of this crisis is created by the politicians and administrators themselves for want of certain theoretical perceptions and practical adjustments. The stress and strain in their relations led to mutual accusations. Their social and educational backgrounds, professional commitment, intellectual abilities, etc., led to differences in outlook and temperament. The survey makes an attempt to look into the researches undertaken on the politico-administrative relations in India, particularly during the last decade. This period is most important because of the post-emergency problems, sudden replacement of strong and experienced leadership by new and inexperienced leadership, tensions between the leadership of the Centre and States and deteriorating conditions of law and order in crucial sectors of the nation. During this period, the representatives of democracy and bureaucracy struggled for the mutual dominance and balance.

Jayant Kumar Ray[123] in his innovative approach to study the current politico-administrative history recorded the views, opinions and experiences of over 50 senior civil servants of the ICS, IAS, IPS and IFS, presented in the form of "sketches", and explained the type of interaction between politics and administration and how bureaucrats respond to vital changes in political circumstances. Commenting about the confusion about the duties of politicians administrators, Ray pointed out that in a "mixed polity", the line of distinction between the duty of a politician and the duty of an administrator remained largely blurred.[124] It was a complex phenomenon to identify each other's role. For, in the present authoritarian milieu of public administration, the idea of partnership is far from reality.[125] This milieu is partly because of the bureaucratic sub-service and partly because of the large discretionary authority vested in the elected representatives.[126]

Authors of administrative memoirs universally complained that politicians were mainly responsible for the failure of Indian administrative system since Independence. Their unwarranted interference in the daily activities of administration was one of the greatest enemies of administrative efficiency. Such interference resulted in blurring the line of distinction to an extent, endangering the goal of good administration.[127]

A great many administrators allow political interference, for they feel secure so long as they can achieve a high degree of collusion with politicians exerting illicit pressures,[128] and, thus, majority of Indian administrative personnel are either "detractors" or "accommodators". It is also observed that the administrative personnel engaged in a scramble for prizes, tend to become camp-followers of the politicians in power instead of their colleagues, candid friends and advisers.

M.N. Buch suggests that when ministers give decisions which are illegal or financially improper, the administrators should refuse to carry out the orders and should place on record reasons for doing so. As they are not subordinates to Legislature, they should not succumb to political pressures.[129] However, it is not healthy for civil service to determine policy, because a civil servant, by training and temperament, is not either fit to understand the aspirations of the people or the best ways of fulfilling them.[130]

However, it is also important to note that in the contemporary Indian society, many politicians are commanding the personal loyalty of a sufficiently large number of administrators who, by their unethical and unfawful activities, shatter the public confidence in administration.[131] Public confidence in the government is further shattered when the guilty politicians and corrupt administrators escape any punishment.[132]

When Indira Gandhi swept back to power in 1980, her government put a premium on loyalty and put professional independence at risk. Senior officers were transferred to remote posts for devoted service to fallen political advisors. After 1980, Indira Gandhi relied increasingly on palace advisors, many of whom were senior civil servants.[133]

S.R. Maheshwari contemplates in years to come politics in India is likely to become both more intensive aggressive and multilinear, accompanied by an increasing traditionalisation of itself, largely as a result of the emergence of new political leadership thrown up by the contemporary political and electoral processes. The civil service, consequently, is apt to face new and novel pressures and in more concentrated dosages; and in the process Max Weber would be discovered to be nearly totally irrelevant. It appears that India is on its way to evolving an East Minister model of role relationship between political executive and permanent executive.[134]

B.K. Nehru, pleading for the restoration of the independence of the civil service, felt it necessary to regulate the powers of transfer, suspension and promotion by law and to raise substantially the emoluments[135] of civil servants. "The whole experience showed generally that the relationship between elected democratic politicians and political administrators representing an older tradition remained a difficult one, produced in part by having retained an ICS tradition of administration in a changed political context."[136]

In very critical notes, Harbhajan Singh Deol,[137] a former Member of the Punjab Public Service Commission, observed:

> Under the present constitutional system, the politicians and bureaucrats, following the careerist approach, do not look beyond their own pays, perks, fringe benefits, salaries and allowances. They seem to have become so selfish and personal that each depends on the other for the fulfilment of narrow selfish motives and not for solving any administrative problems. If bureaucracy is so tight, stiff-necked, lackadaisical and indolent, then the political parties are also guided by the "iron law of oligarchy". Party organisations have become bureaucratic and elitist, with only a formal relation with the masses, that too during election time. In such circumstances, only garrulous individuals and erratic characters, clearly piercing through the thick crust of administrative and political control come to dominate the socio-political scene on the national level.

Thus, according to P.D. Sharma,[138] the perfect politico-bureaucratic combination or collusion have defined public interest and evolved and implemented public policies that brought the country to the present state of political decay and economic stagnation.

Administrative Reforms

From the above discussion of the Indian exercise in developing capable administrative system, we learn a lesson that any amount of tinkering with the colonial model of bureaucracy cannot produce a suitable bureaucracy, particularly the development personnel. Therefore, what is advocated is a "bold rendering of the total administrative system—its foundation, structure, culture, classification, procedure and style, to make it an appropriate instrument for development."[139] The redesigning of administrative system and administrative change in the Indian political context is only possible through efforts of administrative reforms. Therefore, a look into the reform effort is undertaken to assess the intentions, execution and results.

The Government of India intends that administrative reforms should make public administration a fit instrument for carrying out social and economic goals of development and also one which is responsive to the people. On an examination of administrative reforms in retrospect since Independence, many critics felt that there was no clearly thought-out strategy of reform and there was only tinkering with the given system as opposed to comprehensive reform.[140] The Indian administrative reforms were characterised as "ideological in conception but incremental in execution."[141] The dilemma in devising a proper relationship between idology and the concrete condition led to many ambiguities and challenges faced by the reformer. The ambiguities and challenges are categorised as "ideological, systemic and social."

For strengthening administrative capability in India since 1947, the Government of India constituted about 25 bodies to suggest administrative reforms. A detailed analysis of measures recommended and steps taken by the government was made by S.R. Maheshwari, P.K. Mattoo and others.[142] It was noted that "in India, administrative reform has rarely emerged above the level of rhetoric; the political leadership has shown consistent passivity." The acceptance and implementation of the recommendations rested almost exclusively on the bureaucratic will. The bureaucracy provessed the recommendations in the light of its own wisdom favouring the status quo.

The Congress Party at the Centre broadly supported the IAS and the ICS tradition of administration and did never believe that radical restructuring of administration was necessary. The ICS/IAS also worked actively to preserve the existing structure of administrative arrangements from their own powerfully entenched position within the State.[143]

The bureaucracy in India generally resists innovations in administrative structural arrangements.[144] It firmly believes in the superiority of the hierarchical organisational structure and its adherence to the numerous administrative routine. It has no commitment for remodelling the administration for nation-building.

> The present administrative situation is aptly described that "the entire administrative machinery is groaning under its own size. It is eating more than it can chew. There is proliferation of

> programmes all round, but not commensurate with the availability of qualified persons; while the line jobs are understaffed, the staff jobs have been indiscriminately proliferated. The staff jobs have an especially irresistible appeal to action-shy, comfort-loving Indians.[145]

With the decline in the quality of leadership, bureaucracy would not allow any administrative reform efforts.[146] The corrupt bureaucracy would not allow any administrative reform for its selfish interests and manipulations.[147]

The government has no organisation specially charged with the responsibility of doing long-range thinking to keep the administrative machinery well-equipped and meet the changing socio-economic environment.[148]

It is important to note that during 1979-88, not much concerted effort was made to introduce administrative reform and change except some isolated attempts, viz., *(a)* to revitalize the panchayati raj system at the grassroot level (Ashok Mehta Committee, 1979) and *(b)* to change the system of economic and fiscal administration.

Most of the recommendations were neither radical nor change-oriented. Further, no serious administrative reform was possible for want of stable political leadership, self-confident and willing to experiment with innovative changes. In March 1985, the Government of India created an independent Ministry of Personnel and Training, Administrative Reforms and Public Grievances and Pensions, but due to frequent Cabinet reshuffling, no stable leadership to this ministry was made available. "The all-pervasive politics of survival has overwhelmed the all-pervasive need for administrative reforms."[149]

During 1986, Rajiv Gandhi, then Prime Minister, attempted to introduce a new style of administration based on managerial orientation of government programmes. Computerisation of data projection into future targets, implementation of strategies, monitoring of results, midcourse adjustments, etc., are the techniques which formed the components of this new administrative style. Strees on long-term objectives, rather than immediate compromises, management of results rather than problems, bold pragmatism rather than illogical wooliness seemed to be the hallmark of this new approach.[150]

These measures were introduced to ensure the professional quality of the services and insulate them from inappropriate political pressure. The government proposed to prevent frequent transfers of officers, protect them against appropriation by local interests, encourage specialisation and break the monopoly of IAS on the highest positions by opening alternative recruitment channels to high quality candidates from technical services and the non-governmental sector.[151]

The main lesson of the administrative reforms in India is that "since administration is value-laden and culture-bound, the reforms presupposes change in the culture and the values of the people themselves."[152] Hence in the future adaptive bureaucracy in India the "perceptions and attitudes of the bureaucracy towards its own group (Civil Servants) ... and towards the people must undergo serious change." Such a change is possible only through a radical administrative reform with a sense of mission, to make the adminsitrative personnel socialised and educated with greater vigour and favour than in the past.[153]

Through the programme of administrative reforms, public administration has to be delinked from "economic pressure groups and loyalties around caste and religion" and it should be made impartial by focussing its attention on efficient implementation of poverty eradication programmes.[154]

The judiciary and the civil service are the two institutions which are expected to protect the democratic rights and provide safety and security to the people respectively. Both are under constant attack from the politicians. They succumb often to the onslaught of the politicians. The civil servants have become subservient to the politicians. With unprecedented majority in the Parliament, the ruling party vested extraordinary authority in the hands of the leader of the party compelling the members to submit to his dictates. In these circumstances, the Parliament has lost its reviewing authority on administration and administration paid little respect to the legislatures and the judiciary. In the name of security, public order and national interest, the access to the government offices has been restricted and the extraordinary secrecy maintained.

During the last decade there has been a tremendous proliferation and multiplication of administrative posts and overstaffing in the higher levels of administration. There was no rationale for creating posts and promoting persons of their choice. It led to top-heavy hierarchy and inefficiency.

Summing Up

During the period of this research survey (1979-88) a number of events occurred in the history of Indian polity. The impact of those events is very important for the evaluation of the administrative system of the country. The events include Mrs. Indira Gandhi's return to power in 1980 leaving the entire parliamentary opposition parties at crossroads. Sanjay Gandhi who was at the helm of affairs extending necessary support to this mother, particularly during the 'emergency', died suddenly in 1980. Then landed Rajiv Gandhi with great reluctance from nine clouds, first to assume the leadership of the party and later to consolidate his position in the government.

Even without much experience of the party politics and administration, Rajiv Gandhi won the Eighth Parliamentary elections in early 1985 with an unprecedented majority in the Parliament. The Parliament, without any opposition, passed the Anti-defection Law in 1985 which further consolidated his power in the party and the government. This law enabled him to get rid of all his opponents in the party and the government.

The new Prime Mnister promised the countrymen in his broadcast and through a number of "accords" (internal and external) a peaceful and secure life to every one by toning up the public administration of India. However, he observed that the government servants "have no work ethics, no feeling for the public cause, no involvement in the future of the nation, no comprehension of the national goals, no commitment to the values of modern India; they have only a grasping, mercenary outlook, devoid of competence, integrity and commitment." These were the features of the Indian administrative system that he inherited from his mother and grandfather. With this kind of groundsmen and crew, he assured the nation for a take-off to the twenty-first century.

New departments were organised, reforms were introduced, training of administrative personnel was undertaken, the computer-technology and managerialism was inducted, public grievances were attended under the very nose of the Prime Minister, and for the first two years of his regime people looked to him as their leader. But, then started cracks in his fort and political instability crept along with the scandals in defence deals. For the next two years, in spite of all the power and majority in the Parliament, he had to allot much of his time and energy to set his house in order. Naturally, the reform measures and the intentions could not be properly attended to. Hence the capabilities of the administrative personnel and the bureaucracy required to be evaluated. A systematic analysis is only possible, when the public administration as a discipline grapples with the socio-political reality of contemporary India.[155]

However, the context has failed to influence many research studies. For, the studies seldom referred to these events and assess their impact properly, except a few macro-studies by David C.Potter, Rudolph and Rudolph, some retired experienced senior civil servants, social scientists like Rajni Kothari, academics like C.P. Bhambri, R.B. Jain, S.R. Maheshwari, J.D. Sethi *et al.,* who have been writing about the politics of bureaucracy and the impact of political development over the administrative machinery. But, to a large extent, the public administrationists in India undertook research studies in public administration, avoiding the study of politics. This politics-avoidance syndrome, the initial thrust of the discipline of public administration, is still dominant. The internal politics and external linkages have not been highlighted in the research studies.Therefore, the causes for the bureaucratic non-performance could not be effectively evaluated.

Some of the research studies (about 30) by young academics were leading to Ph. D. degrees. They were micro-studies with limited scope. Further, without much research experience and knowledge of administration, they investigated only the selected problems. Not many of them have discussed with a particular theoretical perspective.

They are mostly descriptive of the structure and narrative of the functions, and seldom made any specific prescription for any change.

Research projects sponsored by the ICSSR, UGC and different ministries of Government of India (about 30) undertaken by the faculty of Indian Institute of Public Administration, Centre for Policy Reesearch and other research institutes, individuals and groups were based on field studies, with a command on resources, personnel, institutional support and better experience in the methodology and tecinques of rapport building, and they probed deep into the selected problems. Their findings and suggestions are based on the obtaining practice but mostly not linked to any theory. They have their own limitations. They are more pathological, and on the dysfunctionalities of the administrative system. They suggested certain structural and behavioural changes in the bureaucratic system and behavioural attitudes. Some studies analysed the issues with certain theoretical propositions and found that the Weberian approach to study the issues was not suitable. Some felt the Riggisian approach be appropriate for the developing societies. Some studies highlighted the Marxian model, but it was not acceptable to them. Some suggested a new model, either "indigenous" or "mixed", perhaps without affecting the basic structure. Some have not touched the theoretical issues as they are "ideological" and "operational", and beyond the "scope" of their study.

Thus, by and large, the studies have been conducted in "structural-functional mould" and are "heavily descriptive and dealt with institutions and their functioning". For, public administration in India, "as usually understood and generally developed has been concerned mostly with administrative structure and administrative functions ... process of formulation of policy and programmes as well as their implementations."[156]

The research studies of academics are "at best instructive and informative . . . neither could they be of high order in terms of basic knowledge, nor could they be any guide to the decision-makers". This is perhaps due to the lack of exposure of the researchers to the administrative reality. [157] There are very few research studies anlysing trends in administration over a period of time (except studies by David C. Potter). Some academics and administrators have been contributing their experiences over a period of years mainly through observation and interacting with one another.

It is true that there is "dearth of innovative studies" and "very few new ideas on administrative restructuring". They have not become leaders of thought and "merely remained contented with responding to the initiatives taken by the government ". This is mainly due to the poor background of the academics and their symbiotic relationship with the public administration. Therefore, the research studies remained imitative and descriptive, much like a comprador discipline.[158]

Writings based on vast and rich administrative experience are the real source of information for many academics in public administration in India. Eminent administrators through their lectures, writings and memoirs better identified the weaknesses of the prevailing bureaucracy.

For them the causes of decline of bureaucratic standard are mainly due to lack of proper training, wrong postings, hasty transfers, and unnecessary political interference in the administration. They suggested better incentives, higher pay and proper conditions of service, training in specialised fields, change in attitudes and appraisal methods but not a radical change in the administrative system. According to them, the administrative personnel are not basically incapable; there is not much of a fault with the selection and recruitment but placement, frequent transfers, political pressures, rigid rules and regulations that make them mainly incapable and ineffective. Nowhere do they state that the regular, revenue bureaucracy is unsuitable for developmental activities, but they plead for the strengthening of the regular bureaucracy and to bring the developmental activities under the leadership of the disrict collector. They claim more autonomy to administrators and less interference by the people's representatives. For them, "representative" bureaucracy, "development" bureaucracy and "committed" bureaucracy are against the merit bureaucracy.

J.D. Sethi reviews the writings on bureaucracy as they have "gone too far off from reality and tasks to be performed". He observed that bureaucracy "behaves like an autonomous class," without being accountable to any one and there is "no clear-cut accountability theory of bureaucracy".[159]

Most of the studies broadly concluded that the imperial legacy or the ICS tradition has been maintained in different ways in the IAS and they survive into the 21st century (David C.Potter). In this process of "continuity" and "change" of the civil service, there is less change and more continuity. "The ICS had gone, but that central feature of their tradition lived on in the 1980s." The forces that have challenged the services, such as the call for "partisan" and "personal commitment" and "regional loyalty" are powerful and long term. "They have taken their toll, but they have not as yet prevailed" (Rudolph and Rudolph).

The dichotomy between the traditional/revenue administration and the development administration is rejected by many studies as administrators in both the fields share similar role perceptions, values and social backgrounds. The structural and operational characteristics of both the departments are more or less the same, viz., the hierarchy, division of labour, rules and impersonality. Therefore, almost every study proved that the prevailing bureaucratic structure as a whole was more successful in maintaining order and internal opposition to their rule, but less successful in implementing the development programmes. It is not that the administrative personnel are in the dissonance with the developmental goals, and are ambivalent but their incompatibility with developmental needs, socialisation process and orientation towards the people are the crucial aspects in which more changes have to be introduced. Thus, certain changes in the structural components of the bureaucracy are suggested to bring desirable changes in the behaviour of the bureaucracy to make the developmental programmes more successful. Whether any structural changes suggested are possible depends upon two major factors: the place of bureaucratic power as a part of Indian political and economic system, i.e., the nature of bureaucratic power. Many research studies did not touch this aspect. But all the studies almost confirmed that the political leadership of the State has been extending its support for the continuation and persistence of the administrative traditions. David Potter concluded his study of two decades that the ICS/IAS "tradition makes them great survivors, politically . . . moving quickly for advantage in political struggle. In any new administrative structure, they or others like them will be there as individuals. Even . . . of their tradition may survive. But the traditions as a whole cannot last much longer."

As per the conclusions of Rudolph and Rudolph, it is possible for "the state in India to be not only relatively autonomous and self-determined but also self-interested." "The self-determining state is in a position to serve itself and like other self-interested actors, to a source of exploitation or injustice."

Rajni Kothari observes that the organised democratic process and the regular bureaucracy is in a state of decline and is being replaced by a new set of actors and a new "order". The Congress Party handed the new order to a rising generation of professional managers and technocrats. With this "the state began to lose its autonomy, because of subservience to the new class and its cohorts in big business and the bureaucracy, and indirectly to latter collaborators and palm-greasers from abroad. "[160] Rajni Kothari further observes that in the new order, the technocrats are taking the place of the politicians at higher levels, and the technology is becoming a substitute politics. India is moving into periods of enormous convulsions and violence, and it may not be possible for the technocracy to handle these.[161]

References

1. See H.V.R. Iyengar, *Administration in India: A Historical Review,* Bharatiya Vidya Bhawan, Bombay, 1967 and Swamy Ranganathananda, *Administrative Efficiency and Human Resource Development,* Government of Andhra Pradesh, Hyderabad, 1986. It is observed that there is no effective system of regular assessment of the capabilities of the administrative system. See K.K. Khanna. *Bureaucratic Blunder World: A Behavioural Profile of the Indian Bureaucracy,* National, New Delhi. 1984, pp.88-89; Subhash Chandra Sarkar, "Anatomy of Central Government Administration". *Commerce,* 2-8 January 1988, pp. 5-15 and R.B. Jain and O.P. Dwivedi in R.B. Jain (ed). *Bureaucratic Politics in the Third World,* Geethanjali, New Delhi, 1989, p. 278.

2. Rajni Kothari, *Politics in India,* Orient Longman, Hyderabad, 1970, p. 14.
3. See, for details, O.P. Dwivedi, R.B. Jain and B.D. Dua, "Imperial Legacy, Bureaucracy and Administrative Change, India 1947-87", *Public Administration and Development,* Vol. 9, 1989, pp. 253-69.
4. See, for details, J.D. Shukla, *Indianisation of All-India Service and its Impact on Administration (1934-47),* Allied, New Delhi, 1982.
5. V. Bhaskara Rao, *Public Administration in India,* Ajanta, New Delhi, 1989, p. 55.
6. Rajni Kothari, *op, cit.,* p. 111.
7. See, for details. B.B. Misra, *The Bureaucracy in India: An Historical Analysis of Development upto 1947,* Oxford University Press, Delhi, 1977, pp. 299-305.
8. *Ibid.*
9. *Ibid.*
10. S.R. Maheshwari, "Strengthening Administrative Capabilities in India, *Public Administration and Development,* Vol. 4, 1984, p. 50.
11. *Ibid.,* p. 51.
12. C.P. Bhambri, *Bureaucracy and Politics in India,* Vikas, Delhi, 1971, p. 54.
13. *Ibid.,* p. 210.
14. O.P. Dwivedi and R.B. Jain, *India's Administrative State,* Gitanjali, New Delhi, 1985, p. 8.
15. *Ibid.*
16. S.L. Verma, "Bureaucratic Culture of Higher Civil Services in India", *Journal of Constitutional and Parliamerntary Studies,* Vol. 12, No. 1, January-March, 1978.
17. R.B. Upadhyaya and K.C. Sharma, *Politicocracy, Bureaucracy and Technology in India,* Sashi, Jaipur, 1987, p. 35.
18. L.K. Jha, "Bureaucracy in India: Internal Weakness and External Pressures" (Second Dr Chandran Devanesan Memorial Lecture), *The Hindu,* 28 December 1985. See also L.K. Jha, *Mr. Red Tape,* Allied, Allahabad, 1987.
19. L.K. Jha, "Economic Administration" in *India: Retrospect and Prospect* (Endowment Lecture), Indian Institute of Public Administration, New Delhi, 1986, p. 18.

20. *Ibid.* See also L.K. Jha, 'The Role of Bureaucracy in a Developing Democracy", *Indian Police Journal,* Vol. 30, No. 2, October-December 1983, pp. 6-18.

21. P.C. Alexander, "Role of Civil Service: Then and Now", *Indian Management,* Vol. 23, No. 7, July 1984, pp. 3-6.

22. T.N. Chaturvedi, *Politics, Bureaucracy and Development* (M.N. Roy Memorial Lecture), Uppal, New Delhi, p. 11.

23. *Ibid.*, p. 21.

24. *Ibid.*, pp. 22-23. Also see Denni J. En Carnation, "The Central Bureaucracy: Responsive to Whom?", *Asian Survey,* Vol. 19, No. 11, November 1979, pp. 1126-45.

25. S.C. Dubey, ed., *Public Services and Social Responsibility,* Vikas, New Delhi, 1979, pp. 263-68.

26. Satya Deva, "Administration in Developing Societies" in Susheela Kaushik, ed., *Public Administration: An Alternative Perspective,* Ajanta, New Delhi, 1984, pp. 83-97.

27. Prabhat Kumar Datta, "Exploring the Character of the Indian State", *The Calcutta Journal of Political Studies,* Vol. 7, No.1, Winter 1987, pp. 11-35. Also see S.C. Patnaik, "Land Reforms Measures in Orissa and Expansion of Production Opportunities" in K. Prasad and S.C. Patnaik, *Rural Development Strategies for Weaker Sections.* Utkal University, Bhubaneshwar, 1984, p. 110.

28. Pradeep Saxena, *Personnel Administration and Management: Towards an Alternative,* Printwell, Jaipur, 1987.

29. *Ibid.* See also S.L. Verma, "Bureaucracy and Political Development in India: An Ideological Perspective", *Political Change,* Vol. 2, No. 2, July-December, 1989, pp. 81-92.

30. K. Rama Moorthy, "How, Relevant is the Civil Services?" *Nirnay.* Vol.1, No. 1, June 1984, pp. 1-6.

31. K.K. Khanna, *Behavioural Approach to Bureaucratic Development.* National, New Delhi, 1983.

32. K.K. Khanna, *Pro-Active Bureaucracy: The Psychology of Change in a Developing Bureaucracy,* National, New Delhi, 1985, pp. 193-208.

33. *The Hindu* (International edn), 27 March 1982.

34. B.S. Appu, "The Decline of the Indian Bureaucracy". *Man and Development,* Vol. 8, No. 1, March 1986, pp. 63-86. See also N.S.

Saksena, "Why IAS and IPS are in Poor Shape?". *Times of India*, 27 December 1989; Nari Rustomji , "Changing the Guard: Unimportance of Being Earnest", *Statesman*, 21 October 1980, p. 6 andd Nishi Sinha, "The IAS—A Much Maligned Monster", *Amrita Bazar Patrika*, 16 December 1980, p. 6.

35. T.K. Moulik, "Bureaucracy, Development and People", *Mainstream*, Vol.20, No. 33, 10 April 1982, pp. 15-19.

36. Krishna Kumar Tummala, "Higher Civil Service in India: 'Commitment' of 'Establishment' ", *Politics, Administration and Change*, Vol.6, No. 2, July-December 1982, pp. 17-40.

37. Krishna K. Tummal, "Higher Civil Service in India" in Krishna K. Tummala, ed., *Administrative Systems Abroad*. University Press of America, Llanham, 1982, p. 111.

38. S.R. Maheshwari, 'The Morale of the Civil Service', *Indian Express*, 28 January 1980.

39. Haridwar Rai, Sakendra Prasad Singh and M .K. Gaur, "Neutrality Vs Commitment: A Futile Debate", *Indian Journal of Political Science*, Vol. 39, No. 2, April-June 1978, pp. 171-87. Also see Dharma Vira, "Civil Services, Living upto Contemporary Reality", *Man and Development*. Vol, 1, No. 4, December 1979, pp. 64-68.

40. Avneet Kumar Ghildiol, "From Steel Frame to Open Structure: Bureaucracy and Change in India", *Administrator*, Vol. 28, No. 1, January-March 1983, pp. 33-40.

41. Mohit Bhattacharya, *Bureaucracy and Development Administration*, Uppal, New Delhi, 1979, p. 14, 116.

42. K.K. Khanna, "Growing Bureaucracy: Some Idiosyncracies", *Economic Times*, 10 July 1981.

43. M. Umapathy, "Designing Bureaucracy for Development", *Indian Journal of Public Administration*, Vol. 28, No. 2, April-June 1982, pp. 276-97.

44. B.R. Sharma, *Motivation Crisis in Indian Administration*, Indian Institute of Public Administration, New Delhi, 1986.

45. B.R. Sharma, *Frustration: Reactions of Government Executives*, Indian Institute of Public Administration, New Delhi, 1988.

46. B.R. Sharma, *Administrative Stress: A Study of Middle Level Government Executives in India*, Indian Institute of Public Administration, New Delhi, 1986.

7

MNCS (MULTI-NATIONAL CORPORATIONS) IN INDIA

Definition of an MNC

An MNC owns and controls income generation assets in more than one country, and in doing so produces goods and services outside its country of origin. Its managerial headquarters are located in the country referred to as the "home country", while the enterprise carries out operations in a number of countries, known as host countries. Thus, it has the character of giant size, international operations, oligopolistic structure, spontaneous evaluation and collective transfer of resources. MNCs are also referred to as TNCs (Trans National Corporations), which implies that their operations extend beyond the boundaries of a nation in which they are originally envisaged.

MNCs in India – Background

India started planning her economy in 1951, with a blend of public and private sectors. It was a so-called "mixed economy". In the 1960s, India became a more or less closed economy, raising tariff walls. Our export-orientation was very limited, and we were very suspicious of foreign investment, and foreign capital, despite facing a domestic resource crunch. Our technology was also outdated, and economy protected and industrial licensing policy, working against rapid industrialization. In the 1970s, our BOP (Balance of Payments) became distorted, and we had to borrow a massive loan of 2.5 billion dollars from the IMF. The MNCs are increasing their hold over the Indian economy since the 1970s, and today control about 53 per cent of the assets of the industrial sector in India. The growth of MNCs through collaboration with Indian industries has been fast during the 1980s. In the 1980s with the coming to power of Rajiv Gandhi, liberalization and deregulation started gaining momentum but gathered full pace only in the 1990s, with the coming to power of Dr. Manmohan singh as Finance Minister and P.V. Narasimha Rao as Prime Minister in 1991. They initiated a process of liberalization, privatization and globalization and transformed the Indian economy, making it vibrant and competitive.

Impact of MNCs on various sectors of the Indian Economy

The impact of MNCs on industrial development of India during the 1980s reveals that during the period 1990-92, the index of industrial production increased from 47.6% in 1970, to 155.8% in 1992. The contribution of manufacturing sector to industrial development increased considerably. The Industrial Policy of 1991 contributed significantly to the rise of MNCs in the Indian economy. The main features of the Industrial Policy of 1991 are:

(*i*) To accelerate the pace of industrial growth, by providing greater freedom in investment decisions, keeping in view the objectives of increasing exports, efficiency and competitiveness of the industry. The policy encourages foreign investment, and provides enhanced access to state-of-the art technology, to enable advances in production techniques, and helps in the attainment of international competitiveness.

(*ii*) Industrial licensing has been abolished for all industries, except for six reserved for the public sector, those reserved for the small sector, and 15 industries that have compulsory licensing.

(*iii*) In order to attract foreign investment in high priority industries, involving large investments and advanced technologies, direct investment upto 51% foreign equity is being freely permitted.

(*iv*) A system of informatic approvals has been introduced for speedy clearance of proposals.

(*v*) Foreign brand names and trade marks of goods is also freely permitted.

74. Padma Ramachandran, ed., *Issues in Indian Public Administration*, Oxford & IBH, New Delhi, 1986, pp. XI-XII.
75. Meena Sogani and R.M. Khandelwal, *State Level Personnel Administration in India*, Printwell, Jaipur, 1987, p. 129. Also see Meena Sogani, *The Chief Secretary in India: A Study of his Role in State Administration in Rajasthan*, Associated, New Delhi, 1984.
76. G.C. Singhvi, "District and State Administrations: A New Leadership for the IAS", *Indian Journal of Public Administration*, Vol. 29, No. 4, October-December 1983, pp. 808-20.
77. B.C. Das and K. Das, "Social Background of Orissan Bureaucracy: A Case Study of Orissa Secretariat Service", *Indian Journal of Political Science*, Vol. 42, No. 4, October-December 1981, pp. 30-44.
78. R.K. Sapru, *Civil Service Administration in India*, Deep and Deep, Jaipur, 1988, pp. 333-34.
79. Rajni Goyal, *State Civil Services Training in India*, RBSA Publishers, Jaipur, 1988, pp. 333-34.
80. Balveer Arora, "Political Control over Administration in the Federal Context", in R.B. Jain, ed, *Public Services in a Democratic Context*, The Indian Institute of Public Administration, New Delhi, 1983, pp. 72-86.
81. Rasheed Talib, "More Unitary than Federal", *India Today*, Vol. 6, No. 16, 16-31 August 1981.
82. Kuldeep Nayyar in *Sunday*, 28 February 1982. See also "Rule by Prime Minister's Secretariat", *Economic and Political Weekly*, 13-20 November 1982.
83. Balveer Arora, *op. cit.*, p. 81. Also see Dipak Rudra, "God, with Feet of Clay: Temptations of the Middle Years", *Statesman*, 9, August 1980. There were attempts by the Prime Minister and her colleagues to get the top echelons of the State bureaucracy in West Bengal to non-cooperate with and conspire against the Left Front Government. See *Economic and Political Weekly*, 29 May 1982, p. 887.
84. See, for details, David Potter, *op. cit.*, pp. 164-66.
85. Letter No. 1407-PMO/80, 19 August 1980.
86. S.K. Goyal, *Bureaucratic Administration in India*, Chugh, Allahabad, p. 251.

87. *Ibid.*, pp. 267-69.
88. S.N. Tawale, P.N. Limaye, V.K. Kshire and N.R. Inamdar, *Leadership and Bureaucracy in Developemental Process* (ICSSR Project), Oxford & IBH, New Delhi 1985, pp. 169-72.
89. L. Dayal, "The District Officer in Bihar: Post-Independence Period" in Edwin James and Paramatma Saran, eds, *District Administration in India,* Vikas, New Delhi, 1988, p. 200.
90. Edwin James and Paramatma Saran, eds, *District Administration in India,* Vikas, New Delhi, 1988, p. 218.
91. *Ibid.*, p. 221.
92. *Ibid.*, p. 222.
93. *Ibid.*, p. 217.
94. H. Bhushan Singh, "District Administration in India (Note I), *Indian Journal of Public Administration,* Vol. XXXII, No. 2, April-June 1986, pp. 348-53.
95. See, for details, Abhimanyu Singh, "Changing Role of the District Officer", *Indian Journal of Public Administration,* Vol. XXXII, No. 2, April-June 1986, pp. 251-67.
96. M.A. Aleem, "Public Personnel Organisation: A Comparative Perspective, "*Prashasanika,* Vol. 12, No. 4, October-December 1983, pp. 11-14.
97. K.K. Katyal, "How Autonomous are the Public Service Commissions?", *The Hindu,* 1 December 1980 and S.L. Goel, *Public Personnel Administration,* Sterling, New Delhi, 1984, pp. 138-41. See for the evaluation of the Bihar Public Service Commission L.P. Srivastava. *Public Personnel System in India,* Janaki, Patna, 1987, pp. 210-15. Also see Pradeep Saxena, *public Policy and Administration and Development,* Printwell, Jaipur, 1988, pp. 213-14 and Niru Hazarika, *Public Service Commission* (A Study of Assam Public Service Commission). Leela Devi, New Delhi, 1979.
98. D.R. Chaudhury, "Public Service Commission under Pressure", *Tribure,* 13 March 1981, p. 4. See also Amarjit Singh Jaj and K.K. Puri, "Government and Public Service Commission (A Case Study of Punjab and Haryana)" is K.K. puri, ed., *Public Administration: Indian Spectrum,* Kitab Mahal, Allahabad, 1985, pp. 214-24.
99. R.K. Sapru, *Civil Service Administration in India,* Deep and Deep, New Delhi, 1985.

100. B.M. Sinha, "Imbalances in Civil Services", *Hindustan Times,* 12 October 1981, p. 9.
101. J.B. D'Souza, "Selection for Civil Services: Changes in the System Vital", *Economic Times,* 9 May 1981.
102. Satya Deva, *op. cit.,* p. 65. See for different views, N. Umapathy, "Recruitment to Public Services, Candidates' Reactions to Interviews as a Technique of Selection to Public Services", *Indian Journal of Public Administration,* Vol. 31, No. 4, October-December 1985, pp. 1279-96. Also see J.D. Sethi, "Bureaucracy and Accountability", *Indian Journal of Public Administration,* Vol. XXIX, No. 3, July-September 1983, p. 535 and Maheshwari, "Civil Service Recruitment," *The Hindu,* 10 March 1981.
103. Ranjit S. Mooshahary, "Towards More Efficient All-India Services", *Administrator,* Vol. 28, Nos. 3-4, September-December 1983, pp. 339-44. Also see S.N. Sinha, "Recruitment of Higher Civil Servants in India : Post-1978 Development", *Administrator,* Vol. 28, No. 1, January-March 1983, pp. 1-10 and G.P. Pilmia and Hoshiar Singh, *Administration and Social Change,* Printwell, Jaipur, 1985, p. 55.
104. B.D. Mansingh, "The Executive in Travail", *Hindustan Times,* 12 June 1979. See also M.A. Muttalib, *Democracy,Bureaucracy and Technocracy,* Concept, New Delhi, 1980.
105. See R.B. Upadhyaya and K.C. Sharma, *op.cit.,* pp. 524-82. See for details Krishna K. Tummala, "Reservations in the Indian Public Service" in Krishna K. Tummala, ed. Equity in Public Employment *Cross Nations* (mimeo), Montana State University, USA, pp. 65-102; W.R. Sharma, "Selection of Civil Services", *Economic and Political Weekly,* January 1979 and Sreekanth Sambrar and Pulin K. Garg, "Brave New World of Young Indian Decision-Making Elite," *Economic and Political Weekly,* August 1979. See also S.N. Singh, "A Study of Recruitment Pattern of the IAS", *Administrator,* Vol. XXVII, No. 2, 1982 and C.P. Bhambri, "IAS and the Secular Goal", *Hindustan Times,* 27 May 1982.
106. C.P. Bhambri, "Mismatch between Theory and Practice in Traning in Public Administration", *Indian Journal of Public Administration,* Vol. XXXIV, No. 3, July-September 1988, pp. 476-81.
107. Krishna Mohan Mathur, "Human Resource Development in Administration". *Indian Journal of Public Administration,* Vol. XXXIII, No. 2, April-June 1987, pp. 230-32.
108. *Ibid.,* p. 232.

109. See Bidhu Mohanty, "Service Before Self: Tasks for India's New Brahmins", *Statesman,* 26 May 1981. Also see Rakesh Hooja, Hen, SIPA and LBSNAA, "The Complementary Role of Training Institutions in Training IAS Regular Rectruits," *Indian Journal of Training and Development,* Vol. 9, No. 4, August 1979, pp. 31-34: Bulbul Pal, "Alber Administrators?" *Hindustan Times,* 17 July 1980 and A.S. Prashar, "Spotlight on Mussoorie Academy", *Tribune,* 21 March 1982.

110. L.K. Jha, *Bureaucracy in India, p. cit.*

111. See, for details, David C. Potter, *op. cit.,* pp. 200-11.

112. A.S. Prashar, *op. cit.* Also see R. Bakshi, "The Indian Aggrieved Service", *Indian Express,* 21 March 1982.

113. Inder Malhotra, "Mussoorie Mess and After—Not the End of the Affairs", *Times of India,* Bombay, 11 March 1982.

114. Arul B. Louis, "The Loyal Servants", *Hindustan Times,* 12 April 1981.

115. K.S. Bhat, "Induction Strategy to Higher Civil Service: A View Point", *Indian Journal of Training and Development,* Vol. 13, No. 4, October-December 1983, pp. 133-36.

116. T.N. Chaturvedi, *Politics, Bureaucracy and Development , op. cit.,* p. 24. Also see P.R. Dubashi, *Administrative Reforms,* B.R., Delhi, 1986, p. 121.

117. J.B. D'Souza, "Training Permanent Politicians", *Times of India,* 23 October 1980.

118. See, for details Hari Mohan Mathur, ed., *Issues in Service Training* (Papers and Reports of a Conference held in New Delhi, 12-14 May 1981), Indian Institute of Public Administration, New Delhi, 1982. After this first conference, training conferences are held every year to take stock of the situation and to help generate new ideas. A National Training Conference on Training of Civil Servants in India was also held in Mussoorie during 21-23 September 1982. For details see David C. Potter, *op. cit.,* pp. 203-4.

119. See, for details, A.P. Saxena, ed., *Training in Government: Objectives and Opportunities.* Indian Institute of Public Administration, New Delhi, 1985.

120. *Ibid.,* pp. 36-40. Also see A.P. Saxena, "Changing Role of the Trainer", *Economic and Political Weekly,* Vol. XVIII, No. 48, 26 November 1983.

121. See, for details, Krishna Mohan Mathur, *Administration of Police Training in India,* Gian, Delhi, 1987.

122. S.N. Sadasivan, "Training for Administrative Excellence", *Indian Journal of Public Administration,* Vol. XXXIII, No. 4. October-December 1987, pp. 833-44. See also Shriram Maheshwari, "Training for Administrators in India", *Indian Journal of Public Administration,* Vol. XXXIII, No. 2, April-June 1987, pp. 242-61.

123. Jayant Kumar Ray, *Administrators in a Mixed Polity,* Macmillan, Delhi, 1981, p. 7.

124. M.A. Muttalib, "Indian Ecology of Bureaucracy" in R.B. Jain, ed., *Public Services in a Democratic Context,* Indian Institute of Public Administration, New Delhi, 1983, pp. 119-22. He recommended the Swedish system as an answer to the maladies of Indian public administration in which the politician is checked, the bureaucracy is accountable and the public interest is better served.

125. See K.K. Khanna, "Indian Bureaucracy: Dangers Flowing from Politicisation", *Economic Times,* 7 May 1980 and Jayant Kumar Ray, *op. cit.,* p. 16.

126. See Anil Bhatt, "Colonial Bureaucratic Culture and Development Administration: Portrait of an Old-fashioned Indian Bureaucrat", *Journal of Commonwealth and Comparative Politics,* Vol. 17, No. 2, July 1979, pp. 159-75.

127. C.D. Deshmukh, *The Course of My Life,* Orient Longman, Delhi, 1974, p. 105.

128. Badruddin Tyabji, *Indian Politics and Practice,* Orient, New Delhi, 1972, p. 107.

129. M.N. Buch, "Constitutional Role of the Civil Servants", *Administrator,* Vol. 27, No. 2. Summer 1982, pp. 191-200. Also see M.N. Buch, "Who is Afraid of the Big Bad Wolf", *Administrator,* Vol. 28, No. 1, January-March 1983, pp. 41-47.

130. R.P. Naronha, *A Tale Told by an Idiot,* Vikas, Delhi, 1976, p. 65.

131. Jayant Kumar Ray, *op. cit.,* pp. 201-2. Also see *Stateman,* 8 January 1979.

132. See Pradeep Saxena and Rajendra Joshi, "Minister-Civil Servant Relationship", *The Indian Journal of Constitutional and Parliamentary Studies,* Vol. 13, No. 2, April-June 1979, pp. 184-96.

133. "India's Interventionist, managerial state can no longer pretend that its bureaucracy is neutral in the sense of being anonymous and voiceless", See for details, Lloyd I. Rudolph and Susanne Hoeber Rudolph, *op. cit.*, pp. 45-48.

134. S.R. Maheshwari, *Political Development in India,* Concept, New Delhi, 1984, pp. 45-48.

135. B.K. Nehru, "The Role of Civil Services in India", *Eastern Economist,* 2 May 1980, pp. 878-81. See also S. Bhatnagar, "Politics of Postings and Transfers of Government Officials", in K.K. Puri, ed., *op. cit.*, pp. 199-213 and Edwin James and Paramathma Saran, eds., *District Administration in India.*

136. See, for details, David C. Potter, *op. cit.*, pp. 156-58.

137. Harbhajan Singh Deol, "Administration and Politicians: A Critique of Their Roles", *The Indian Journal of Public Administration,* Vol. XXX, No. 2, April-June 1984, pp. 311-20.

138. P.D. Sharma, "Public Interest and Politics in India" in R.B. Jain, ed., *op. cit.*, pp. 180-182. Also see S.N. Mishra, *Civil Services at the Grassroots Level* (A Study in Conflict between Local Police and Rural Elites), *op. cit.*, pp. 184-192.

139. Krishna Kumar Tummala, *The Ambiguity of Ideology and Administrative Reform,* Allied, Bombay, 1979, pp. 138-39.

140. M.A. Muttalib, "Philosophy of Indian Administrative-Reforms", *Indian Journal of Public Administration,* Vol. XXI, No. 3, July-Sep. 1985, pp. 485-86. Also see M.A. Muttalib, "Academic Culture of Public Administration: The Indian Experience", *Journal of Public Administration,* Vol. XXXIII, No. 2, April-June 1987, pp. 190-92.

141. Krishna Kumar Tummala, *The Ambiguity of Ideology and Administrative Reforms, op. cit.*, pp. 286-98.

142. S.R. Maheshwari, "Strengthening Administrative Capabilities in India ", *Public Administration and Development,* Vol. 4, 1984, pp. 49-62. Also see P.K. Mattoo, "Administrative Reforms at the Central Level", *Indian Journal of Public Administration,* Vol. XXXI, No. 4, July-Sept. 1985, pp. 535-47 and O.P. Dwivedi *et. al., Imperial Legacy Bureaucracy.*

143. See, for details, David C. Potter, *op. cit.*, pp. 150-78. See also G.P. Pilanic and Hoshiar Singh, *Administration and Social Change,* Printweel, Jaipur, 1985, pp. 42-43.

144. L.K. Jha, " Bureaicracy in India: Intemal Weaknesses and External Pressures", *The Hindu,* 28 December 1985.

145. R.B. Jain and O.P. Dwivedi, "Bureaucracy in India: The Development Context" in R.B. Jain, ed., *Bureaucratic Politics in the Third World,* Geethanjali, New Delhi, 1989, pp. 296-97.

146. Sisir K. Chaudhury, "Bureaucrats vs. Technocrats: Why Administrative Reform has Never Taken Off,' *Capital,* 10 November 1980, pp. 15-17.

147. See S.R. Maheshwari, "Towards Better Administrative System" in K.K. Puri, ed., *Public Administration: Indian Spectrum,* Kitab Mahal, Allahabad, 1985, pp. 61-71 and S.R. Maheshwari, *Administrative Reforms in India,* Macmillan, New Delhi, 1981, pp. 106-14.

148. *Ibid.,* p. 61.

149. O.P. Dwivedi *et al., op. cit.,* pp. 262-63.

150. Susheela Kaushik in her Foreword to Malathi Subramanian, *Management of Public Administration: Patterns in the Generalist vs. Specialist Debate,* Delhi, 1987, p. vi.

151. See, for details, Lloyd I. Rudolph and Susanne Hoeber Rudoph, *op. cit.,* pp. 180-82 and 433.

152. M.A. Muttalib, *Academic Culture of Public Administration, op. cit.,* p. 192 and P.S. Bhatnagar, "Planning and Administrative Development", *Indian Journal of Public Administration,* Vol. XXXI, No. 2. April-June 1985, p. 317.

153. Noorjahan Bawa, "Changing Role of Bureaucracy in India", *Indian Journal of Public Administration,* Vol. XXXI, No. 2, April-June 1985.

154. C.P. Bhambri, "Basic Issues in Administrative Reforms", *Indian Journal of Public Administration,* Vol. XXXI, No. 3, July-September 1985, pp. 408-503.

155. Mohit Bhattacharya, "Public Administration in India: A Discipline in Bondage", *Indian Journal of Public Administration,* Vol. XXXII, No. 2, April-June 1986, p. 228.

156. Kamta Prasad, "Public Administration Research and the Problem of Inequality", *Indian Journal of Public Administration,* Vol. XXXIV, No. 1, January-March 1988, p. 2.

157. M.A. Muttalib, *Academic Culture of Public Administration, op. cit.*, pp. 192-93.

158. Mohit Bhattacharya, "Public Administration in India", *op. cit.*, p. 228.

159. J.D. Sethi, "Bureaucracy and Accountability", *Indian Journal of Public Administration.* Vol. XXIX, No. 3, July-September 1983, p. 525.

160. Rajni Kothari, *State Against Democracy : In Search of Humane Governance,* Ajanta, New Delhi, 1988, pp. 44 and 95.

161. *Ibid.*, p. 229.

to GCA (general currency areas) have increased. With the collapse of the Soviet Union and the growing turmoil in the newly liberated economies of Eastern Europe, both our exports and imports to and from this region have drastically declined. As a result foreign trade in Rupee terms has virtually disappeared. One favourable aspect of this development is that we now earn more hard currencies. Besides we have been obliged to improve the quality of our products greatly.

While we should strengthen our position in the US and Western Europe, it is now high time for Indian business to fan out to new regions of the world. In SouthEast Asia, Malaysia is becoming saturated with Indian ventures and hence we should make further inroads into Thailand, Singapore and the Indo-Chinese countries. In Africa, the Francophone West African countries have been almost ignored; though there does exist scope for an Indian commercial presence. South America and the Caribbean countries can also be explored for Indian expertise and manegerial contributions particularly in regard to small-scale industries. Similarly there are good prospects once Russia opens up Siberia for international ventures. Eastern Europe offers immense possibilities for our private sector companies to establish production-sharing arrangements.

The government of India has identified 34 export thrust areas where Indian products should do well, such as marine products, horticulture, floriculture, jewellery, bicycles and granite. Export units in these areas are being provided infrastructural support and development assistance to increase their existing strengths. It is important to concentrate on a few products where we have a competitive advantage rather than try to make market inroads with an amorphous group of products. It has to be kept in mind that in the new EU (European Union) there will be an increasing demand for "branded goods" with appeal to specific categories of consumers. At the same time, customers around the world will look for products with special fashion appeal. Thus "niche marketing" will become increasingly important. In our view India has the potential to carve out exclusive "niches" for itself in leather garments for up-market consumers in Europe and in designer cotton wear for the younger generation in the US and Western Europe.Food processing and computer software are also areas which hold a lot of promise for India's overseas business forays.

2. Right Selection of Personnel

Besides, the product profile and country spectrum, an important aspect in globalisation efforts is manpower training. The selection of personnel to go abroad should be very carefully done. Only the best managers who have worked competently in various functional areas at home should be sent abroad. The mindset of people sent abroad should be such that they are equally competent to work in an alien milieu. Thus a common complaint among Japanese and South Korean business undertakings is that Indian businessmen are overbearing in their dealings and have a supercilious attitude. It has to be realised that while keeping pace with the West may be important, the grace of the East has to be given due consideration if we want to succeed in East Asia.This requires proper orientation and cross-cultural training prior to an overseas assignment. The manager working abroad has to deal with people with different value systems, inter-personal behaviour patterns and work practices. He has to interact with such business associates in a culturally appropriate manner. This calls for adequate orientation and training in languages, legal procedures, and customs and above all in suitable reactions and responses so that the sensitivities of the host are always respected.

3. Monitoring and Feedback

A major weakness in our globalisation strategies is improper monitoring and inadequate feedback. Our diplomatic missions through the commercial attaches should take greater interest in our foreign business presence. They should constantly give feedback to the government of India on the progress of business ventures so that appropriate policy redirections can be attempted. "Country Risk Analysis" should be an integral part of the international business divisions of companies global checklist of the performance of enterprises in various regions of the world should be made, so that lessons can be learnt from both successes and failures coordinated country-specific policy evaluation of both private and public sector overseas ventures should be made, so that lessons can be learnt from completely premature. For a successful system of arbitration presumes a comparatively small margin of difference where agreements cannot be reached; where differences are large or fundamental in nature, compulsory arbitration imposes a strain which may, in the long run, be found to be equally irksome to both the sides.It was also felt that the existence of compulsory arbitration deprives the parties of the incentive to compromise at the discussion stage.

The Second Pay Commission also recommended compulsory arbitration as a method of settling differences unsolved by negotiation and as a necessary complement to a joint machinery for negotiation, and to make the Whitley machinery for negotiation work more equitably. It felt that by accepting compulsory arbitration on pay and allowances, leave and hours of work, government would be discharging its obligation towards employees, if they were to give up the right to withhold their labour.[9]

In 1960, some sections of Central Government employees went on strike for five days from July 11-16, on the question of need-based minimum wage and dearness allowance formula. The strike forced the government to realise the need for a proper negotiating machinery and decided in 1960 to set up a Joint Consultative Machinery with a provision of compulsory arbitration. The government wanted to give statutory effect to the proposed JCM Scheme and ban the strikes by government employees. The employees organisations refused to give up their right to strike and dis-associate outsiders with their unions.

On October 7, 1963, the government announced its decision to set-up a scheme for Joint Consultative Machinery and Compulsory Arbitration to provide a machinery and to create conditions which would render strikes superfluous.

THE JCM SCHEME

The Scheme is the result of the protracted discussions between the Ministers of the Government and the Leaders of the Employees' Organisations. An agreement was reached between the Government and the employees by declaring a joint intent regarding the common approach of the government and the employees' organisations.

The Scheme broadly covers more than three million regular Group C and Group D employees of the Central Government, including Industrial Employees working in the departmentally run undertakings like the Railways and workshops and production units of various Ministries.

The Scheme provides for a three-tier structure of Joint Councils at the national, departmental, and regional office levels. The apex body in the structure is the National Council.

The National Council of the JCM deals with matters of general nature, such as minimum remuneration, DA and pay of certain common categories. The Departmental Councils deal only with matters affecting the employees in the Departments concerned. The Regional Councils deal with regional and local questions.

Agreements arrived at between the Official Side and the Staff Side of the Council become operative subject to the final authority of the Cabinet. Should a final disagreement be recorded, arbitration is available at the National and Departmental Council levels.

Compulsory Arbitration

The JCM Scheme provides[10] for compulsory arbitration, but its scope is limited to the following: *(a)* Pay and Allowances, *(b)* Weekly hours of work, and *(c)* Leave of a class or grade of employees.

The definition and scope of the two terms used as "a class" or "a grade" of employees led to controversy and different viewpoints between the official side and staff side. Due to this, the employees went on a token strike[11] for one day on September 19, 1968 protesting against the attitude of the government[12] towards the demands of the employees for the need based minimum wage and merger of dearness allowance with basic pay. The government maintained that these two demands were not arbitrable as they did not relate to a "class or grade of Employees" as laid down in the Scheme. Thus, the government exercised power to decide whether a particular item relates to a "class or grade" of employees.

Clause 17 stipulates that cases of individuals shall not be subject to Compulsory Arbitration.

The government has the final authority in deciding whether an issue can or cannot go for arbitration, in case the Joint Councils do not succeed in their efforts to settle differences through negotiations. On this issue, the National Commission on Labour considered that government's discretion requires to be fettered. It is the arbitrator who should decide whether an issue is or not arbitrable within the framework of the Constitution of the JCM. One of the parties to the dispute cannot be an arbiter on this point.[13]

Issue of Non-arbitrable Items

The JCM Scheme was silent about the arbitrability of non-arbitrable issues of a dispute. According to Clause 18 of the JCM Scheme, no dispute can be referred to arbitration unless it was considered by the National Council or the appropriate Departmental Council and final disagreement between two sides was recorded. Disputes relating to arbitrable matters in lower councils may be placed before the concerned departmental council.

There were complaints that the government has been delaying in decision on arbitrability of an issue and refusing to refer it to the Board of Arbitration. In this regard, a convention was evolved in 1969 that the Staff Side may put forward their viewpoint before a Committee of Ministers consisting of the Home Minister (now Minister for Personnel), the Labour Minister and the Minister administratively concerned with the matter.

If the Committee of Ministers is satisfied with the views of the Staff Side, it may accept to refer the issue to arbitration.[14]

It was informed at a meeting of the sub-committee on the review of the JCM Scheme, that the group of Ministers in 1988 decided to refer the dispute about arbitrability of an issue to the advice of the Attorney General, which would be binding on both the sides. It was agreed to incorporate this recommendation in the JCM Scheme.[15]

Clause-20 (*ii*) of JCM Scheme

According to Clause-20 *(ii)* of the JCM Scheme, matters determined by the government in accordance with the recommendations of a commission will not be subject to arbitration for a period of five years from the date of the recommendations, after which they will become arbitrable with reference as far as possible to the factors referred to in Clause-20 (*i*).

Clause-20 (*i*) suggests that "in determining a dispute the Board of Arbitration shall examine the merits of the case presented by both the Official and Staff Sides, and take into account all other relevant factors including the principles enunciated in any recent report of a Commission of enquiry etc".

Employees' Organisations represented that the Board of Arbitration should be free to take independent decisions and not be bound down to any principles contained in a report of a Commission which may have been accepted by the government. The government's contention was that the Board of Arbitration should decide specific disputes rather than going into more fundamental questions of economic, social and political implications.

However, the government explained that the restriction on the Board of Arbitration need not be as rigid as had been provided for in the JCM Scheme and the Board may take into account all other relevant factors, including such principles as might have been enunciated in any recent report of a Commission of Enquiry, etc. Thus, the employees and the government recognised the necessity of freedom to the Board of Arbitration to take independent decisions.

There were seven issues relating to disagreements recorded before November 16, 1973 in the National Council and certain Departmental Councils which had not been referred to the Board of Arbitration as the government applied a ban on arbitration in terms of Clause-20 (*ii*) of the JCM Scheme. The argument of the government was that the recommendations of the Third Pay Commission were accepted with effect from November 1, 1973.

As such the government refused to refer the cases to arbitration, though disagreements were recorded well in advance of the submission of the report of the Third Pay Commission, as the matters were under the consideration of the Pay Commission. The government filed applications before the Board of Arbitration for abatement of the pending references as on November 16, 1973. The Staff Side challenged the abatement applications-after hearing the arguments and interpretations of both the Sides about the scope for the Clause-20 (*ii*) of the JCM Scheme, the Board of Arbitration passed 'Order' as Clause-20 (*ii*) does not apply to references made before the date of the decision of government, viz., November 16, 1973. In this regard, miscellaneous applications 94 & 95 of 1973, 5 of 1974 and 15 to 17 of 1974 were disposed of by the Board as the arguments of the Official Side were not tenable in interpreting Clause-20 (*ii*).

BOARD OF ARBITRATION

A Board of Arbitration under Clause-19 of the JCM Scheme was constituted in July 1968. The Board consists of three members, one drawn from a panel of five names submitted by the Official Side, one from a similar panel submitted by the Staff Side of the National Council and a Chairman who is an independent person. The members and the Chairman are selected by the Minister of Labour.

Terms of Reference

Arbitration claims are referred to the Board of Arbitration by the Ministry of Labour at the request of the Department of Personnel on behalf of the National Council or the departmental councils. The Ministry of Labour should forward the reference to the Board of Arbitration within a period of 15 days alongwith the "terms of reference". In few cases, as there was no mutual agreement between the Official Side and Staff Side, both sides maintained separate terms of reference to the Board.

Notice to the Parties

The Board issues notices about the reference to the concerned parties. The nature of the reference and the categories and number of employees to be affected by the reference are also provided. The parties concerned submit their claims and counter-claims along with the history of the disagreement between the two sides, a detailed statement of the case is presented to the Board.

Though, time limits are fixed by the Rules of Procedure, yet in practice the parties usually took more time in submission of necessary information and filing documents.[16] The Staff Side faced difficulties in collection of official information in support of their claims for reasons of organisational difficulties, non-cooperation by the departments and for want of information on certain items. The government representatives also faced difficulties in getting data from different sources as data banks do not exist. Even on a simple matter, like the number of employees involved in a particular reference, each Side provided different numbers and in some cases even a number could not be provided. Proper census of employees and other information is also not readily available in a particular department.

Hearings

After submission of the statement by the parties, the Board fixes dates of hearing of the case in consultation with the parties. The Chairman alone takes all the necessary steps to get the case prepared for hearing by the Board.

The procedure of the Board in conducting the arbitration has not been very formal. Each side has their spokesman usually, the Staff Side was represented by one of the office bearers of the Union/ Association, a member of the National Council or Department Council, Leaders of the Staff Side to the reference and an officer of the government represented the Official Side. No Counsel is permitted to appear before the Board to represent a party to the reference.

Spokesmen of both the Sides argue their case based on statements of the case submitted by them. They are allowed to make comments the other's statement. The parties, in support of their case, may produce oral evidence, at the discretion of the Board. The Staff Side brings witnesses in certain cases. The Chairman and Members of the Board interject questions during the course of the presentation of the case.

Normally, the hearing takes place only for few hours on a single day. But in some cases the Board takes one to three days.

Award

After hearing the parties, careful consideration of the material placed on record, and the merits of the case and taking into account all the relevant factors, the Board gives its Award. If the members of the Board disagree, the Chairman makes an umpire's award. Except in four references, all the awards were unanimous. The contents of award may include: The Claim is allowed in its original form or modified form. The claim might be partially allowed by rejecting a certain part of it, or the claim might be rejected out right. The Board gives no reasons for its decisions. The Award provides the date from which the Award comes into effect. It may be retrospect, prospect, or from the date of issue of award. The award is signed by the Chairman and the Members, attested by the Secretary, Board of Arbitration and transmitted to the concerned departments and parties.

Chairman

The Chairman plays a very crucial role in Arbitration. Until 1990, seven persons[17] have acted as Chairmen of the Board. All of them were retired Judges of the High Courts and the Supreme Court. The independent nature of the Chairman is thus protected by appointing experienced and reputed legal luminaries, which enhances confidence in arbitration.

It is important to note that from the beginning, the adjudicators, the Chairmen of Pay Commissions, Dearness Allowance Committees and Commissions, National Labour Commission, the Chairman of the Ad hoc-Tribunals and the Chairmen of the Board of the Arbitration are retired Judges of the Supreme Court or High Courts. Though, their appointments are semi-political, their assignments are almost Judicial. They are eminent in their field and independent. The pre- and post-independence governments in India, it appears, approached the whole issue as a legal one to provide legitimacy to their findings. Though, the bodies are not statutory, but due to the reports of the Commissions chaired by the Judges, the Governments were required to honour the reports as awards without any difficulty. Anomalies were rectified through further negotiations between the Government and the Unions. Thus, settlement of disputes in public employment through Pay Review Bodies or voluntary or compulsory arbitration gained respect and seldom questioned their authority.

Members (Staff Side)

A close observation of the panels of the Staff Side reveals that they selected outstanding personalities to represent as the members of the Staff Side on the Board of Arbitration. They were leaders[18] of life-long experience in the trade union movement of the country having deep insight into the problems of the employees.

Some of them were seasoned negotiators, having good relations with the authorities in the government. Before becoming members of the Staff Side on the Board they represented the Staff Side in different capacities in the Joint Councils of the JCM. They enjoyed the patronage of well organised political parties and national trade unions. Some of them were recognised leaders of the workers and employees represented in the Parliament. However, as in the UK academic experts on labour and industrial relations were not given any opportunity.

Arbitration Awards

All the awards given by the Board were unanimous except in four references, where the members of the Official Side and Staff Side expressed dissenting view making the Chairman to give an umpire's award. The CA 7/1980 was referred to the Board to make a distinction between ex-audit UDCs and the present UDCs working in the P & T Department, wherein 40 employees were involved. The Chairman, was driven to make an umpire's award in terms of the Standing Rules of procedures in view of the disagreement between the Members of Staff Side and Official Side. The Staff Side member pleaded on the principle of equal pay for equal work, while the Official Side member argued that officials performing the same duties do not get the same pay scale. The Chairman, as an umpire, declared that the subsistence of the distinction would not be valid.

In reference four of 83, also, the Chairman acted as umpire wherein 117 employees involved for the revision of pay scales. The

Chairman, partly accepted the claim of the Staff Side, when there was disagreement between the members.

In reference 2 of 83, wherein 2, 25, 215 employees were involved, the Staff Side demanded parity in Half Pay Leave between Industrial and non-industrial employees other than Railways. There was no agreement between the members. The Chairman in his umpire's award accepted the claim of the Staff Side. In all the cases, the Chairman's awards either fully or partly favoured the claim of the Staff Side.

The Board of Arbitration is a very small organisation with limited staff and accommodation functions on the support of the Ministry of Labour. The parties to the references, it appears could not extend their full cooperation in presenting the statements and counter statements and appearing before the hearings. It resulted in the delay of the disposal of the reference. But it is all the part of the game of the arbitration process. Each side attempts to delay the case depending upon their own prospects of winning or loosing the case. Nobody wants to loose the case without much effort. Thus, there is some delay in finalising the references.

ARBITRATION IN PRACTICE

In the 24 years of history of compulsory arbitration a total of 204 references were made to the Board of Arbitration. Most of these (83) references were made during 1968-74 in the initial years of compulsory arbitration while the Third Pay Commission was sitting. Again many cases (104) were referred during 1980-86, while the Fourth Pay Commission was sitting. After the submission of the reports of the Pay Commissions, the number of references have become very less. During 1975-79, there were only six references and none[19] during 1975-77. Likewise, during 1987-91, there were only 19 references, one each in 1987, 1988 and 1989 and two in 1990, but suddenly the number increased to 15 in 1991. Most of the cases were referred during 1968(17), 1971(19), 1973(21), 1982(19), 1986(16) and 1991(15).

The total number or the average number of references per year are not many. For, a number of Departmental Councils were not constituted for a number of years.[20] Some departmental Councils could not record disagreements for want of acceptance of the Official

Side. Some disagreements were not recorded and referred to the arbitration as the government felt, they were not arbitrable. The number was also less due to the appointment of two Pay Commissions and a number of items were settled through special negotiations to consider the recommendations of the Pay Commissions.

Results of Arbitration

Out of the 204 references, 189 (93%) were decided by the Board, of which 13 (7%) were withdrawn by the Staff Side and four (2%) were amicably settled by both the sides.

In 144 (76%) references, the claims of the staff were either partly or fully accepted and 31 (16%) were outrightly rejected. 135 Awards were implemented by the government while five were rejected. The rest are yet to be implemented by the government. The Staff could not win their claims in 26 per cent of the references, as some were withdrawn by them, some rejected by the Board and some rejected by the government.

Compulsory arbitration benefitted the staff on a large scale and strengthened the Staff Side in joint consultation. It is a victory to the Staff Side and trade unionism which enhances the faith in the joint consultation. The Official Side has to learn from the awards of the arbitration and must acquire positive culture in solving the problems through mutual discussions. Despite the partial victory to the Staff Side, they were at times harassed by the arbitration procedure and process, as many references were pending with the Board for a long time.[21] Quick disposal of the references must have given a fair trial to the process of arbitration. However, the fault is not always with the Board. At many levels, the delay occurred for various reasons.

Nature of Subjects

More than 50 per cent of the references were on revision of pay scales, grant of higher scales or sanction of selection grades. Majority of them were referred to the Board while the Third and the Fourth Pay Commissions were enquiring into the matters respectively. In 10 per cent of the references, Staff Side claimed special pay or consolidated pay to certain categories of employees due to their specific nature of duties.

In 30 per cent of the references, the Staff Side demanded revision of Allowances, particularly over-time allowance to many categories in Railways and P&T, revision of House Rent Allowance and City Compensatory Allowance to many employees or allowances to a particular project area or state, or place due to high cost of living in those places. However, about 92 per cent were on pay allowances and increments. Such a large number of disagreements were recorded, in spite of the recommendations of the Two Pay Commissions.

At least in about 15 references, they were demanding parity with employees in other departments or places. For example, the Staff Side demanded HRA and CCA to the Central employees, working in Chandigarh on per with the State Government employees of Haryana and Punjab. There were anomalies of pay scales and treatment of certain categories of employees differently in different departments. This shows that job evaluation and rationalisation of work are still not done effectively on certain categories of some departments.

The claims of the staff on pay, leave and working hours are more justifiable compared to allowances. For 40 per cent of the claims on allowances were rejected by the Board. The claims of the Staff on all items except on leave are only partly acceptable to the Board.

Number of Employees Involved

Information is available in 110 awards about the number of employees in the references. In some references, no Side could provide the number of employees to be affected by the references. In some cases, there was difference of opinion about the number of employees, between the two Sides, the official side stating more number of employees. It shows that there are no regular census about the number and grades of employees in different departments.

It is interesting to note that in 10 per cent (11) of the references, the total staff involved in each case was under 10 only. In one reference (13 of 1973), there was no employee involved as the post was unfilled. The Board accepted the claim of the Staff Side to revise the pay scale from Rs. 95-110 to Rs. 110-131 of Head Book Binder in Survey of India. In such a simple cases also, the Departmental Council could not negotiate effectively, where there is not much burden on the government immediately, or even at a later stage. It not only leads to the wasting the time of the Board and loss of faith in joint consultation and negotiation.

In four references, only one employee was involved in each reference. In nine of 1982, revision of pay scale of Map Curator from Rs. 425-700 to Rs. 550-800, the Board accepted the claim of the Staff Side, but it took about three years from the date of disagreement recorded (August 28, 1980 to October 1, 1983). In 11/72, revision of pay scale of an Accountant from Rs. 130-300 to Rs. 210-425, the Board did not accept the claim but offered a special pay of Rs. 30 per month. In another case of 14/82, the revision of pay scale of Accountant from Rs. 350-500 to Rs. 425-700 was rejected but the Official side assured to take positive action in further negotiations. In reference 8/83, revision of pay scale from Rs. 260-350 to Rs. 380-560, the Board partly accepted the claim but only after 33 months. In two cases there were only two employees, in another two, only three employees and in the rest more than three but below ten. In almost all cases the employees benefited, but it could have been done by negotiation to enhance the mutual trust and faith in negotiations.

In 28 per cent of the references less than 100 employees were involved and less than 500 in 48 per cent of the references. In fact, in 86 (78%) cases only about 15,000 employees were affected out of which, the claims of the staff in 27 cases were fully accepted and in 40 cases partly accepted by the Board.

In 10 per cent of the references three to seven lakh of employees were involved. However, in three cases all the employees of Government of India, *i.e.*, 32 lakhs who come under the jurisdiction of the JCM Scheme were involved.

Reference 3 of 86, involved 32 lakhs of employees, demanding the facility to enable encashment of earned leave when the employees were in active service on par with some state governments. It is interesting to note that in India, generally, the State Governments follow the Central Government as a model employer. But, in this regard, the State Government became a model for the Government of India. The demand was under discussion during 1979-85. As both sides failed to negotiate, disagreement was recorded on January 14, 1986 in the National Council. The government did not accept the demand on the plea that it costs heavy expenditure of about Rs. 330 crore per annum. The Board of Arbitration gave its award on March 31, 1989 after about 35 months. The Board accepted the claim of the Staff Side with slight modification with effect from April 1, 1989. Accordingly, each employee was enabled to encash earned leave for a period of 15 days, if leave credit exceeded 60 days.

In the same way, through reference eight of 86, there was a claim of the Staff Side for revision of House Rent Allowance and City Compensatory Allowance to all the 32 lakh employees. The government did not accept the demand in view of heavy estimated expenditure. But the employees insisted on the demand in view of the rise in the cost of living particularly in towns and cities. The Board partly accepted the claim after full three years on January 1, 1989, with effect from the date of disagreement recorded *i.e.,* on January 15, 1986.

It is understandable from the point of long term and large scale financial implications, where lakhs of employees were involved when the Official Side delayed and dodged to negotiate and agree to the Staff Side. In one case (encashment of earned leave) after six years of negotiation, the Official Side almost agreed to a draft scheme, but at the government level, it was rejected for want of finances. When it was referred to the arbitration, it took three years, but almost accepted the claim of the Staff Side as it was agreed to by the Official Side on the negotiation table in the National Council. Thus, the government acquired more time but finally, the matter could be clinched only after ten years.

In three cases, where millions of employees were involved, the Board of Arbitration definitely favoured the Staff Side, with slight modification of the claim, but not at the loss of prestige of the Official

Side. The Official Side might be well aware of the implications of referring the issues to the Arbitration. Yet, they were referred to the arbitration, as the government did not accept them for want of finances but not prestige. Thus, the Staff Side might appear to have gained through but, the arbitration has not treated roughly the stand of the Official Side. An estimate of gains and losses in the final analysis may be very difficult. The point is the rules of the game are accepted, while maintaining the principles of negotiation, in which the balancing role has been very affectively played by the fairness of the arbitration. Thus, some sort of balance is maintained by the arbitration for furtherance of mutual negotiations. The awards of the Board, though clearly favoured the Staff Side yet finally, more than 50 per cent of cases fell in the "Zone of Compromise"[22] as they were partly accepted.

Implementation of Awards

According to clause 21 of the JCM Scheme, the recommendations of the Board to Arbitration are binding on both the sides, subject to the over-riding authority of Parliament.

If, for reasons to be recorded in writing, the government is of opinion that the recommendations of Board of Arbitration should, on grounds affecting 'national economy' or 'social justice' be modified, the government as soon as possible shall lay before each House of the Parliament, the report of the Board containing such recommendations together with the modifications proposed and the reasons therefore, and there upon Parliament may make such modification in the recommendations as it may deem fit. Modification may extend to the rejection of a recommendation. Thus, the theory of the sovereignty of the State is retained vesting the final right with Parliament to reject or modify any of the awards of the Board of Arbitration. While the details of the JCM Scheme were discussed by the Ministers and the leaders of various employees' organisations, nobody expressed any doubt about this final authority of Parliament, as this Clause was borrowed in letter and spirit from the theory and practice of Whitley System in UK.

The Staff Side of the National Council, in the meeting of the standing committee held on April 12, 1985 raised the issue of non-implementation of arbitration awards in letter and spirit of JCM Scheme and particularly referred to the award in respect of overtime allowance to administrative staff, which the government had neither rejected nor modified as required by the JCM Scheme. The government informed Parliament that the award would be referred to Pay Commission. Though it neither amounts to rejection nor modification yet it is not proper in the spirit of the JCM Scheme.

The Staff Side also complained that some awards of the Board were pending for final decision of the government for more than six months. The JCM Scheme did not specifically lay down any time-frame for implementation of the recommendations of the Board of Arbitration. The Staff Side expressed at length about the inordinate delays in arriving at a final conclusion by the government and urged that the JCM Scheme needed to be clarified in regard to the time frame for implementation of the awards.[23]

The Official Side agreed to take decision to implement or reject an award within six months of the receipt of the award. It was reported that a number of awards were treated as rejected by placing statement on the Table of the House. However, the government assured to re-examine the whole issue and take a final decision.[24]

Majority of the awards of the Board were effective from the date of signing of the disagreement. But in many cases, the recording of disagreement could not be completed before the third meeting of the Council from the date of first meeting in which the item was first discussed. Therefore, the Staff Side demanded that the date of third meeting should be taken as the date of recording disagreement.[25]

The Staff Side also complained that the Defence Ministry had issued orders modifying two awards without completing the procedure for such modification obtaining the necessary approval of the Parliament.[26]

Till 1984, only two cases concerning the Overtime Allowance and Working Hours are reported to have been taken to Parliament for modification of the Board's recommendation despite the fact that more than 81 per cent of the cases referred to the Board of Arbitration till August 1985 have really gone against the Government.[27]

Five awards[28] were not accepted by the Government and statements required under the JCM Scheme have been laid on the tables of both the Houses of Parliament.[29]

The Awards were:

(a) Overtime Allowance to the staff during Parliament Sessions in the Central Secretariat and allied offices;

(b) Raising of the upper pay limit from Rs. 750 to Rs. 900 for admissibility to Overtime Allowance to government employees holding non-gazetted post and enhancement of the rates of Overtime Allowance;

(c) Working Hours of operative staff and payment of OTA to the P&T Staff;

(d) Cash incentive to Postmen; and

(e) Encashment of half-pay leave on superannuation.

The Staff Side may not show much enthusiasm for JCM and arbitration unless all the awards are fully honoured. The government should go as far as they can to see the awards are honoured in the interest of the staff.

Time Taken by the Arbitration

Either the time taken in the government (between the concerned department and the Ministry of Labour) or time taken in submitting the statements by the parties or time taken for *hearing,* or time taken by the Board to issue the Award after *hearing,* whatever it may be, on an average the time taken to get an award was 20 months. In 25 per cent of the cases the time taken was about 40 months for each reference. It is unduly a very long time. However, in most cases, the benefit of the references was given with retrospective effective from the date of disagreement recorded.

An analysis of 64 Awards (during 1968-73), the Board of Arbitration took on an average 13 months in each case to give its award. In 27 (42 per cent) cases, it took more than 13 months and in One-Third of the cases more than 18 months.[30] The delay was mostly due to the long time taken by both the parties to submit their statements and presenting their case as it involved collection of information from different agencies which was not readily available at one place. From the date of reference to the date of hearing in more than 50 per cent of the references it took more than twelve months. However, after the final hearing by the Board, it took about one month on an average in each case to give its award.

In the final analysis, in 64 per cent of the references, the time taken was more than two years in each case. Though, the time taken was too long, no displeasure was expressed from the Staff Side. The duration of the reference and the award can be reduced over a period of time, when much of the information is made available in the departments and from the Staff Side. The delay can be reduced further in the Board of Arbitration by making both sides expedite submission of their statements. Eventhough many awards were given with retrospective effect from the case of disagreement recorded, the benefit given after much delay would not reduce the strained relations between the two Sides and not increase faith in the practice of Compulsory Arbitration. Therefore, it is imperative to reduce unnecessary delay at every level of arbitration.

To sum up, compulsory arbitration in practice[32] under the JCM Scheme yielded good results to the Staff Side as the awards of arbitration clearly favoured the claims of the Staff Side and benefited lakhs of employees.

The Board of Arbitration could not decide the cases quickly for variety of reasons, particularly lack of cooperation from both the parties to the case.

The Staff Side avoided confrontation at Board's level and wisely withdrew the cases from the Board and settled some of them amicably outside the Board.

The Government, on its part, though did not reject outright the awards, it delayed the implementation part. Therefore, it may be desirable to stipulate the maximum period for implementation.

A perusal of the references and the analysis of awards indicate that many cases could have been settled at the negotitation level to avoid unnecessary arbitration. Therefore, to resolve the disputes more effectively by better Joint Consultation and Negotiation rather than by resorting to Compulsory Arbitration.

References

1. S.J. Frankel, "Arbitration in the British Civil Service", *Public Administration,* Vol. XXXVIII, Autumn 1960.
2. A.W.R. Carrothers, *Labour Arbitration in Canada,* Toronto, Butterworths, 1961, p.178.
3. K.N. Subramanian, *Labour Management Relations in India,* London, Asia Publishing House, 1967, p. 362.
4. *Ibid.,* Also see *Report of the National Commission on Labour,* New Delhi, Government of India, 1969, pp. 373-74.
5. At the instance of the All-India Railwaymen's Federation (AIRF), the government set up a one-men ad hoc Tribunal in 1953, consisting of Shri Sanker Saran, Retired Judge of the Allahabad High Court. It submitted its report in October, 1958. The award on all items was accepted by the government. The Second Tribunal was appointed in 1969 to report on eight items of differences between the National Federation of Indian Railwaymen (NFIR) and the Railway Board. The Railway Labour Tribunal was presided over by Shri Miabhoy, retired Chief Justice of the Gujarat High Court, as one-man Tribunal. The report was presented in August, 1972. All the recommendations of the tribunal were accepted. In 1973, the Third Tribunal was set up to adjudicate upon five issues between AIRF and the Railway Board.
6. *Report of the Central Pay Commission,* New Delhi, Government of India Press, 1950, p. 118.
7. *Ibid.,* p. 128.
8. For details see V. Bhaskara Rao, *Employer-Employee Relations,* Delhi, Concept Publications, 1978, pp. 30-31.
9. *Report of the Commission of Enquiry on Emoluments and Conditions of Service of Central Government Employees, 1957-59.* New Delhi, Ministry of Finance, Government of India, pp. 549-50.
10. Clause 7(*i*), (*ii*) and (*iii*) of the JCM Scheme.
11. For details, see P.A. James and V. Bhaskara Rao, "The Second Strike by Central Government Employees: Some Demands", *Journal of National Academy of Administration,* Vol. IV, No. 7, January-March 1970, pp. 37-42.
12. For details, see P.A. James and V. Bhaskara Rao, "The Second Strike by Central Government Employees: Some Issues", *Indian Journal of Industrial Relations,* Vol. 5, No. 1, July 1969.
13. *Report of the National Commission on Labour, op. cit.,* p. 376.
14. For details, see V. Bhaskara Rao, "Civil Service Staff Relations in Government of India", *Administrative Change,* Vol. 4, No. 2, January/June, 1973.

15. *Report of the Sub-Committee of the National Council,* September 11, 1989.
16. In one reference (*i.e.*, 3 of 1990), the Staff Side failed to submit its statement even after two years. After repeated reminders, the Board decided the reference as 'No Dispute' case.
17. Justice K.N. Wanchoo (1968-75); Justice J.S. Bedi (1976-78); Justice Jaswanth Singh (1989-81); Justice H.N. Kapoor (1982-84); Justice M.L. Jain (1984-85); Justice K. Bhaskaran (1985-90) and Justice Mahesh Chandra (1990).
18. G Ramanujam, Homi F. Daji, S.M. Joshi, Peter Alvares, K.H. Kulkarni, Bagaram Tulpule, S.R. Vasavada, Shanti G Patel, (Mrs.) Maitreyee, and Gopeshwar.
19. During 1974, the All-India Railwaymen Federation (AIRF), went on strike from May 8 to 28, 1974. National 'Emergency' was declared during 1975-77. Consequently, the JCM at different levels was not active.
20. Only 14 Department Councils were constituted against 21, till 1974. But many have not functioned effectively due to 1968 strike and 1974 strike by Railway Employees. By 1991, 25 Departmental Councils have been constituted.
21. Cases pending in 1971 (17), 1972 (15), 1973 (30), 1982 (30), 1983 (28), 1984 (15) and 13 during 1987-89 and 15 in 1992.
22. Frankel designated these awards as the "Zone of Compromise" between the Official and Staff Sides. See S.J. Frankel, *Arbitration in the British Civil Service, op. cit.*, p. 206.
23. *Minutes of the 27th Ordinary Meeting of the National Council,* July 10-11, 1985.
24. *Minutes of the Meeting of the Standing Committee* held on March 7, 1990. For details, see *JCM Bulletin,* June 1990.
25. *JCM Bulletin.* January 1990, pp. 5-7.
26. *Ibid., pp. 5-6; and Minutes of the Standing Committee* held on October 3, 1989.
27. Bata K. Dey, "Conflict-Management in Government—JCM Style", *Indian Journal of Public Administration,* Vol. XXXI, No. 3, July-September, 1985, p. 621.
28. These were: 3/80, 9(*a*)/80, 6/81, 14/81 and 1/88.
29. On 16-12-83, 25-8-84, 18-8-87, 19-11-87, 1-3-88 and 29-3-88.
30. V. Bhaskara Rao, *Employer-Employee Relations, op. cit.*, pp. 179-80.
31. *Ibid.*, pp. 182-83.
32. For details, V. Bhaskara Rao, *Arbitration in Public Service,* Khama Publishers, New Delhi, 1995.

3

Intellectuals' Perception and Attitudes Towards a Public Policy : A Study of Six Point Formula in Andhra Pradesh*

The state of Andhra Pradesh was formed in 1956 as a result of the states reorganisation on the linguistic basis, by integrating the nine districts of erstwhile Hyderabad state, popularly known as Telangana with the State of Andhra. The struggle for a united state for Telugu speaking people was a long cherished desire and ultimately resulted in the formation of Andhra Pradesh, yet there were a few lurking doubts in the minds of Telangana people and their leaders about the cultural and economic gaps between advanced Andhras and backward Telanganites. With all inhibitions in their minds the Telangana leaders accepted the united state, partly due to charismatic leadership of Nehru and partly due to certain safeguards to protect the interests of Telangana people in the shape of a "Gentleman's Agreement".[1]

The inhibitions that were lingering continued to pervade the Telangana people even after fifteen years. It appears, that the linguistic, and cultural homogenity have failed to serve as the basis for the state systems, the common language and history were found not enough to keep the people of the state together. The backward regions could not be developed; implying that the state leadership had not paid due attention to the development of backward regions. Hence separation of such regions is considered essential for the development.[2] It may be observed that the sentimental unity based on the common language failed under the strain of interacting group interests, and revealed powerfully the sub-regional rivalries generated by economic imbalances and genuine accumulated grievances.[3]

* Co-authored with Shri M. Kistaiah.

In 1968 the safeguards were due to expire and there was a peaceful agitation for their renewal, but both the Andhra Pradesh High Court and the Supreme Court decided that the safeguards were constitutionally invalid. This added fuel to mounting agitation as by that time the demand for a separate Telangana State became dominant and the call for reinforced safeguards was overshadowed.[4]

To start with the agitation was peaceful and passive but took violent turn for various reasons, notable being the active participation of the students, the Government Employees, and the dissatisfied politicians forcing K. Brahmananda Reddy to resign his Chief Ministership in spite of the Eight Point Formula.[5] He handed over the power to P.V. Narasimha Rao, a Telanganite, to preserve the unity of the State.

In the short regime of Narasimha Rao two important events took place. One was that the High Court of Andhra Pradesh struck down the Mulki Rules as void of the Constitution. The other one was an appeal preferred to the Supreme Court, by the Government of Andhra Pradesh against the judgement of the High Court which was reversed by upholding the Mulki Rules. This opportunity was availed of by various interests of the Andhra region to agitate for the scrapping of the Mulki Rules, which ultimately turned into an agitation for separate Andhra.[6] The violent situation compelled the Government of India to persuade the leadership of the state to accept the Five Point Formula[7] as a solution to protect the integrated state. However, the leaders of the Andhra Region gave up the formula under the influence of mass reaction and most of the Ministers of Andhra region resigned. As a result of uncontrollable agitation in Andhra area, the President's Rule was imposed in the State in January 1973.[8]

The popular government was installed ending the one year President's Rule after protracted discussions between the State and Central party Leaders and relentless persuation by the central leadership to solve the problems of the state through the Six Point Formula.

The Six Point Formula envisages :[9]

(1) Accelerated development of backward areas of the state by constituting a Planning Board at the State level and Sub-Committee for different backward areas.

(2) Preference to the local candidates in the matter of admission to educational institutions and establishment of a new Central University at Hyderabad.

(3) Local candidates should be given preference to specified extent in the matter of direct recruitment subject to the requirements of the state as a whole.

(4) Constitution of high power administrative tribunal to deal with grievances of services regarding appointments, promotion and other allied matters.

(5) Amendment of the Constitution suitably to ensure the implementation of the above principles.

(6) Abolition of Mulki Rules and Telangana Regional Committee.

The decision of the Government of India to solve the vexed problem of Andhra and Telangana through the Six Point Formula has wider implications. The people and the leaders of both the regions tried their strength separately in the streets as well as in the legislature for the bifurcation of the state and they were vexed with the problem. Solution to such an important problem like the Mulki Rules should have been properly diagnosed after careful study of the pulse of the people. The Mulki Rules dispute was discussed and solution obtained through the channels of the political party not through the administrative machinery; nor from direct sources *i.e.*, the public.[10]

In view of the above observations, the study seeks to survey and evaluate conclusions of a research, based on a limited but a comparative sample of college teachers at two places. The study has three parts and the comparative data has been processed and the analysed in an overall research design, seeking to answer the following three questions :

(1) How far the people at large and intellectuals in particular have understood the formula with all its attendant implications ?

(2) What is their reaction to the Formula ?

(3) What according to them are their preferences for integration or bifurcation and about the future of the State.

The study in our knowledge is first of its kind in evaluating attitudes and the perception of the elite towards the Six Point Formula as a solution to the problem of the bifurcation demand of the people from both the regions.

The teachers[11] in Arts and Science Colleges of different disciplines are selected for the purpose of this study, since they represent one of the most powerful segments of the society, as they are highly educated, working in the centres of knowledge and responsible for moulding the future citizens of the nation. As academicians, the teachers are expected to keep abreast of the current social problems in different walks of life. Although, they do not play an active role in the day to day events, yet, their contribution in solving the problems through debate, discussions and analysis has its own impact, for, they are expected to give an intellectual lead to the community.

For the purposes of a comparative study two towns have been selected, Warangal and Khammam in the Telangana region of Andhra Pradesh, to highlight the issues in a comprehensive manner. Warangal and Khammam are the district Head Quarters of Warangal and Khammam districts respectively. Warangal is the second biggest city in Telangana region next to the capital of Andhra Pradesh, while Khammam bordering the Andhra region, is small in size. The city of Warangal has been recognized as a centre of higher education having Medical, Engineering and several Arts and Science and other Technical Colleges and the Post Graduate Centre, whereas in Khammam there are only four colleges of Arts and Sciences.

There are about 250 college teachers working in three university colleges—(P.G. Centre, two Arts Colleges), three Government Colleges (One College of Education, Two Degree Colleges—one for boys and one for women) and two private colleges in Warangal. In Khammam, there are 125 college teachers spread over in two Government and two private colleges (one for women).

The city of Warangal and the college teachers in particular were selected for the study because, both the people of the city and the college teachers[12] along with the students and government NGO's agitated for separate Telangana state in 1968-1970.

Various relationship factors with the Andhra region made the people of Khammam to play a prominent role for the movement of Vishalandra. A hunger strike in Khammam by college student in 1969 for the Telangana safeguards, incidentally spread the seeds of agitation for bifurcation all over the Telangana region. However, the vigour and the impact of the agitation was not felt much, because, mostly they were either indifferent or inclined towards difurcation of the state. It is pertinent to note that the present Chief Minister, J. Vengal Rao, hails from the same district. It was alleged that he was connected with the hunger strike.[13] Subsequently, he became the Home Minister in the thick of the agitation and was known for his ruthless suppression of the agitation. Emerging as a strong leader he accepted the onerous responsibility of implementing the Six Point Formula for the protection of the integrated state.

Out of the 250 college teachers from Warangal we interviewed in privacy, as ample of 150 [60 per cent and 100 (80 per cent)] from Khammam at random through a structured questionnaire which is partly close ended and partly open ended.

Table 1 explains the satisfaction of the solution and preference of the state either for integration or for bifurcation, age-wise. It can be seen from the table that in Warangal teachers of all the age groups were dissatisfied with the formula, more so, in the age brackets of 26-50. The general dissatisfaction among them constitute about 71 per cent of the sample. While in Khammam the dissatisfaction is only 49 per cent, it is very high in the age groups of 36-45. It is important to note that at both the places, 9 per cent at Khammam and about 3 per cent at Warangal do not know anything about the solution. Although this is not significant, it may be attributed, either to their indifference towards the problem or most of the respondents in this category were women.[14]

In spite of the general dissatisfaction at both the places, it is interesting to note about 47 per cent and 77 per cent of the respondent at Warangal and Khammam respectively preferred the united state. The remaining i.e. 53 per cent and 23 per cent wanted a bifurcated state.

Tables 2 and 2 'A' explain caste-wise satisfaction of the solution, degree of participation in the agitation and preference of the state.

In both the agitations the caste groups participated and agitated for their vested interests.[15] A considerable sample reacted sharply towards the relevance of the caste to the problem. In Warangal about 57 per cent belonged to forward castes of which 27 per cent constituted Brahmins, followed by Reddies with 14 per cent. About 68 per cent Brahmins did not participate in the agitation, yet were dissatisfied with the solution but 56 percent preferred a united state. Though 66 percent of Kammas participated in the agitation only 50 per cent of them were dissatisfied with the solution and surprisingly 66 per cent of them preferred a united state. True to the fact that 62 per cent of Reddies participated in the agitation, 85 percent were not satisfied with the solution and obiviously 71 percent preferred bifurcation. Another powerful caste, Velamas did not participate (62 per cent), at the same time were not satisfied with the solution, but preferred bifurcation. The Vysya participation is negligible but their dissatisfaction and preference for bifurcation is very high. The remaining 43 per cent belonging to the minority communities, are dissatisfied. But about 6 per cent (Kapu and Padmashali), participated in the agitation and their preference for bifurcation is noticeable.

At Khammam 70 per cent of our sample is dominated by the forward castes, led by Brahmins with 39 per cent and Kammas with 16 percent. Except Kammas all caste groups were dissatisfied with the solution. The participation in the agitation of all the castes is practically nil. Surprisingly, all the castes, forward and backward preferred an united state except 1 per cent of the Velamas.

A comparative study of the two Tables reveals that the general impression of attributing motives to the forward castes for the agitation is not correct. Because, the caste groups, at least intellectuals belonging to such castes reacted differently at two places. In this respect, it appears, that the earlier writers on the agitation were carried

Table 1

Satisfaction of the Solution and Preference of the State—age-wise

Sl. No.	Age	Warangal						Khammam					
			Satisfaction			Preference			Satisfaction			Preference	
		N	Yes %	No %	Dk %	United %	Bifur-cated	N %	Yes %	No %	Dk %	United %	Bifurcated %
1	2	3	4	5	6	7	8	9	10	11	12	13	14
1.	21-25	20	45.00	55.00	Nil	60.00	40.00	21	47.61	33.33	19.04	76.19	23.81
2.	26-30	54	25.92	74.08	Nil	40.74	59.26	23	43.47	43.47	13.04	95.65	4.35
3.	31-35	26	26.92	69.23	3.84	50.00	50.00	20	45.00	45.00	10.00	75.00	25.00
4.	36-40	30	16.66	76.66	6.66	46.66	53.34	17	29.41	70.59	Nil	70.59	29.41
5.	41-45	10	10.00	80.00	10.00	50.00	50.00	13	15.38	84.61	Nil	53.84	46.16
6.	46-50	8	12.50	75.00	12.50	37.50	62.50	5	100.00	Nil	Nil	100.00	Nil
7.	51-55	2	50.00	50.00	Nil	50.00	50.00	1	100.00	Nil	Nil	Nil	100.00
	Total	150	25.33	71.33	3.33	46.66	53.34	100	42.00	49.00	9.00	77.00	23.00

Table 2

Satisfaction of the Solution, Participation in the Agitation and Preference of the State—Caste-wise

Sl.No.	*Caste*	*Satisfaction*			*Participation in the Agiration*			*Preference of the State*		
		Warangal			*Warangal*			*Warangal*		
		DK %	*Yes %*	*No %*	*Active %*	*Passive %*	*No. %*	*United %*	*Bifurcated %*	*Total N=150 %*
1	*2*	*3*	*4*	*5*	*6*	*7*	*8*	*9*	*10*	*11*
1.	Brahmin	Nil	31.71	68.30	2.44	29.27	68.29	56.09	43.91	27.34
2.	Khamma	16.66	33.34	50.00	16.66	50.00	33.34	66.66	33.34	4.00
3.	Reddy	Nil	14.28	85.72	33.33	28.57	38.09	28.58	71.42	14.00
4.	Velama	Nil	37.50	62.50	25.00	12.50	62.50	50.00	50.00	5.34
5.	Vysya	11.12	Nil	88.88	Nil	33.34	66.66	22.23	77.77	6.00
6.	Kapu	20.00	Nil	80.00	20.00	80.00	Nil	Nil	100.00	3.33
7.	Padmasali	Nil	Nil	100.00	60.00	20.00	20.00	20.00	80.00	3.33
8.	Others	2.23	31.11	66.66	17.79	33.33	48.88	51.11	48.89	30.00
9.	Christians	Nil	25.00	75.00	Nil	Nil	100.00	100.00	Nil	2.66
10.	Muslims	16.67	33.33	50.00	16.67	33.33	50.00	50.00	50.00	4.00
	Total	3.33	25.33	71.33	16.00	31.33	52.66	46.66	53.34	100.00

Table 2 'A'

Satisfaction of the Solution, Participation in the Agitation and Preference of the State—Caste-wise

Sl.No.	*Caste*	*Satisfaction*			*Participation in the Agiration*			*Preference of the State*		
		Khammam			*Khammam*			*Khammam*		
		DK %	*Yes %*	*No %*	*Active %*	*Passive %*	*No. %*	*United %*	*Bifurcated %*	*Total N=100 %*
1	*2*	*3*	*4*	*5*	*6*	*7*	*8*	*9*	*10*	*11*
1.	Brahmin	7.69	43.58	48.71	5.12	15.40	79.48	76.92	23.08	39.00
2.	Khamma	12.50	50.00	37.50	Nil	6.25	93.75	87.50	12.50	16.00
3.	Reddy	Nil	25.00	75.00	Nil	Nil	100.00	75.00	25.00	4.00
4.	Velama	Nil	Nil	100.00	Nil	100.00	Nil	Nil	100.00	1.00
5.	Vysya	10.00	30.00	60.00	10.00	10.00	80.00	60.00	40.00	10.00
6.	Kapu	Nil	42.85	57.14	Nil	Nil	100.00	85.71	14.29	7.00
7.	Others	6.25	50.00	43.75	6.25	Nil	93.75	81.25	18.75	16.00
8.	Christians	40.00	20.00	40.00	Nil	Nil	100.00	60.00	40.00	5.00
	Total :	9.00	42.00	49.00	4.00	9.00	87.00	77.00	23.00	100.00

away by the general mass impressions. In our view, caste is only one of the several factors for the agitation but not the major factor.

Table 3 identifies the university degrees obtained before 1968 and after 1968. It was assumed that there should be some different reaction towards the problem between the degree holders before 68 and after 68, for, those who have taken degrees after 1968 witnessed the process of din and bustle of the agitation, but to our surprise respondents in both the categories at both the places reacted almost equally. At the same time it is to be noted that in Warangal, 53 per cent of degree holders before 1968 opted for a united state, and 63 per cent degree holders after 1968 opted bifurcation. While in Khammam, it is interesting to note that 85 per cent degree holders after 1968 preferred united state showing a significant improvement of 15 per cent over pre-1968 degree holders.

Table 4 reveals that 75 per cent of the respondents at Warangal are natives of Telangana while the percentage of dissatisfaction among the total respondents is 77 per cent. Not only in natives but also those who settled down 10 years back and earlier were also dissatisfied both at Warangal and Khammam to the extent of 66 per cent and 57 per cent respectively. Except the natives at Warangal, all other categories are for promoting the cause of a united state while in Khammam the natives and the settlers (75 per cent) wish to live in a united state. About 24 per cent and 45 per cent of the sample at Warangal and Khammam respectively, are non-Mulkies who came from outside the Telangana region, mostly from the Andhra area in search of employment, preferred united state. A close observation of the table indicates that 45 per cent of the teachers, working mostly in the Private Colleges are Non-Mulkies. 25 per cent of them at Khammam came to the place during and after the agitation and altogether 16 per cent of them did not have any idea about the solution, but 76 per cent preferred a united state.

Table 3
Satisfaction of the Solution, Preference of the State, Degree Obtained

Sl.No.	Name of the University	Warangal						Khammam						
		N	DK %	Satisfied %	Dissatisfied %	United %	Bifurcated %	N	DK %	Satisfied %	Dissatisfied %	United %	Bifurcated %	Total %
1	2	3	4	5	6	7	8	9	10	11	12	13	14	15
	BEFORE 1968													
1.	Osmania	71	5.63	19.71	74.66	50.70	49.30	40	Nil	45.00	55.00	70.00	30.00	75.51
2.	Andhra & S.V.	9	Nil	22.22	77.78	55.55	44.55	6	20.00	30.00	50.00	60.00	40.00	10.20
3.	Southern Universities	3	Nil	66.66	33.34	66.66	33.34	4	Nil	50.00	50.00	50.00	50.00	4.76
4.	Northern Universities	5	20.00	20.20	60.00	80.00	20.00	9	11.11	55.55	33.34	88.88	11.12	9.52
	Total	88	5.68	21.59	72.73	53.40	46.60	59	3.38	45.76	50.86	71.18	28.82	100.00
	AFTER 1968													
1.	Osmania	60	Nil	28.33	71.67	35.00	65.00	10	30.00	30.00	40.00	100.00	Nil	67.96
2.	Andhra & S.V.	Nil	Nil	Nil	Nil	Nil	Nil	18	Nil	55.55	44.45	83.33	16.17	17.47
3.	Southern Universities	Nil	Nil	Nil	Nil	Nil	Nil	1	Nil	Nil	100.00	10.00	Nil	0.97
4.	Northern Universities	2	Nil	100.00	Nil	100.00	Nil	12	33.33	16.66	51.01	75.00	25.00	13.59
	Total	62	Nil	30.64	69.36	37.09	62.91	41	17.07	36.58	46.34	85.36	14.64	100.00

Table 4

Satisfaction of the Solution and Preference of the State—Residence-wise

Sl. No.	*Length of Residence*	*Satisfaction*			*Preference*		
		DK %	*Yes %*	*No %*	*United %*	*Bifur-cated %*	*Total N=150 %*
1	*2*	*3*	*4*	*5*	*6*	*7*	*8*
Warangal							
1.	Below 5 years	Nil	66.66	33.34	66.66	33.34	2.00
2.	Between 5 and 10 years	Nil	60.00	40.00	80.00	20.00	6.66
3.	Above 10 years	8.34	25.00	66.66	62.50	37.50	16.00
4.	Since birth	2.66	21.24	77.10	39.82	60.18	75.34
Khammam							
							Total N=100
1.	Below 5 years	16.00	40.00	44.00	76.00	24.00	25.00
2.	Between 5 and 10 years	Nil	50.00	50.00	100.00	Nil	6.00
3.	Above 10 years	7.11	35.55	57.34	78.57	21.43	14.00
4.	Since birth	7.27	43.63	49.10	74.54	25.46	55.00

Table 5

Media of Awareness

Sl.No.	*Media of Awareness*	*Warangal N=150 %*	*Khammam N=100 %*
1	*2*	*3*	*4*
1.	Radio	72.00	65
2.	News Papers	90.66	95
3.	Friends	14.66	16
4.	Formal Leaders like M.L.A., M.P. etc.	8.00	1

Note: Percentage do not tally because of multiple answers.

Table 6
Knowledge of the Six Point Formula

Sl. No.	*Knowledge of the Six Points*	*Warangal N=150 %*	*Khammam N=100 %*	*Total N=250 %*
1	*2*	*3*	*4*	*5*
1.	All the six points	Nil	Nil	Nil
2.	Five points	2.66	7	4.40
3.	Four points	20.00	16	18.40
4.	Three points	20.67	17	19.20
5.	Two points	26.67	11	20.40
6.	One point	10.00	10	10.00
7.	None	20.00	39	27.60
	Total	100.00	100.00	100.00

It is interesting to observe from Table 6 that out of our 250 respondents none has the complete knowledge of the six points. At the same time 20 per cent and 39 per cent Warangal and Khammam respectively do not have the knowledge of any of the points in the formula. 20 per cent and 16 per cent could explain only four points. 10 per cent in both the places could recollect only one point in the Formula. It may be seen from Table 5, that though more than 90 per cent had the privilege of going through the newspapers and more than 65 per cent of them were listeners of Radio, it appears that they did not give a serious thought to a very important public problem.

Time and again the State and Central Leaders made public statements to the effect that the formula was accepted by one and all. That prompted us to know the reasons for the satisfaction and the dissatisfaction of the intellectuals about the Formula. As explained earlier in Table 1, there is large scale general dissatisfaction at both the places and more at Warangal.

Table 7 indicates the near unanimity among those satisfied with the formula. They felt that the formula would maintain the integration

Table 7

Reasons for Satisfaction/Dissatisfaction of the Six Point Formula

Sl. No.	*Satisfied with the solution*			*Not-satisfied with the solution*		
	Reasons	*Warangal N=38 %*	*Khammam N=42 %*	*Reasons*	*Warangal N=107 %*	*Khammam N=49 %*
1	*2*	*3*	*4*	*5*	*6*	*7*
1.	Maintains Integration	52.63	52.38	Temporary measure	38.31	40.81
2.	Satisfied the people	10.52	9.52	Politically motivated	31.77	36.73
3.	All round development	26.31	9.52	Does't fulfil desires of Telangana people	39.25	38.77
4.	More Employment opportunities	13.15	4.76	Divided the state into Blocks (21)	6.54	4.08
5.	Avoid disturbances in the state	2.63	7.14	Not practicable	2.80	4.08
6.	No definite reasons	15.78	14.28	No definite reasons	8.41	Nil

Note: The total does not tally because of multiple answers.

of the State, because it satisfied the people, ensured more development, would provide ample employment opportunities and avoid possible disturbances. Some even felt that it would lead to abolition of anchronistic Mulki Rules which prevented the emotional integration among Telugu people. Yet some others are satisfied with the solution preferring the larger states as it appeared to be the best under the present circumstances.

There is equal unanimity among those dissatisfied with the solution. They stated that it a temporary measure, politically motivated and does not fulfil the desires of Telangana people. Some of them also felt bad because the formula would result in the creation of 21 employment zones almost blocking the desired mobility.

The intellectuals who are expected to give lead through discussion and debate to the pressing problems of the society, appear to be totally apathetic towards the formula and its implications, because it could be observed from Table 8 a large percentage (more than 40 per cent) have not discussed the problem with anybody. A microscopic minority had the privilege of discussing the issue with

Table 8

The Problem Discussed

Sl. No.	*Discussed with*	*Agreed with the Respondent*		*Opinion Divided*	
		Warangal N = 89 %	*Khammam N = 56 %*	*Warangal N = 89 %*	*Khammam N=56 %*
1	*2*	*3*	*4*	*5*	*6*
1.	Formal political leaders like M.L.A., M.P., etc.	8.99	3.57	5.62	3.57
2.	Friends	62.92	55.35	34.83	33.93
3.	Relations	23.59	19.80	15.73	18.20
4.	Service Unions	8.99	9.10	6.74	12.53
5.	Others	10.11	7.14	4.49	5.35
6.	None	40.66*	40.00**		

Note : * N = 150, **N = 100.

The total does not tally because of multiple answers.

Table 9

The most appealing point in the Formula

Sl. No.	*Preferred Point*	*Warangal N = 150 %*	*Khammam N = 100 %*	*Total N = 250 %*
1	*2*	*3*	*4*	*5*
1.	Development Boards	11.33	16.00	13.20
2.	Central University	16.66	14.00	15.60
3.	Regional Employment	16.00	11.00	14.00
4.	Administrative Tribunals	0.67	1.00	0.80
5.	Constitutional Amendment	Nil	Nil	Nil
6.	Abolition of Mulki and T.R.C.	4.67	7.00	5.60
7.	None	30.67	12.00	23.20
8.	Do not know	20.00	39.00	27.60
	Total	100.00	100.00	100.00

the politicians. Majority of the sample, however, discussed the problem in a closed circle of friends and relations, who have agreed to the respondents barring a negligible section that held a divided opinion.

Table No. 9 makes clear that a greater percentage of the sample did not know anything of the formula, and for some, no point in the formula was an attraction. Among those who understood the forumla as solution, some mentioned the Central University, Regionwise Employment and Development Boards, as salient but a minor section was attracted by the abolition of Mulki Rules and the Telangana Regional Committee. None seem to be convinced about two of the Six Points like setting up of an Administrative Tribunal and Constitutional Amendment.

To disentangle the vexed problem of Andhra and Telangana several solutions were offered from time to time by the central leaders. In order to assess the attitudes of the respondents towards the solutions, we administered a question whether the Six Point

Formula was an improvement over the earlier Formulae. Surprisingly, it could be seen from Table 10, the response was very poor, because about 24 per cent and 33 per cent of them, from Warangal and Khammam respectively did not have any knowledge of the earlier Formulae. Among those who said Six Point Formula was an improvement felt that it would benefit the people in the shape of providing more educational facilities, more development and solve the problems of unemployment and that of the employees in an integrated state.

For many all formulae meant the same thing and they felt that the problem could only be solved through separation of the state. Their percentage is very high at both the places exceeding 85 per cent at Warangal and 74 per cent at Khammam. This 85 per cent and 74 per cent includes three categories viz, none of the points is acceptable, all formulae are same and no definite reasons are given.

We asked our respondents, irrespective of their participation in the agitation about their reaction to an imaginary agitation against the Six Point Formula. The non-participation in the last agitation at Khammam is very high compared to Warangal where the participation is 47 per cent. Table 11 shows that except those who participated in the agitation actively, by giving lectures, courting arrest etc., others preferred to oppose or be indifferent or be neutral to the agitation against Six Point Formula. An equal percentage of them could not decide about their attitude towards the agitation right now and felt that depending on the issues at stake and circumstances they would decide about it.

Since mass reaction about the formula was difficult to ascertain, it was felt desirable to gather the attitude of the masses through our intelligentia. Although it suffers with certain limitations, Table 12 depicts the intellectuals' impressions about the mass attitude. It is interesting to note that about 23 per cent and 28 per cent of our respondents at both the places have not maintained any contact with the masses and as such they are oblivious to mass reaction. At both the places respondents opined that the people were not aware of the formula or its implications because they were either indifferent or influenced more by politicians.

Table 10

The Perception of the Respondents whether the Six Point Formula is an Improvement over the earlier ones like Eight Point and Five Point Formulae

Sl. No.	YES (It benefits the people) Reasons	Warangal N = 46 %	Khammam N = 36 %	NO (Which point is acceptable in all the three formulae)	Warangal N = 68 %	DK about 8 and 5: Kham-mam N =31	DK about 8 and 5: Warangal N = 36 %	DK about 8 and 5: Kham-mam N = 33 %
1	*2*	*3*	*4*	*5*	*6*	*7*	*8*	*9*
1.	More educational facilities	32.61	Nil	None	28.21	32.26	24.00	33.00
2.	More Development	32.61	25.00	All are same and wants total separation	39.71	Nil		
3.	Total Integration/satisfied both the regions	26.08	33.33	Regional Development Boards	2.94	9.67		
4.	Solves the employees problems	17.39	8.33	Regionwise employment	5.88	6.93		
5.	Solves the employment through regionalisation	15.22	27.77	Central University	2.94	19.35		
6.	Abolition of Mulki Rules	13.04	8.33	Abolition of Mulki Rules	1.47	9.67		
7.	No definite reasons	4.35	11.11	No definite reasons	17.65	41.13		
	Total	30.66 N = 150	36.00 N = 100		45.34 N = 150	31.00 N = 100	24.00 N = 150	33.00 N = 100

Note : The Total does not tally because of multiple answers.

Table 11

Degree of Participation in the Last Agitation for Bifurcation and their Reaction towards the Agitation against the Six Point Formula

Sl. No.	*Degree of Participation in the agitation*	*Reaction towards the agitation against the 6 point formula*												*Total of cols. 13%14*
		Positive		*Oppose*		*Neutal*		*Indifferent*		*Can't Say*		*Total*		
		Warangal N = 35	*Khammam N = 8*	*Warangal N = 20*	*Khammam N = 19*	*Warangal N = 38*	*Khammam N = 28*	*Warangal N = 16*	*Khammam N = 17*	*Warangal N = 41*	*Khammam N = 28*	*Warangal N = 150*	*Khammam N =100*	*N = 250*
		%	%	%	%	%	%	%	%	%	%	%	%	%
1	*2*	*3*	*4*	*5*	*6*	*7*	*8*	*9*	*10*	*11*	*12*	*13*	*14*	*15*
1.	Active	58.33	25.00	12.50	25.00	8.33	25.00	8.33	Nil	12.50	25.00	16.00	4.00	11.20
2.	Passive	23.40	11.11	12.76	22.22	17.02	22.22	8.60	11.11	38.29	33.33	31.33	9.00	22.40
3.	Not participated	12.65	6.89	13.92	18.39	35.44	28.73	12.65	18.39	25.30	27.58	52.67	97.04	66.40
	Total	23.33	8.00	13.33	19.00	25.33	28.00	10.66	17.00	27.33	28.00	100.00	100.00	100.00

Table 12

Impressions about the Attitudes of Masses towards the Formula

Sl. No.	*Reaction of the Mass*	*Warangal N = 150 %*	*Khammam N = 100 %*	*Total N = 250 %*
1	*2*	*3*	*4*	*5*
1.	Satisfied	9.33	15	11.60
2.	Dissatisfied	26.66	18.	23.20
3.	Indifferent	13.34	12	12.80
4.	Not Aware	20.00	20.	20.00
5.	Led by Politicians	8.00	7	7.60
6.	Do not know the Mass reaction	22.67	28	24.80
	Total	100.00	100	100.00

Table 13

Problem of Andhra and Telangana

Sl. No.	*Problem of the State*	*Warangal N = 150 %*	*Khammam N = 100 %*
1.	Cannot say	10.67	19.00
2.	Settle down	20.66	30.00
3.	Settle down provided the Formula is implemented properly	4.00	8.00
4.	Erupt again	64.67	43.00
	Total	100.00	100.00

One of our most important questions was whether the Six Point Formula would settle the long pending problem of Andhra and Telangana or would there be an agitation in the future ? As mentioned earlier about the general dissatisfaction over the solution. Tables 13 and 13 'A' show that a greater percentage stated that the problem would erupt again in one form or the other because of the

Table 13 'A'

Problem of Andhra and Telangana

Sl. No.	*Problem of the State (Erupt Again)*	*Warangal N = 97 %*	*Khammam N = 43 %*
1	*2*	*3*	*4*
1.	General Mass Dissatisfaction	48.44	18.61
2.	Dissatisfied Politicians	37.11	27.91
3.	Government Employees	5.15	11.63
4.	Students and Intellectuals	9.27	Nil
5.	Government fails to implement the Formula as it happened earlier	2.06	23.26
6.	If the Formula is not implemented properly	1.03	11.63
7.	No definite Reasons	10.30	11.63

Note: Total does not tally because of the multiple answers.

Table 14

Prediction about the Future of the State and their Preference

S.No.	*Prediction and Preference*	*Warangal N=150 %*	*Khammam N=100 %*	*Total N=250 %*
1	*2*	*3*	*4*	*5*
1.	Remain united, prefers united	33.33	60	44.00
2.	Remain united, prefers bifurcated	6.67	3	5.20
3.	Have to be bifurcated, prefers united	8.67	10	9.20
4.	Have to be bifurcated, prefers bifurcated	41.33	20	32.80
5.	Cannot predict, prefers united	5.33	7	6.00
6.	Cannot predict, prefers bifurcated	4.67	nil	2.80
	Total	100.00	100	100.00

dissatisfaction among the general mass, the politicians, the Government employees and the proven inability of the Government in implementing the earlier Formulae and agreements successfully, leading to an agitation in future. Some of the staunch integrationists, though satisfied with the solution to some extent, expressed their doubts about likely intricacies that may arise in the settlement of the problem. Those who believed in a satisfactory settlement of the problem are of the opinion that the strong leadership at the Centre and the State, and the disinterestedness and the virtual loss of faith in the people to participate in further agitations would in course of time, lead to a fairly satisfactory solution of the problem to the supression and possible elimination of any untoward and unexpected eruption.

After a long, serious and violent agitation in both the regions of Andhra and Telangana for separation of the State, the people's reaction towards the Six Point Formula was in a way dismal. This situation prompted us to enquire how the respondents predict the future of the state and indicate their preference. Although certain section of the sample prefer bifurcated state, mostly at Warangal, their prediction appears contrary to their preference. Table 14 indicates, that at Khammam, the preference for the united state was as high as 77 per cent but 30 per cent predicted that the state had to be bifurcated. On the whole out of 59 per cent who preferred an united state only 49 per cent could predict that the state would remain united. Contrary to the above observation an equal percentage of about 41 and 42 preferred the bifurcated state and predicted that the state will have to be bifurcated.

Conclusion

In all respects distinct perceptions and attitudes are perceivable in the solution of the problem between Warangal and Khammam. The people at large and the intellectuals in particular have been utterly dissatisfied with the Formula. Perhaps the solution did not receive the due publicity to educate and convince the people. In our view, the earlier impressionistic analysis about the dominant role of the caste groups does not stand the test of the study. At both the places the college teachers did not evince keen interest in the Formula. Dissatisfaction to the solution is very much prevalent at both the places and it is evident that the formula is not at any rate a people's solution but one politically motivated. It is interesting to note that the reaction of the mass was dismal, and most of the respondents even though did not have any knowledge of the earlier or the present Formula, with all the dissatisfaction predict the possibility of an agitation in future. The supporters of the Formula neither have faith in the proper implementation of the Formula nor any clear understanding of its implications. The revealing point of our study is that despite the general dissatisfaction in regard to the formula, lack of faith in the politicians and the expectation of an agitation in future, there is a marked preference to live in an integrated state, at Khammam and with a little difference at Warangal.

References

1. For a detailed discussion see, K.V. Narayana Rao, *Telangana: A Study in the Regional Committees in India,* The Minerva Associates, Calcutta, 1972, and also Shriram Maheshwari," "Regionalism in India: Political and Administrative Response", *The Indian Journal of Public Administration,* Vol. XIX, No. 4. Oct-Dec. 1973, pp. 441-471.
2. C.P. Bhambhari : "The Limits", *Seminar* (164) April 1973, p. 29.
3. Rasheeduddin Khan, "The Regional Dimension", *Seminar* (164) April 1973, p. 35.
4. For detailed discussion see, Hugh Gray, "The Demand for a Separate Telangana State in India" *Asian Survey,* Vol. XII, No. 5. May 1971, pp. 463-474, Duncan B. Forrester, "Subregionalism in India: The Case of Telangana", *Pacific Affairs,* Vol. XLIII, No. 1, Spring 1970, pp. 5-21.
5. K.V. Narayana Rao *op. cit,* for Eight Point Formula, See, Appendix VI, pp. 388-91.
6. A complete and exhaustive narration of events about the Andhra agitation, was made by M.V, Rama Murthy, see, "Prathyeka Andhra Rastrodyamam", *Prasaritha,* (Telugu) Social Sciences Quarterly, Hyderabad, No. 13, July-Sept. 1973, pp. 1-136.
7. *The Hindu,* November 28, 1972, p. 9.
8. For a detailed study see, Dagmar Bernstorff, "Eclipse of "Reddy Raj?" : The Attempted Restructuring of the Congress Party Leadership in Andhra Pradesh", *Asian Survey,* Vol. XIII, No. 10, October 1973, pp. 959-979.
9. Statement issued by the leaders of Andhra Pradesh on 21 September, 1973, see *The Hindu,* 22nd September, 1973.
10. Ishwar Dayal, "Organisation for Public Policy in Government" *Indian Journal of Public Administration,* Vol. XIX, Oct.-Dec. 1973, p. 431.

11. College teachers include Professors, Principals, Readers and Lecturers.
12. The college teachers organised seminars and symposia and brought out booklets highlighting the problem of Andhra and Telangana, supporting the issue of bifurcation. See, *Telangana: A Challenge of the Masses,* Telangana Graduates Convention, Hanamakonda, July 1969.
13. K. Seshadri, "The Telangana Agitation and the Politics of Andhra Pradesh", *Indian Journal of Political Science* Jan-March 1970 and "The Rise and Fall of Telangana Praja Samithi—A Case Study", *Journal of Constitutional and Parliamentary Studies* Vol. V, No. 4, Oct-Dec. 1971, p. 680 and also "Telangana Praja Samithi: "Avirbhavam, Anthardhanam", *Prasaritha,* No. 9, July-Sept 1972, pp. 71-78, N. Innaiah, "Sarin Salahalanundi Vengala Rao Velugu Needalloki", *Prasaritha,* No. 15, Jan-March 1974, pp. 84-86, and N. Innaiah, "Power Politics in Andhra Pradesh—A News Letter" *Radical Humanist,* March 1974, pp. 1-2.
14. Generally females do not evince interest in political issues, see, G. Di. Palma, *Apathy and Participation.* The Free Press, New York, 1970, p. 137.
15. Hugh Gray, *op. cit.,* p. 467-8, and Dagmar Bernstori, *op. cit.*

4

Civil Service Staff Relations in Government of India

The need for joint consultation and staff co-operation was first recognized in India after the Second World War. The strike notices by the employees of the Railways and the P & T, immediately after the War, compelled the Government to promote a formal and a permanent negotiating machinery which will bring about cordial relations between employers and employees.

The present note examines the evolution of the civil service staff relations in the Government of India during the post-independence years, and discusses how far the government and the employees' organizations are able to deal with the complicated task of maintaining harmonious staff relations. Our analysis is devoted to the assessment and evaluation of the functioning of the Joint Consultation and Compulsory Arbitration Scheme that is operating at the National and Departmental levels.

Staff Committees and Staff Councils

The Government has been considering the question of establishing a Whitley type of machinery from time to time. In 1954, it had introduced on an experimental basis a system of appointing in various ministries, Staff Committees on the model of Whitley Councils which, in 1957, were renamed as the Staff Councils. Accordingly, some 30 Staff Councils were set up in the various ministries, departments and attached offices of the Government of India. But the associations/unions of employees rejected, and disassociated themselves from these councils, as they were merely *ad-hoc* and advisory bodies without any power and means for effecting final settlement. The Staff Committees and Councils had suffered from ideological, constitutional and functional shortcomings.

The Second Pay Commission had, therefore, recommended the setting up of a Joint Consultative Machinery on the lines of the Whitley Councils in the U.K. along with a provision for compulsory arbitration.

In 1960, the Central government employees went on a general strike over the unresolved dispute regarding the need-based minimum wage and dearness allowance formula. The strikers demanded the establishment of a machinery for joint consultation and negotiation on the Whitley pattern. Immediately after the strike, the Government recognized the necessity for setting up of a new machinery. In 1963, announcing its acceptance of the recommendation of the Second Pay Commission, the Government made a decision to establish a Joint Consultation and Arbitration Machinery. After a series of protracted discussions between the Government and the representatives of the employees' organizations, an agreement was reached for starting the present scheme for the settlement of issues between the Government and the employees.

As is well-known, joint consultation in civil service staff relations is the recognition of the rights of government employees to associate and participate in the decision-making process that affects the working conditions of civil service. Keeping this idea in view, the Government of India introduced a scheme in 1966 for Joint Consultative Machinery and Compulsory Arbitration (JCM) for Central government employees.

It may be noted at this stage that separate arrangements were made for negotiation and consultation in the Ministries of Railways, Defence, and the P. & T. Department. While the Ministry of Railways (1952) and the Defence (1954) had established a Permanent Negotiating Machinery (PNM) in their departments, the P & T Department, since 1954, had been following a system of holding, on a regular basis, monthly and bi-monthly meetings. The systems of negotiation and the working of the machinery in these departments were somewhat more satisfactory than the other departments. It is interesting to note that excepting the Ministry of Defence, the other two ministries decided to retain the existing arrangements alongwith the new scheme of JCM.

The JCM Scheme

The JCM scheme, inaugurated at the national level in October 1966, was considered a landmark in the history of staff relations. It was expected that the scheme would initiate a new era of fruitful co-operation between the government and the employees. Further, it was hoped it would lead to the creation of mutual goodwill and promote congenial atmosphere for the resolution of disputes through peaceful means. The scheme is regarded as an outcome of new developments in the fields of civil service unionism, the changing social environment, the changing concept of the government and the evolution of human relations approach.[1] It is an *ad hoc,* voluntary and a supplementary arrangement to the existing facilities. It came into existence as a result of the declaration of a joint intent by the Government and employees' organisations.[2]

> The scheme which covers both the industrial and non-industrial employees of the Government of India, has been designed with the object of promoting harmonious relations and of securing the greatest measure of co-operation between the Government in its capacity as employer and the general body of its employees in matters of common concern and with the object of further increasing the efficiency of public service combined with the well being of those employed.[3]

The present scheme provides for a three tier structure of Joint Councils at the national, departmental, regional and office levels. The Joint Councils deal with all the matters relating to conditions of work, welfare of employees, standards of work and efficiency. In the matters of recruitment, promotion and discipline, however, consultation is limited only to matters of general principles and the individual cases are not considered.

In the total JCM structure, the National Council is the apex body. It deals with matters affecting the service conditions of Central government employees, such as minimum remuneration and allowances and pay of certain common categories. The Departmental Councils deal only with matters affecting the employees in the departments concerned. The Regional and Office Councils look into the regional or local issues.

The JCM is a bi-partite body consisting of the representatives of the Government of India (the official side) and those of the employees' organizations (the staff side). The officials are nominated by the Government. Notably, only a government official can function as the chairman of a Joint Council. The staff side is represented by members nominated by the employees' organizations recognized by the Government. Thus, any organization of the employees which wants to participate in the scheme, has to fulfil two conditions. First, it should satisfy the test of a broad and adequate representation of at least 15 per cent of the categories of employees it seeks to represent. Second, it should be recognized by the Government.

The seats on the staff side are distributed among the various organizations on the basis of strength of the respective categories of staff concerned and on the respective membership of each organization. The scheme permits only an employee or an honourably retired employee to be a member of the staff side. The Government may, however, permit an ex-employee to be a member after examining the merits of each individual case.

Discussions, consultations and negotiations help the Joint Councils function at various levels. The official side is expected to conclude matters at the meetings of the councils without reserving them for a later decision by the Government. The councils may appoint committees to study and report on matters falling within their jurisdiction. All the agreements arrived at between the two sides of a council become operative subject to the final authority of the cabinet. In case of failure to reach any agreement, the matter may be referred to arbitration, if any one party so desires.

In cases of disagreement, which are not arbitrable, the Government acts on its discretion. But in all such cases, by convention, the staff side has a chance to put forward its views before a Committee of Ministers consisting of the Minister for Home Affairs, the Minister for Labour and the Minister administratively concerned with the matter. The convention enables the staff side to present its viewpoint at the highest level.

The National Council

The National Council is one of the largest Joint Councils membered by the officials and staff personnel. The official side with a maximum membership of 25 is appointed by the Government. The staff side, nominated by the employees'organizations, may consist of 60 members.[4] The Cabinet Secretary of India is the Chairman of the Council. There is no vice-chairman nor any provision exists as to who should preside in the absence of the Chairman of the National Council, acts as the chief spokesman of the Government policies and as the leader of the official side. The staff side elects by a simple majority one of its members as its leader for a term of one year. The official and staff sides appoint secretaries from amongst their members. The constitution of the Council provides for a permanent secretariat of the Council, which functions under the supervision and control of the Chairman.

The JCM scheme recognizes the peculiarities and differences between the problems of industrial and the non-industrial employees. The constitution of the National Council provides for the setting up of two standing committees, one for the industrial staff and the other for non-industrial employees to deal with their respective matters. The Council and its standing committees may appoint other committees composed of their members to study and report on any matter within their jurisdiction. Thus, provision is made for permanent committees which are expected to deal with most of the business of the council which, in turn, formally meets only once in four months. Ironically, however, the Council has so far not set up the two proposed standing committees.

Working of the National Council

An attempt is being made here to assess the working of the National Council by analyzing minutes of its meetings. The Council in its 16 meetings held from 1967 to January 1974 discussed 178 items and took final decision on 130 (73.13 per cent) of the items. But agreements were reached between both the sides only in 79 (44.7 per cent) of the finalized items. Although, agreements were not reached on 19 (10.7 per cent) of the items, disagreements were recorded only in 10 (5.6 per cent) cases. Only three were referred for compulsory arbitration.

Out of 178 items discussed by the Council, about 85 (48 per cent) items were referred to the committees of the Council for study and report. Of the 61 items on which the committees reported, there was agreement between the two sides on 52 cases. The reports of the committees were adopted by the Council without any change.

Departmental Councils

Under the JCM Scheme, there is a provision for the formation of one Departmental Council for each department. There may, however, be a single council for two or more small departments under a Ministry, especially if the nature of duties in the departments are similar. The Councils deal with problems of employees who are working in a ministry department and in the subordinate and attached offices of a department.

The official representatives are nominated by the Government or the head of the department. The Secretary of a ministry represents official side and acts as the Chairman of the Departmental Council. The strength of the official side together with the Chairman and permanent members is 10. The membership on the staff side varies from 20 to 30, depending upon the strength of the staff and the number of grades of services in the departments.

According to the provisions of scheme, in all 21 Departmental Councils were proposed to be constituted. But till 1974, only 14 Departmental Councils could be set up.[5] A few Councils out of the 14 had chequered records and at times slowed down or stopped functioning. A mojority of the councils were suspended by the Government on some issue or the other.

Working of the Departmental Councils

It has been noticed that the meetings of the Departmental councils are not held regularly in many departments. The effectiveness of the councils depended upon the personalities involved in the joint consultation and negotiation. In this regard, the Chairman and the leader of the staff sides play key roles. It was observed that the Chairman who believed in civil service staff relations could lead their councils nearer to the accomplishment of its objectives.

The minutes of the 97 meetings held by the seven Departmental Councils[6] from 1967 to 1974 were analyzed by the author to study the nature of the items discussed in the meetings. The councils discussed about 1,119 items and a large number of them pertained to the promotion (245), revision of pay (155) and allowances (170). It shows that promotion is a matter of prime concern to the staff. The staff preferred promotion by seniority to that by merit, and filling up of vacancies through promotion rather than by direct recruitment.

The councils could not take decisions quickly on account of lack of authentic data and readily available information on different issues. Data collection and its examination took more than the usual time. Therefore it is suggested that for the effective functioning of the councils, data banks should be set up in every department; this will help provide information on the strength of each class, grade, recruitment rules, promotion channels, transfer policies, pay scales, work-load, working hours, co-ordinative procedures and other related areas.

Undue delay has been observed in the disposal of items that were referred for clarification and consideration to the Ministries of Finance, Works and Housing and the Department of Personnel. It appears that under the present system of administration with diffusion of power and responsibility, it is not possible for any department to take quick decision without consulting some other departments. Therefore, in order to make the scheme successful, some of the powers in regard to finance and personnel should be decentralized to the operational departments.

Notably, the councils have not worked effectively in small departments, particularly where the employees' organizations were not strong, their leadership was not adequately enlightened or where the staff side lacked unity. Generally, it was found that the members on the staff side possessed no knowledge and training in the art of joint consultation and negotiation. Above all, it appears that both the sides had little faith in the participative management and industrial democracy. Therefore, for an effective system of collective bargaining, office bearers of trade unions and the personnel managers of government need to be educated and trained in the philosophy and mechanics of joint consultation, negotiation, collective bargaining and participative management techniques.

Compulsory Arbitration

Compulsory arbitration is the essence of the JCM scheme. If final disagreements are recorded in cases pertaining to pay and allowances, weekly hours of work, leave of a class or grade of employees, compulsory arbitration may be sought by either sides. For this purpose, a Board of Arbitration was constituted in 1968. The Board consists of three members;one nominated by the official side, one by the staff side of the National Council, while the third is the Chairman of the Board who is an independent member. Although the recommendations of the Board are binding on both the sides, the Government is vested with the final authority to decide the 'arbitrality' of an issue. Besides, the Parliament may modify or reject the recommendations of the Board on grounds of the exigencies of national economy and social justice.

Till 1974, only 83 cases were referred to the Board of Arbitration by the National Council and the various Departmental Councils. A majority of them were from the Railways (38), the P & T (12) and the Science and Technology (13) departments. Out of these, the Board gave awards in 69 references. The claim of the staff were fully accepted by the Board in 25 cases and only partly in 23 cases; 16 cases were rejected, five were permitted to be withdrawn and the remaining were kept pending. In the 60 awards, about 2.8 million employees were involved. Out of these, about 2 lacs employees benefited fully, about 18 lacs benefited partly and only about 50 thousand employees did not get any benefit, since their claims were rejected by the Board. The employees of the Railways, the P & T, and the Finance ministries were the most highly benefited. Majority of the cases referred to the Board pertained to the pay scales (48), and allowances (30); only four cases related to hours of work; and one concerned the leave privileges. The Board rejected 13 cases pertaining to allowances and accepted 22 claims relating to pay matters.

In 1974, on Government's refusal to refer disputed matters like need-based minimum wage and merger of dearness allowance with pay for compulsory arbitration, Government employees went on a strike. As a result of a deadlock, the National Council ceased to function for more than a year. At the departmental level, the scheme was partially implemented and the councils in many department could not work effectively. At times they ceased to function, for either they were suspended by the Government or were boycotted by the unions. The Government could not constitute Departmental Councils in seven departments for want of cooperation by the employees' organizations. Besides, the Government failed to set up the Regional and Office Councils, except in the Defence Ministry and at some headquarter offices.

The major achievement of the JCM scheme was that it brought the departments and the representatives of the employees' unions together and afforded them with an opportunity to know each other's point of view. The scheme also brought together a motley crowd of unions representing different ideologies and political affiliations. Despite its stunted growth so far, the joint consultative machinery needs to be given further support and encouragement. In the changing political climate, their operation on sounder lines appears to be important imperative.

References

1. Manjulika Koshal and Ramesh C. Singh, "Joint Consultation at the Government Level— The Case in the Posts and Telegraphs Departments," a paper submitted to the Seminar on Participative Management in Public Enterprises, January 15 to 19, 1972, New Delhi.
2. Both sides agreed to give a fair trial to the scheme for a period of five years and during this period all the disputes were expected to be settled by the use of machinery in a peaceful manner.

3. Scheme for Joint Consultative Machinery and Compulsory Arbitration for Central Government Employees, Annexure I and II, pp. 3 and 7, Department of Personnel and Administrative Reform, Cabinet Secretariat, Government of India, 8 September, 1971.
4. The staff side could fill up 49 seats only till the end of 1974.
5. This was attributed either to the absence of the employees' organizations or to the existence of inter-union rivalries.
6. Railways, P & T, Defence, Finance, Civil Aviation and Tourism, Works and Housing and Personnel and Administrative Reforms.

5

Paradox of Public Administration in India : Emerging Issues

Public administration, in the broader context, is understood as an instrument of action, as a profession and an academic discipline (teaching and research).[1] The contradiction between its intent and content, the context and the text, the distinction between the constitutional ideals and the operational goals is paradoxical. This article attempts to analyse the challenges set off by this paradoxical situation and makes an effort to propose a future course of action in order to provide a solution to the paradox.

The nature, scope and importance of Public Administration in India is generally determined[2] by the historical, social, cultural, political, economic and several other external factors. But today, the last three factors, particularly, the external factor seems to be playing a dominant role. In fact, it is this factor which has been shaping the destinies of Public Administration in India, both before and after Independence. Whether the extent of external factor can be reduced by adopting inter-nation or global perspective to serve the cause of emerging India in all respects, needs to be examined in the light of the past and the present experience of Public Administration in India.

Thus, Public Administration in India has been an instrument of the government and a creation of a political philosophy. It is different that at times, the governments might not have a clear-cut political ideology. Public Administration as an academic discipline has been "non-political", but in matters of governance, Public Administration, by and large, is committed to the ruling political elite. The ruling elite in India with the willing cooperation of the bureaucracy, maintained the colonial structure that indeed paved the way for development of a capitalist order, but not without sermonising the socialist rhetoric, culminating in the emergence and concretisation of a dominantly Hindu state in essence,[3] thus marring the very spirit of the Constitution of India. The role of Public Administration in the whole process of such developments in India has been enormous, possessing regulating functions.

In the light of the above, the most important change in the Public Administration in India in the recent years (1990s) is its reduced scope and significance. It has been asked to change itself in the nature of its dealings with certain 'Public'.

RECENT CHANGES

The recent widespread changes have altered the international, social and economic order, which demands the administration, including economic planning,[4] to "respond and adjust to the changes quickly and creatively to the market economy" "without tearing out socio-cultural fabric".

The recent changes are enlisted for a better understanding of the paradox and the emerging issues:

1. New Economic Policy – Privatisation—Market friendly economy—GATT Agreement.
2. New Social Policy – More percentage of reservations, facilities to BCs/ OBCs.
3. New Political Policy – Constitutional status to the local governments and reservations to women, BCs/ SCs, and STs.
4. New Educational Policy – Science, computer, professional and Management education through private institutions.

5. New Labour Policy – Golden Shakehand, Exit policy.
6. New Administrative Policy – Deregulation, delicensing
   – Use of Para-Military forces and TADA Act.

Implications of New Policies

All these 'new' policies need to be carried on by the administration "without tearing the socio-cultural fabric". Till the beginning of the 1990s, the Indian socio-economic fabric had been essentially anti-market and its 'populist concern' was for the poor, the weak and the backward. There was greater emphasis on social justice and development. But neither social justice nor the development was possible without change in the "socio-cultural fabric". Therefore, if the new policies are to be effectively implemented, one of the first tasks would be to educate the people and the ruling elite that the economic and political restructuring requires restructuring of the traditional values and behaviour in all the fields.[5]

There are strong feelings against some aspects of privatisation[6] and the market philosophy for the new economic policy has in a way whittled down the power of the State and the poor who continue to expect that they can use state power and policies for uplifting themselves. "In fact, their hope and ambition to do so are now riding higher than before".[7]

Privatisation or liberalisation of economy would result in less government in one field, but it requires to have a better state (Social State) particularly in India. For the Constitution of India entrusted the state with special obligation for achieving the "socio-economic transformation" to ensure "socio-economic justice" to the masses.

The new policies in a way reduce the role of the positive state and at the same time enhance the scope of the negative state. The negative state and its administration cannot achieve the aims and objectives enshrined in the Constitution. It may also lead to more executive powers further reducing the parliamentary democracy.

Even now, the contemporary democratic state could not devise proper mechanism to control administration and make bureaucracy accountable.[8] Despite all this, the role of the state and bureaucracy cannot be minimised.

Privatisation may lead to a better performance of economy, but the Indian private sector, which has not proved in ample terms its social responsibility so far, may cause problems in distribution leading to more inequality. Bureaucracy will have to play an important new role changing its past attitudes in tune with the new economic policy and securing socio-economic justice through market forces. As such, in the new context, state intervention becomes further necessary in a large number of areas of human concern. In this changed context, Public Administration needs to play a large role in economic development, while searching solutions for the unsatisfactory performance of the administration.[9] If it fails to improve to meet the new demands and leaves the matters to the market forces, the police will have more jobs, duties and powers to control the discontended mobs and suppress mass movements, the underworld and the underground trying to gain control over the public. To maintain the security, para-military forces and armed services may gradually replace the police and the civil service and the civilian administration. The roots of the Rule of Law, democracy, and equity would be threatened. Already in some places, violent gang behaviour has made the mark of fascism.[10]

The administration is required to meet the challenges of the 'changing' state. The state and bureaucracy are now much less concerned with the principles of democracy, equity and fair distribution. It is not that socialistic and that secular. It has become a capitalistic-oriented with the native socio-cultural fabric, *i.e.,* the caste, the inequalities and the oppression, the characteristics of an undemocratic society. The polity, though 'democratic', is in the muddle of severe imbalance between the concentration of economic and social power in the hands of a relatively few and the enormous spread of ballot-box power.[11]

Public Administration of India in the past might have responded to organised pressure, agitations and revolts. It may not respond much today, as there is less scope for organised agitations and revolts. Even if there are any, the administration has been given full powers to suppress them.

The appointment of the National Human Rights Commission in 1994 at the instance of certain external factors to maintain internal order indicates many events that are taking place during recent years. The Commission in its recent visits to states expressed its displeasure against the misuse of the TADA Act and irregularities in the system.[12]

Bureaucracy might not have been very effective and efficient but to argue that public servants are not interested in efficiency and effectiveness of the public sector is not logical.[13] If bureaucracy proved to be incompetent in the discharge of certain tasks (economic) and a further clear-cut division of functions between public and private sector administration on principles of economy is felt necessary to reduce the unnecessary burden on the public exchequer, it is some thing different to think over. But, such a division cannot absolve the government of its ultimate responsibility in such activities, where private sector is also permitted alongwith the public sector. The government is required to monitor the privatised economy and its effects. If this leads to a New Public Management Approach,[14] it needs to be thoroughly examined. The new division of functions between public and private sector and between politics and administration is expected to defend the public interests and the tradition of financial incorruptibility and lead to better state-society relations. Even in this approach, increasing interpenetration may not be possible to avoid between the politics and administration.

Public Administration in India as an instrument and a profession faces many constraints: *First,* its own background and upbringing; *Second,* its technical incapacity; *Third,* ideological dilemma on what governments should do and should not do; and *finally* the divisive forces of ethnicity, religion and regional imbalances in socio-economic and political development. Added to these, the politicians at the helm of affairs not only lacked the political will/skill and could not evolve a political consensus, leading to political divisions and institutional instability. It is for these reasons, in addition to its acquired maladies, the bureaucracy can be accused, but in certain other respects it acted not as a 'hidden' government but as a means to democracy and development as an end.[15]

PUBLIC ADMINISTRATION AS A DISCIPLINE

Public Administration discipline is essentially an American product. It has developed alongside the growth of capitalism in USA. Alongwith many other countries, India also could not escape the Americanisation of Public Administration. It appears, India was caught in a web of circumstances and did not attempt to get out of it.[16]

Contemporary Public Administration discipline in India is at crossroads. To decide upon the core of the discipline, there were meetings/seminars/workshops in recent years (1989-92) at the national level organised in collaboration with the University Grants Commission, the Indian Institute of Public Administration and Universities. The Indian Council of Social Science Research completed its third survey[17] of Research in Public Administration (1979-89) in 1993. Even after the existence of about six decades in India, it has not expanded quantitively or qualitatively as the profession of Public Administration proliferated. Above all, there was no consensus about the nature of its development and achievement. Some scholars preferred it to be a profession and others a discipline. In the absence of a national/regional consensus, it appears many universities are following the syllabus prescribed for the All-India Services by the Union Public Service Commission and the National Education Test (NET) mode of the University Grants Commission for all practical purposes.

It is beyond doubt that the healthy growth of Public Administration discipline would necessitate a close interaction between the academics and practitioners. But to a large extent, such an interaction is felt not only conspicuously absent, but there is also no mutual understanding, cooperation and ideology.

Public Administration in India, as an instrument or as an academic discipline, largely preferred to be a part of the

'Administration' due to the socio-economic and political backgrounds of their members. Despite this, as a discipline, it has not lost sight of the realities of the system. Yet, it supports the system as the system supports it. In the light of the recent changes in the government's policies, the nature, scope and importance of both the profession and the discipline need to be redefined and its field to be rediscovered, new paradigms of governance and administration have to be found and new solutions evolved and a new administrative culture developed.[18]

The policies of the government can be effectively carried with better understanding between the practitioners and the academics. The Indian Institute of Public Administration at New Delhi, the Institutes of Public Administration in the state capitals and a number of All-India training institutes of different departments must interact with the academics in the universities and research institutes to enrich them with their problems and seeking in turn, certain possible solutions from their research findings.

A new Public Administration with unmistakable identity should grow on the basis of socio-economic realities of contemporary India and by a better suited global perspective. India being a traditional society, its socio-political reality is very complex. At least the present model of administration is declared unsuitable. We, therefore, need a new kind of conceptual framework to understand our reality.

Governance of India as a New Focus

Public administration in India must act as a means of mobilising political power, functions and democratic ways of thinking. So far, it was responsible to implement the public law and as a servant of the executive branch of the government. Now, to be more suitable to the new century, it is felt necessary that Public Administration need emerge as a "teacher of governance to society",[19] which implies a different and more crucial role for Public Administration than it has played in the past. It is "a search of ways and means of managing the affairs of the State". The approach to governance go "beyond the technology of Public Administration and even beyond the realm of the executive arm of the government". It is a measure of the nature and quality of the "policy choices of the state". It deals with providing "good government of society" and "exercise of political power to manage a nation's affairs".

Public Administration must be ready to teach on-going lessons of governance and it must possess a capacity to direct society with respect to both the "substantive knowledge and normative ideals" of governance.[20] As the discipline is not fully ready for this role, three ways are suggested in which the discipline could begin to prepare for its impending responsibility. First, the establishment of the teachers' credibility; second, development of adequate forums to perform the teaching function, particularly between careerists and political appointees and the level of citizenry as a whole; and third, improving a language of dialogue for teaching governance. All this is expected to elevate the status of Public Administration of full partner in the process of democratic governance.[21]

Political and Administrative Reforms/Changes

In this direction, it is necessary to get on to the chosen path of democratic decentralisation and socialist economic planning. We have to work towards the success of the new local governments which empower the people at the grassroot level. The success of the new social policy (reservations), the new economic policy depends mostly on the relations between politics and the administration in order to maintain the balance of power between the contending social groups. This is a very difficult task. This calls for certain reforms/changes in the existing politico-administrative set-up. The list of such radical reforms may be very exhaustive. But, important changes needed immediately are stated below :

1. Introduction of electoral reforms for cleaner and free elections at all levels to all public bodies and to eschew influence of money and muscle power.

2. Amendments in the Anti-Defection Law to prevent defections of whatever nature.

3. Ensuring inner-democracy in every party/body/organisation/society/association/union which is registered or recognised.

4. Strengthen and permit all the constitutional and statutory bodies ensuring necessary autonomy to enable them to discharge their duties/obligations.
5. Demystification of the 'Black-Box' (Policy-making Process) and bringing amendments in the Official Secrets Act.
6. Effective exposer of the unholy nexus among politicians, bureaúcrats and criminals.
7. Creation of quasi-judicial bodies in every statutory organisation to regularly and constantly resolve the organisational conflict.
8. Creation of effective public grievance redressal system at all levels.
9. Creation of permanent/regular Human Rights Protection Commissions at all levels.
10. Conscious effort on the part of the academic discipline of Public Administration to educate and train the students/ citizens to be an effective human resource.
11. To certain extent, training of professionals and education of semi-professionals by giving them considerable doses of theory of public administration.
12. Need for rethinking of Public Policy Theory and practice by public policy makers and introduce the subject in the universities for teaching and research.

SUMMARY

It may be very difficult to introduce the suggested reforms/ changes in the existing system. But, it is the only hard way that we can go alongwith. Therefore, the present model of Public Administration in India needs to be changed. It is pertinent to note that nothing much is possible immediately "without tearing the socio-cultural fabric". Therefore, the role of the State cannot be minimised based on the external factors. In fact, it should be a better State and making the bureaucracy accountable. A more open government is suggested for better participation of all the concerned in the policy process. An urgent need is to evolve the political consensus and develop the political will and the skill. The governance will deal mainly with democracy, human rights and the institutional functioning, particularly the new panchayati raj and urban local governments. Toward these aims, the public administration in India should strive to utilise its energies. At least now at this crucial hour of our transition, Public Administration as a discipline should realise and rise to meet the crucial situation. If this opportunity is missed for any reason, the very survival of the polity, the democracy, the constitutional guarantees and the administration of social justice may be difficult leading to further crisis in the Indian political system. In such circumstances, Public Administration alone as a machinery cannot do any thing for the social good.

References

1. See for details, V. Bhaskara Rao, *Public Administration in India,* New Delhi, Ajanta Publications, 1989; and Shriram Maheshwari (ed.), *Education in Public Administration in India,* New Delhi, Indian Institute of Public Administration, 1992.
2. See for details, Muhammad A. Hakim, "Determinants of Administration in Developing Countries: A Review and a Basis for Analysis", *Indian Journal of Public Administration,* Vol. XXXIX, No. 2, April-June, 1993, pp. 111-22.
3. "V. Bhaskara Rao, Colonial Structure, Capitalist Policy, Socialist Slogan, Hindu State: Indian Administration in Nineteen Eighties", *op. cit.,* pp. 249-54.
4. See for details, V.M. Dandekar, "Role of Economic Planning in India in the 1990s and Beyond", *Economic and Political Weekly,* June II, 1994, pp. 1457-1664.
5. See, V.M. Davdekar, *op. cit.*
6. Ken Rasmussen, "Public Enterprise and Privatisation: A Study of Canada and India", in Pradeep Saxena (ed.), *Comparative Public Policy,* Jaipur, Rawat Publications, 1993, pp. 167-72.
7. Pran Chopra, "The Crisis of Democracy", *The Hindu,* August 24, 1994.

8. See for details, Kuldeep Mathur, "Bureaucracy in India: Development and Pursuit of Self-interest", *Indian Journal of Public Administration,* Vol. XXXVI, No. 4, October-December, 1991, pp. 637-48.
9. See for details, H. Elsenhans, "On the Political Economy of Development Administration: Why There cannot be Weberian Administration in the Third World", in Pradeep Saxena (ed.), *op. cit.,* pp. 83-124.
10. Pran Chopra, *op. cit.*
11. *Ibid.*
12. See for details, Amit Baruah, "The 'Harsh' Side of the Law", *The Hindu,* August 28, 1994, p. 7.
13. Bola Dauda, "Toward a Reconstruction of Public Policy: Theory and Practice", in Pradeep Saxena (ed.), *op. cit.,* p. 14.
14. See for details, Rainer Pitschas, "Aspects of the Max Weber's Theory on Bureaucracy and New Public Management Approach", *Indian Journal of Public Administration,* Vol. XXXIX, No. 4, October-December 1993, pp. 643-51.
15. See for details, David C. Potter, *India's Political Administrators,* (1919-83), Oxford Clarendon Press, 1986, pp. 236-45.
16. See for details, V. Bhaskara Rao, "Public Administration in India: Retrospect and Prospect", in C.P. Barthwal (ed.), *Public Administration in India,* New Delhi, Ashish Publishing House, 1993, pp. 68-76.
17. The Survey was conducted with a view to take a comprehensive look at the problems of 'governance' in India.
18. T.N. Dhar, "Proceedings and Recommendations", *Seminar on "Re-Investing Government,* Lucknow, May 1994.
19. Charles T. Goodsell, "Emerging Issues in Public Administration", in Naomi B. Lymn and Aaron Wildavsky (eds.), *Public Administration,* New Delhi, 1992, pp. 503-54.
20. *Ibid.,* pp. 504-05.
21. *Ibid.,* p. 507.

6

Ethics in Indian Public Services : A Note

Ethics is a discipline that studies morality and attempts to find the source of moral ideas. Moral principles are elaborated in the process of social practices and experiences of many generations of a people. Moral ideas and standards, for some, are mere conventions. They negate the possibility of creating scientific ethics. They do not believe that morality is dependent on the social background and is determined on the objective historical laws.[1] Therefore, ethics require to be taken into account the motives as well as the social consequences of the people's actions. Moral norms and ethical standards regulate people's conduct through general prescriptions and prohibit certain actions. In contrast to the legal norms, moral norms are not sanctioned by the State authority. Depending on the moral consciousness of society, these are formed on the basis of force of habit and public opinion. Moral norms cannot sufficiently control the human behaviour.

PUBLIC SERVICE AND THEIR ETHICAL OBLIGATIONS

Public personnel as a class/group entrusted with the duty and responsibility of transaction of public business with speed, integrity and efficiency. The duties and responsibilities of the public serivces can be better discussed in a changing social and historical setting.[2]

About 200 years back the British rulers in India designed for the first time two important measures to promote administrative morality by introducing Rule of Law and the system of open competition as a method of recruitment. Even now, in the changed historical context, these two measures remain very important for the maintenance of discipline and integrity of the Public Service in India.

Ethics and morality in Public Services depend upon the ideals and principles involved in serving national and social causes. Democratic India expected from Public services a high sense of public duty, humanism, Rule of Law, Parliamentarianism, Democracy and Development.[3]

The ethical obligations of public servants are listed and explained by O.P. Dwivedi.[4] But the gap between the expected norms and the extent of deviation was well explained by P.R. Dubhashi in a tabular form.[5]

There is a vast amount of literature on the causes and consequences of corruption and maladministration. Many high-powered committees and commissions investigated and recommended the remedies.[6] Public Service Commissions, Election Commission, The Comptroller and Auditor General of India, Anti-Corruption Bureaus, Vigilance Commissions, Lok-Ayuktas, Human Rights Commission, Judicial/Magisterial enquiries, Parliamentary Committees, Departmental enquiries, Public Forums, Civil Liberties Organisations and a number of other agencies have been combating with the corruption and amorality in the public services for maintaining integrity and morality in Public Administration.

Despite these, the spread of corruption, and the resultant demoralisation, indiscipline, and misuse of power could not be curbed and prevented. In fact, all the malpractices have become methodical and systematic. Unfortunately, it is now recognised as a necessary evil. The wheels of the administrative machinery cannot be moved even with a minimum speed without 'greasing and oiling' every joint, each nut and bolt. Percentages, commissions, bakshis, mamools, kick-backs, tips, gifts, expenses, bribes are just paid by the publicmen and people as a very routine part of post-Independent developmental process. Colonial past of the civil service and the political independence of the ruling elite joined hands for private gain through public agencies. It is patrimonial at best and corrupt at worst.[7]

With this brief note on the present ethical setting, it is now (once again) attempted to list out the main causes of demoralisation of Public Services in India. Certain possible remedies (once more) are also suggested only to minimise the loot, check the mis-behaviour, and maintain limited confidence of common man in Public Services.

Causes of Demoralisation

1. While Institutionalisation process has not completely developed to direct and manage the administration, the institutions are under constant attack.
2. 'Teleguided'[8] administration—Central control (political and administrative).
3. Feudal character of Indian bureaucracy.
4. Authoritarian milieu of Public Administration.[9]
5. The Audit system and investigative journalism.[10]
6. Collusion between businessmen, politicians and the bureaucracy.
7. 'Administrative Lawlessness'[11] wide discretionary powers.
8. Lack of sufficient theoretical exposure to Public Administration and Law.
9. Exploitative nature of the State/polity.
10. 'Neo-Patrimonialism' and 'Clientelism'.[12]
11. Poor leadership, both administrative and political, and poor enforcement of law of prevention of corruption.[13]
12. Unsettling politics, the declining political, and moral standards.
13. The Hindu false mythology[14] and the traits of Indian character ("unlimited capacity for self-abasement and to be a villain of the worst kind").
14. The ideology or the Indian Socialism (Licence Permit Raj).
15. Contradictions inherent in the process of capitalist development.[15]

Remedies Suggested

1. Emergency political morality in the society[16] (Utopian remedy).
2. Creation of administrative resilience within the services—Democratisation of administration.
3. Smashing the 'black-box' and reducing the secrecy in administration.
4. Providing more freedom of expression—participation in managing public services.
5. Enforcement of conduct rules and providing citizenary rights to the employees.
6. Organised administrative resistance to protect services from political victimisation.
7. Closer-interaction between Public Services and other sections of intelligentsia.[17]
8. Peoples participation in administration.
9. The guilty should be punished setting an example to others.
10. Proper direction and motivation.
11. Ideological change for more self-government[18] and creation of a favourable social climate.
12. Establishment of Lokpal and Lok-Ayuktas to deal with complaints against Ministers and Civil Servants.

References

1. I. Frolov (ed.), *Dictionary of Philosophy,* Moscow, Progress Publishers, 1967, pp. 132-34.
2. For an eloborate discussion see, B.B. Misra, *Government and Bureaucracy in India. 1947-76,* Delhi, Oxford University Press, 1986, pp. 267-317.
3. For details, R.B. Jain (ed), *Public Services in a Democratic Context,* New Delhi, Indian Institute of Public Administration, 1983.
4. O.P. Dwivedi, in R.B. Jain, *op.cit.,* pp. 231-36.
5. *Ibid.,* pp. 12-14.

6. For a detailed discussion, B.B. Misra, *op.cit.*, pp. 273-317.
7. Kirshna K. Tummala, *Public Administration in India,* Singapore, Times Academic Press, 1994, p. 325.
8. Balveer Arora, "Political Control over Administration in the Federal Context", in R.B. Jain, *op.cit.*, pp. 80-83.
9. M.A. Muttalib, "Indian Ecology of Bureaucracy", in R.B. Jain, *op.cit.*, pp. 118-119.
10. B.G. Deshmukh, "Why Blame Bureaucracy Alone?" *Administrative Change,* Vol. XXI, Nos. 1-2, July 1993-June 1994, pp. 5-6.
11. S.S. Singh, "Administrative Lawlessness: Concept and Concern", *The Indian Journal of Public Administration,* Vol. XL, No. *2,* April-June, 1994, p. 135.
12. Mobasser Monem, "Consequences of Neo-Patrimonialism in the Developing Countries", *Administrative Change,* Vol XXI, Nos. 1-2, July 1993-June 1994, pp. 120-125.
13. Krishna K. Tummala, *Public Administration in India,* Singapore, Times Academic Press, 1994, pp. 205-215.
14. For details, G. Haragopal and V.S. Prasad, "Social Bases of Administrative Culture in India", *Indian Journal of Public Administration,* July-September, 1990, pp. 384-97.
15. For details, Satya Deva, "Bureaucracy and Morality", in R.B. Jain, *op. cit.,* pp. 270-71 and Ralph Clark Chandler, "The Ethics of Managing Scarcity; Approaches to Economy and Prudence in a Consuming Society", *International Journal of Public Administration,* Vol. 17, No. 12, 1994, pp. 2343-65.
16. A.K. Chaturvedi, "Tinkering with the Rule of Law", in R.B. Jain, *op. cit,* pp. 24-31.
17. A.K. Chaturvedi, *op.cit.*
18. S.S. Singh, *op.cit.*, p. 151.

7

The Andhra Pradesh Government Employees' Strike : An Experiment in Civil Service Unionism*

In the recent history of civil servants' strikes in India, the strike by Andhra Pradesh Government employees in the year 1971 is most unique. One of the striking features was the unprecedented solidarity and unity[1] in the strike for promotion and continuation of the strike and the spirited fight put up by the employees for their demands. The decision of the employees to go on strike only after the mid-term elections to Parliament, unlike employees of other States who used strike as a pre-election weapon to achieve their demands, renders the strike very conspicuous. Yet another distinguishing feature was the apparent apathy and absolute indifference of the public towards the strike. The strike is a hallmark in the history of civil service unionism, considered from the high level political maturity and diplomatic shrewdness with which the Chief Minister dealt with the strike. The strike lasted for an unusually long period of 56 days, second only to the 63 days strike by the Uttar Pradesh employees.[2]

In a short article like this it is not possible to deal elaborately with various aspects of the strike. Hence, it states briefly the stages of development of the strike, presents the uncompromising stand taken by the employees and the Government, reviews the events indicating the repercussions and gravity of the situation and outlines the lessons which both parties may profitably learn from experiences of the strike.

* Co-authored with Prof. P.A. James.

Stages of Development

Before discussing the various stages of development of the strike, it may be pertinent to note that employees of the two regions have organised themselves separately under two Joint Councils of Action.[3]

The employees of the Andhra Pradesh State went on strike for 17 days in 1970 but it was called off on the specific assurance by the Chief Minister that issues connected with the revision of House Rent Allowance, grant of City Allowance at Central rates, and provision of suitable scales of pay to those who were not covered by the pay revision of 1969 and 1970 would be resolved within one month.[4] However, the assurance remained only an assurance.

At this stage, the Andhra Pradesh employees were very much influenced by the decision of the Government of India to pay interim relief to its employees and payment of such an interim relief had become one of their most important demands.

The Chief Minister assured the leaders of employees at Eluru, in February 1971, while inaugurating the annual conference of the Andhra Pradesh Non-Gazetted Officers' Association that the Government would have talks on various demands and that the decision of the Government would be announced during the Budget Session of the Legislature.

In the Budget Session the Government did not commit itself to pay interim relief. The dissatisfied employees informed the Government on February 11, 1971 and later on March 23, 1971 that they would be forced to go on strike if their demands were not settled before April 11, 1971.[5]

Negotiations on 6th April between the Government and the employees failed because the Government refused to pay interim relief at Central rates. Other demands could not be taken up for discussion as the problem of interim relief remained unsettled.

Since nothing notable transpired, the burning cause was in the melting pot, the employees, numbering about 4.5 lakhs[6] struck work indefinitely from 12th April, 1971. The strike went on relentlessly gaining momentum every day.

To understand and appreciate the uncompromising stands adopted by both the parties, it becomes necessary to note the demands put forward by the employees. Briefly stated, the demands of the employees were (*a*) the payment of interim relief on par with the Central Government employees; (*b*) the payment of House Rent Allowance and City Allowance at Central rates for all cities and towns; (*c*) the adoption of a modified scheme of House Rent Allowance for all places in the State irrespective of population and types of employees; (*d*) the immediate implementation of the terms of agreement entered into with various Service Associations; (*e*) the immediate rectification of anamolies in pay scales; (*f*) the absorption of all temporary, work-charged and contingent employees as full members of their respective services by creating necessary cadres; and (*g*) the application of all Government Orders regarding pay scales, weightages, leave and pension relating to the Government employees, to all categories of employees working in local bodies.

The demands of J.C.E. and J.C.A. were more or less the same but with the difference that the J.C.A. of Telangana employees wanted, in addition, the immediate implementation of the High Court Judgement on Mulki Rules and regionalisation of services.

Among others, payment of Interim Relief and House Rent Allowance and City Allowance at Central rates may be considered as the main demands.

As already stated, the demand for payment of interim relief to the State employees is indirectly but vitally linked up with the announcements and payments of interim relief by the Government of India to its own employees. The Government of India being fully convinced of the recommendation[7] of the Third Pay Commission, announced an interim relief ranging from Rs. 15 to Rs. 45 to its employees on September 30, 1970 with retrospective effect from March 1, 1970.

It is important to note that the State employees would be highly motivated by the benefits being enjoyed by the Central Government employees. Probably for the same reason some State Governments sanctioned interim relief to their employees in the form of Dearness

Allowance (D.A.) when their employees threatened to go on strike or actually struck work before the elections. For example, the Government of Orissa granted an increase ranging between Rs. 11 to Rs. 32. In West Bengal the employees secured an increase between Rs. 15 to Rs. 25, the Government of Kerala granted Rs. 10 to Rs. 17.50. In Maharashtra the employees got between Rs. 10 to Rs. 22.50. The Governments of Mysore, and Tamil Nadu revised pay scales, and other State Governments such as Rajasthan, Bihar, Madhya Pradesh and Gujarat followed suit.

The Government of Andhra Pradesh rejected the demand on the ground that its implementation would cost the State exchequer Rs. 12 crores a year. Further, it argued that the State Government employees could not claim any interim relief because of recent pay revision.[8]

The other important demands were, payment of House Rent Allowance and City Allowance at Central rates. Under the State Scheme of House Rent Allowance, only employees whose basic pay did not exceed Rs. 320 were paid the allowance. Under the Central scheme, Dearness Pay is being treated as pay for purposes of calculation of House Rent Allowance. The employees of Andhra Pradesh desired that in calculating H.R.A., the principle of treating Dearness Pay as part of the pay, as obtaining in the States of Tamil Nadu, Mysore and Maharashtra, should also be extended to the State of Andhra Pradesh.

The Central Government employees in Hyderabad are being paid City Compensatory Allowance at the rate of $7^1/_2$% of their pay whereas the State employees were getting only between Rs. 4 to Rs. 8. It may be noted in this context that the Tamil Nadu Government has granted City Allowance at rates higher than the Central rates, viz., 10% of the pay.

The Uncompromising Stands

The Government Stand—At Eluru, the Chief Minister said that in his view State Government employees should get the pay of Central employees, but for the fact that the State's resources were limited. Recourse to abnormal overdrafts from Reserve Bank was reported to be the cause for Government's inability to meet the demands. Government pointed out that since 1967, the Dearness Allowance of Government employees was revised five times. These miscellaneous adjustments had already cost the Government Rs. 30 crores a year. Further, pay revision in 1969 and similar other measures, meant an additional burden of Rs. 12.5 crores per year to the Government. The Government was of the view that it had been incurring financial burden to the tune of Rs. 43 crores on additional emoluments payable to its employees and if further increases were to be effected there would be a cut in the development expenditure. In the opinion of the Government there was no point in conceding the demands of the employees because, there has been an increase of 242% in expenditure on civil administration, while the increase in revenue income was only 185%.[10] Similarly, the Government stated that while the per capita income had gone up by 74%, there was a substantial rise of 130% in the pay of the lowest paid employees.[11]

The Employees' Stand—Mr. A. Sreeramulu, the President of Andhra Pradesh N.G.Os. Association and the General Secretary of All India State Governments Employees Federation, has not accepted the Government's plea of lack of resources. He was sure if Government could recover dues from marketing societies[12] advances and loans given to Panchayati Raj Bodies[13] and collect arrears of taxes properly, problems of over-drafts and lack of resources will have been automatically solved. Further, he argued that Central Government should provide financial assistance to State Government to enable it to pay interim relief to its employees at Central rates.

The employees were unable to appreciate the stand of the Government because other States, in spite of their unsound financial position, provided relief to their employees. Moreover, the Government of Andhra Pradesh gained Rs. 25 crores by scrapping prohibition and got Rs. 13 crores per year by way of grant-in-aid and is expected to receive a greater share in Central taxes as a result of the Finance Commission's recommendations. The employees feel that it should be possible for the Government, in view of its improved financial position, to concede their demands.

The employees held that as the percentage of expenditure on civil administration had gone down in recent years, it should not be difficult for the Government to accede to employees' demands.[14] The Government was of the view that the pay of the lowest paid employee had increased from Rs. 792 to Rs. 1,824. But the employees argued that if the per capita income were to be taken as Rs. 478, then, for a family, consisting on an average of four persons, the minimum salary of the lowest paid employee ought to be Rs. 1,912 per year. Thus the employees felt that the allegedly high salary of the lowest paid employees, i.e., Rs. 1,824 fell short of the minimum required, i.e., Rs. 1,912.

The Strike in Operation

The Government prohibited strikes in essential services by promptly promulgating an Ordinance[15] on the eve of the strike, and issued a communique stating that those employees who participate in the strike would be liable for disciplinary action, under Rule 4 of the Andhra Pradesh Civil Service (Conduct) Rules, 1964. The Chief Minister gave an ultimatum to the employees that all those employees failing to report to duty by April 24, 1971 would incur break in service.[16] Ignoring all these threats the employees continued the strike. All the employees participated in the strike for the entire period of 56 days. By and large, the strike was peaceful.

The striking employees had the full sympathy and support of some of the opposition political parties like the Communist Party of India, Telangana Praja Samithi and Swatantra Party. A few of the legislators represented the matter to the Government. Central and other State Governments employees' Associations and Unions of Bank employees, and industrial workers, expressed their support for the striking employees in unequivocal terms.

The employees adopted the following methods to ventilate their grievances. They organised rallies and demonstrations, held public meetings, picketted Government offices, staged 'dharna' before the residence of the Chief Minister; observed relay hunger fasts; submitted petitions to all the Ministers; and appealed to the Governor and to the President of All India Congress Committee.

In addition to the normal daily demonstrations, a state-wide Hartal Call was given on May 12, 1971. The hartal supported by the Communist Party of India, Telangana Praja Samithi and other sympathisers was very successful. However, the hartal at Tirupathi resulted in police firing and unfortunately two persons were killed.

During the strike period, the Government had arrested 3,851, convicted 475 and suspended 229 employees. But none was dismissed from service. In order to maintain the essential services, Government recruited 1904 persons of whom 1832 were later discharged.[17] Further, the services of thousands of temporary employees were terminated. The stalemate continued unabated. Both the parties seemed to have contributed their due share to the disturbing situation. The Chief Minister, as far as he was concerned, felt that he was not responsible for such a dead-lock. Moreover, the Government at one stage declared that it would do no rethinking on the matter. As far as the employees were concerned, no doubt, they tried their best to end the dead-lock. They appealed to the Prime Minister to intervene. The opposition parties, seized of the problem, represented to the Government to explore means of ending the impasse satisfactorily. Time and again the office bearers of the All India State Government Employees Federation, on behalf of the employees, met and had talks with the Chief Minister, but it was of no avail.

As the Andhra Pradesh Government maintained its rigid attitude, the scope for negotiations was crippled. It looked as though the strength of striking employees were ebbing. Therefore, they were driven to a state of requesting the Government for bilateral talks, perhaps, for the following reasons. First, they struck work without adequate planning and so they could not expect the strike to continue for long. Second, the management of the strike was not sound, as there were pulls and counterpulls in different directions. This could be seen by the fact that after the strike, some of the employees blamed leaders for their defective leadership. Third, the employees expected that the prolonged strike would very adversely affect sanitation, and cause such public nuisance and inconvenience that the public would demand an immediate reconciliation which unfortunately was conspicuous by its absence. Finally, it was but natural that the morale of the employees slowly but progressively deteriorated with the lapse of time for want of salaries to keep the families going. At last, bilateral talks commenced on the 44th day of the strike. Government offered Rs. 3 crores as the total quantum of relief which the employees rejected outright. The Government continued to maintain its unhelpful stand that salaries of employees would not be paid for the strike period and ousted temporary employees would not be taken back into the service of the Government.

The Government at one stage offered a rise in D.A. of between Rs. 6 and Rs. 11 on condition that 50% of it would be credited to the Provident Fund and the whole would be paid in cash with effect from 1-1-1972. If strike were called off, Government agreed to reinstate all the ousted employees, but refused to pay the salaries of the employees. Instead, it offered a month's pay as advance to be recovered in 12 monthly instalments.

Afterwards, the events took a dramatic turn to the surprise of the employees and the public. As an anti-climax to what had occurred so far to the agonising strikers, the strike was suddenly called off,[18] on the 56th day leaving all demands to the discretion of the Chief Minister.

The effects of the strike were far-reaching and disastrous. The strike paralysed the entire administration, upset the school year, caused postponement of public examinations, dislocated the work of courts, districts and taluqs, hampered work in government hospitals, created health hazards in all local bodies. In no small way it affected lakhs of people solely dependent on the employees. The employees and their families underwent severe hardship and privation because of non-payment of salaries for two months and lack of outside resources to make both ends meet. Business turnover of the order of crores of Rupees was jeopardised because the total salary bill of all the employees was out of circulation. On the whole, it had a total depressing effect on society.

In order to alleviate the hardship of the employees, the Government announced the following relief measures. First, an ad-hoc increase of Rs. 6 per month in Dearness Allowance was sanctioned to all employees drawing pay upto Rs. 575 p.m.[19] Second, House Rent Allowance[20] was given to the gazetted and non-gazetted employees. Third, the existing rate of the City Compensatory Allowance was enhanced by 50%.[21] Fourth, the Government also enhanced the special pay of Typists and Stenographers.[22] The aforesaid measures entailed an additional expenditure of Rs. 7 crores to the Government. The Government condoned break in service, on compassionate grounds and dropped all cases of disciplinary proceedings against the employees.[23]

Later on, the Government, which had decided earlier not to pay the employees, paid salaries for the strike period, treating the period of absence from 12th April to 6th June, 1971 as earned leave.[24]

The Lessons

In a way the strike may be regarded as an experiment in Civil Service Unionism. The strike offers valuable lessons to both the parties. It would appear they have put their respective strengths to trial.

The employees have to learn that their demands must be reasonable; that they must properly time the strike; and have sound planning and effective organisation. Further, they must realise that to continue a strike if necessary, for a comparatively long period and to make it a success, they must be economically above want and financially sound. Unfortunately, as was amply demonstrated, this was not the case in practice. Moreover, if the strike were to result in a stalemate, there was not much for the Government to lose but the employees only would be put to untold misery. In the final analysis, the employees may note that fight against organised Governments headed by powerful Chief Ministers is not that simple as some of the employees and leaders assume.

The Government can also profitably learn some lessons. It would be wise if the Government were to be a bit restrained in making promises to the already dissatisfied employees on their personal matters about which the employees are bound to be sensitive and even emotionally charged. Perhaps if such promises were not made in many cases, there would be no basis for a strike at all.

When the Central and other State Governments have raised the D.A. or paid interim relief to their employees it is not quite right for the Government of Andhra Pradesh to be unwilling to do so. It would be a desirable policy for any State Government to profit by the experience of Central or other State Governments which have already favourably dealt with similar strike situations. One would even expect a wise Government to properly visualise, anticipate and also adopt cordial measures and policies, specially when the issue under consideration happened to be both a pressing and identical one. Of course, in dealing with problems like increasing D.A. or payment of interin relief, it may be difficult to evolve a common policy for Central and State Governments. Such a step, in the long run, it is hoped, would eliminate the undesirable consequences and help curb the irritant but reasonable behaviour of the employees.

Promulgation of ordinances, termination of service of temporary employees, disciplinary actions, imposition of prohibitary and regulatory orders, etc. would seem stale gimmicks that would not suit the rapidly changing times and their complex administrative situations. Government has to realise the need for a dynamic strategy in dealing with strike situations and endeavour to be liberal to the extent the situation warrants.

Government should have foresight and vision to prevent strikes. Probably it would have avoided the strike by giving the employees a chance for a second round of talks before promulgating an ordinance prohibiting strikes in essential services.[25] It is for the Government to give serious and prompt consideration to the question whether they were always sure that by such precipitate action they would not be further provoking the employees towards recklessness.

Governments in all advanced countries have accepted joint consultation as a method to resolve problems between the Government and its employees. Although Andhra Pradesh Government had been trying to solve problems through the Joint Staff Council,[26] it proved ineffective. It is therefore necessary that Government should show a positive attitude towards the problems of employees and give weight to their point of view before arriving at a conclusion.

Some do not see why the Government should refuse to consider the demands in the beginning and concede the same after the strike. Many attribute such apparently inexplicable decisions of the Government to the fact that they are perhaps motivated by the ensuing elections to State Legislature.

Since the the Andhra Pradesh employees are getting dissatisfied with the unfulfilled nature of their demands and the Government attitude, it is high time for the Government to evolve a clear policy on personnel matters.

References

1. Employees were divided on the regional basis of Telangana and Andhra and reunited for the purpose of the Strike.
2. Employees' representatives, however, claimed that in Uttar Pradesh the strike did not involve simultaneously all the districts of the State. They said the strike was held as Relay strike, while in this State it was "total and complete" involving Government employees in all the 21 districts. '"The Decan Chronicle", Secunderabad, dated 7-6-1971.
3. The Joint Council of Employees' Unions and Associations (J.C.E.) represented 46 unions of the Andhra Non-Gazetted Officers (N.G.Os.) Elementary and Higher Secondary, Teachers of Andhra region, and the Municipal, the Medical, the Government Printing Press, and the Public Works Department workers of the entire State. The Joint Council of Action of Telangana Employees (J.C.A.) represented 16 unions of N.G.Os. and teachers of Telangana
4. See "White Collar Voice", official organ of the Andhra Pradesh N.G.Os. Association April 1971, p. 3. Also see, The Indian Express, Vijayawada, dated 1-7-1971.
5. Employees could not go on strike prior to elections to Parliament as in other States because a section of employees were not ready for the strike in February, 1971 and the majority of the employees favoured an indefinite Strike rather than a day's token strike on 26-2-1971 as contemplated by others and some considered that'it would be improper to disturb the election schedule.

6. They include about 2,30,000 non-gazetted employees, 1,42,000 school teachers, 25,000 employees working in Panchayati Raj institutions, 25,000 work-charged employees and 19,000 municipal employees.
7. The basis of the Commission's recommendation was that the minimum remuneration has not kept pace with the per capita increase in national income, and the real earnings of Central Government employees generally have also lagged behind those of industrial employees. The Commission also observed that while the index of real earnings of factory workers has diminished from 103 in 1962 to 95 in 1968 the diminution in respect of employees has been more marked, thns, the Government employees earning up to Rs. 400 have experienced a fall in the real earnings from an index number of 103 in 1962 to 88 in 1968. The Commission also stated that a review may be called for when the 12 monthly average reaches 228 points in cost of living index. Quoted in "White Collar Voice", *op. cit.*, pp. 3-4.
8. Pay revision was effected in 1969, on the recommendations of the One-Man Pay Commission, and the same pay revision was modified partially in 1970.
9. The Hindu, Madras, dated 19-2-1971, p. 13.
10. The revenue income rose from 79-27 crores in 1958-59 to 222-38 crores in 1969-70.
11. The per capita income rose from Rs. 275 in 1960-61 to Rs. 478 in 1968-69.
12. Amounting to Rs. 36 crores—The Hindu, Madras, dated 21-2-1971, p.4.
13. Amounting to Rs. 20 crores—The Hindu, Madras, dated 21-2-1971, p.4.
14. The expenditure on Civil administration is Rs. 12- 5 crores on 1958-59 forms 19-1% of the total expenditure, while in 1969-70 expenditure was Rs. 34 crores, the percentage being 14.
15. Andhra Pradesh 'Ordinance' No. 1 of 1971 later repealed by the Andhra Pradesh Essential Service Maintenance Act, 1971.
16. The Indian Express, Vijayawada, dated 22-4-1971, p. 1
17. The Indian Express, Vijayawada, dated 27-8-1971, p. 5.

18. *The* leaders believed no useful purpose would be served by further talks and that the Strike would fizzle out as some employees expressed a desire to join duty.
19. G.O.Ms. No. 204, Finance (Pay Commission) Department, Government of Andhra Pradesh, Hyderabad, dated 23-6-1971.
20. About three-fourths of the Dearness Pay (Dearness Pay is a part of Dearness Allowance) was taken into account to calculate H.R.A. G.O.Ms. No. 207. Finance (Pay Commission) Department, Government of Andhra Pradesh, Hyderabad, dated 23-6-1971.
21. G.O.Ms. 158, Finance (T.A.) Department, Goverment of Andhra Pradesh, Hyderabad dated 23-6-1971.
22. Rs. 10 for Typists (lower grade); us. 15 for higher grade; Rs. 20 for Stenographers (lower grade); Rs. 35 for higher grade. The Indian Express, Vijayawada, dated 25-9-1971.
23. The Indian Express, Vijayawada, dated 27-8-1971, p. 5.
24. G.O.M.s. No. 262, Finance (Pay Commission) Department, Government of Andhra Pradesh, Hyderabad, dated 30-7-1971.
25. The J.C.A. of Telangana employees expressed similar view. See the Hindu, Madras dated 17-4-1971, p. 8.
26. See for details, Sri N. Umapathy & Sri A. Amrutha Rao, "Organisation of Joint Staff Council in Andhra Pradesh", Community Development and Panchayati Raj Digest, Vol. 2, No. III, January, 1971, pp. 306—317, National Institute of Community Development, Hyderabad.

8

Strikes by State Governments Employees : an All India Problem*

Employees of most of the State Governments in India have either struck or threatened to strike work a few days before the scheduled dates for the conduct of mid-term elections to Parliament. Strikes by State Governments employees cease to be a mere state problem. The issues posed, the policies involved, and the solutions to be arrived at are so interwoven that their perimeters are hardly confined to the exclusive domain of the States. The intricacies involved are so complex and variant that the only pragmatic way is to consider them as an all India problem. The problem transforms itself into an All India one, and is bound to change the constitutional and organisational structure of Central and State services, impinge upon the established net work of Central State financial relations and disturb the process of planning. Further, it poses social problems questioning the ethics of social justice. Hence, in future any approach by Governments to deal with strikes must be based entirely on new grounds keeping in view the National trends, policies and interests.

The scope of the paper is confined to a brief review of the pre-election trends in strikes all over the states and to an examination of how the issues involved make strikes no less an all India problem.

It is a fact that the State employees are highly motivated by the benefits granted to Central Government employees. On the recommendation of the Third Pay Commission, the Government of India announced an interim relief ranging from Rs. 15 to 45 to its employees on September 30, 1970 with retrospective effect from March 1, 1970. The basis of the Commission's recommendation is

---

* Co-authored with Prof. P.A. James.

that the minimum remuneration has not kept pace with the per capita increase in national income, and the real earnings of Central Government employees generally have also lagged behind those of industrial employees.

Prior to the announcement of interim relief to the Central employees, the Maharashtra State Government employees went on mass casual leave for three days in August 1970 demanding increase in the rates of dearness allowance to maintain parity with Central employees. Since the Government did not respond they went on an indefinite strike for 12 days in November 1970. However, the emphasis has now shifted to grant of interim relief on par with central employees. Dissatisfied with rigid attitude of, and poor response from the Government, the employees with cooperation of other trade unions and political parties threatened with "Bombay Bundh" on 24-11-1970. Perhaps, afraid of the proposed Bundh the Government promptly released the arrested leaders and the strike was called off on Government's assurance to consider their demands. As the assurances were not given effect to, the employees again threatened to strike before elections. Only then did the government after consultations with leaders announce ad hoc interim relief, ranging from Rs. 10 to Rs. 22.50 per month with effect from January 1, 1971 which benefited five lakhs employees, entailing an additional expenditure of about Rs. 11 crores per year.

Soon after the Maharashtra strike, the General Secretary of the All India State Governments Employees' Federation in a press statement announced that more than 40 lakhs State Governments' employees all over the country might resort to strike in January-February 1971, to press their claims for a national wage policy.[1]

The mid-term elections, luckily came in handy for the employees and they started agitating in different ways for their demands, and payment of interim relief at Central rates. The Governments of Tamil Nadu and Mysore being prudent, sensed the pre-election mood of their employees and to satisfy them implemented the pay commission's recommendations.

In the State of Kerala, the employees went on a pre-election indefinite strike for 12 days in February 1971. The main demand was interim relief on par with the Central rates. The Government was not so rigid, for it conceded the demand partially to pay at the rate of Rs. 10 for all those drawing a salary upto Rs. 600 amounting to Rs. 4 crores. But employees wanted full payment, estimated to cost annually about Rs. 9 crores. The strike was a success and complete. Government promulgated ordinance banning strikes in essential services although, those belonging to such did not participate in the strike. There was considerable public reaction against the strike. Doubts were even expressed over the future of the government.

The Election Commissioner requested the employees to call off the strike to conduct elections as per the dates fixed. Apprehending dislocation in election work the Kerala government sought poll postponement. Finally, an agreement was reached sanctioning to all the employees relief ranging from Rs. 11 to Rs. 17 with effect from January 1, 1971. As per the terms of the agreement three and half lakhs of employees benefited and the extra burden on the state exchequer estimated to be Rs. 5 crores. The strike was called off after 12 days, but the gimmicks resulted in postponement of elections, by three days.

In other states like, Uttar Pradesh, Madhya Pradesh, Bihar, Punjab, Orissa and Rajasthan, employees went on strike or on mass casual leave for a day or two. Many of the State governments as though not to displease their employees before the poll either sanctioned some relief or assured to appoint Pay Commissions.

The story of strike in Andhra Pradesh presents a different picture. Only in this State, unlike employees in other States, the employees could not go on strike prior to elections, perhaps, for the following reasons:—

(1) The employees were not quite prepared for the strike by the time, the leaders wanted them to go on strike.

(2) Majority of the employees favoured an indefinite strike rather than a day's token strike on February 26, 1971 as contemplated by others.

(3) The Chief Minister assured the leaders of employees that the Government will have talks on various demands and

decisions arrived at would be announced in the Budget Session of the Legislature.

(4) A section of the employees felt that it would be improper to disturb the election schedule.

Employees of Andhra Pradesh Government were also agitating for grant of interim relief, House Rent Allowance and City Compensatory Allowance on par with Central Government employees. Because of the rigid attitude of the Government, about 4.5 lakhs of Non-Gazetted employees, teachers, Class IV employees, Staff of Local Bodies, industrial workers, contingent and work charged staff were forced to go on an indefinite strike from April 12, 1971.

The Government promptly banned the strike in essential services by promulgating an ordinance and issued a communique stating that the employees were liable for disciplinary action. The Chief Minister warned that all those employees failing to report to duty by April 24, 1971 would incur a break in service. Ignoring all these threats, the employees continued the strike.

A State-wide hartal call, in addition to the normal daily demonstrations, was given on May 12, 1971. The hartal supported by the Opposition parties was almost a success. The hartal at Tirupathi resulted in police firing and unfortunately, two persons had lost their lives. The striking employees had the full sympathy and support of other State Government employees, Central Government employees, different trade unions and Opposition parties.

Bi-lateral talks commenced on the 44th day of the strike. Government offered Rs. 3 crores as the total quantum of relief, but the employees rejected the offer. The Government maintained its stand that the salary would not be paid for the strike period and termination orders served on the temporary, employees would not be withdrawn.

The protracted talks and strike continued. The strike at last was called off on the 56th day leaving all the demands to the discretion of the Chief Minister. But at the same time the Government agreed to reinstate all the temporary employees whose services were terminated and to pay one month's salary as advance to be recovered in 12 monthly instalments. However, break in service was condoned by the Government on compassionate grounds.

Afterwards the Government announced an ad hoc increase of Rs. 6 per month in Dearness Allowance and House Rent Allowance for all employees drawing a basic pay upto Rs. 1,000 and an increase of 50 per cent of the existing City Compensatory Allowance. All this entails an additional expenditure of Rs. 6 crores per annum.

Some peculiar features to be noted in this strike are the solidarity exhibited by the employees, the uncompromising stand taken by the contending parties and the unduly long period over which the strike was allowed to be prolonged without any apparent signs of settlement. Incidentally, it may be noted that although so many lakhs of employees struck work for such a long period, it appears, they did not derive substantial benefits. Whereas employees of other States, did win their cause and achieve some benefit because the strikes were pre-election strikes. Thus, the failure of strike in Andhra Pradesh could be attributed to its characteristics—namely a post-election strike and an ill-timed one.

The timing to strike work stems to be quite opportune except in Andhra Pradesh. Strikes by State Governments employees, no doubt, have had a long history. But the employees appear to have had planned well to make their demands imperative just before elections to put the governments in an uncomfortable position. If the governments were to disagree, the employees would strike dislocating the conduct of midterm elections to Parliament as has actually happened in Kerala. Thus, the employees have mostly succeeded in forcing the government to concede partially to their demands. While election strategy of employees to enhance their bargaining power is commendable, it must be observed, that such things go against the accepted ethics of civil service.

Almost all the State Governments irrespective of their ruling political party, the Congress (Ruling) governments in Maharashtra and Rajasthan, and Andhra Pradesh, the Communist led coalition government in Kerala, the Congress (Organisation) governments in Gujarat and Mysore, the Samyuktha Vidhayak Dal Governments in Bihar and Uttar Pradesh, Akali Dal Government in Punjab and Orissa with President's rule considered the issue in more or less the same manner. The underlined common approach pursued by the State Governments may be seen in their resort to arrest of leaders, promulgation of ordinances banning the strikes in essential services and adoption of the 'pay-cut' policy,[2] for the days of mass casual leave or for the strike period.

Federal Theory No Solution

In India, under the Federal set up the Central Government is responsible for the management of all India Services, Central Services and other Subordinate Services and the States for the State Services. Organisationally and constitutionally it appears to be sound but strikes by state governments employees are primarily based on unsatisfactory service conditions and emoluments. There is imperative need to maintain high levels of efficiency and morale by the government which could be realised only when satisfactory service conditions are guaranteed. Further, indiscipline among the services if not checked and prevented would itself be a threat to democracy. A potent cause for strikes has been the existence of disparity in emoluments between the Central and State Governments employees.

Autonomy of the States is also involved because the States cannot or need not pay their employees always on par with the Central employees. No sooner a rise in emoluments is announced in the Centre than employees of all the State Governments, expect a corresponding rise. Unilateral rise affected by the centre is a sort of indirect dictation to the States in matter of their services—a State subject and hence affecting their autonomy. In a federation it must be understood that there cannot be absolute equality and, therefore, the question of parity should not arise. But the hardship faced by employees cannot be explained away only on the basis of a federal theory. The practical solution appears to be one of fixing for all the employees, on a rational basis, a national minimum wage for which they have been demanding for the last two decades. Thereafter, it should be possible, if conditions so demand, to pay differentially the Central employees. Even then, it would be necessary in national interest to restrict the range of disparity in emoluments between the Centre and State Government employees. It would be advantageous to set up a machinery to review periodically the personnel problems of Centre and State employees and to recommend uniform policy on an integrated basis to reduce their heart-burning.

Financial Implications

Since the announcement of elections to the Parliament, nine State Governments have either revised the rates of dearness allowance or offered interim relief to their employees. The employees expected to benefit by such relief number about 30 lakhs. The total commitments of State Governments, annually, are shown state-wise as under:

Serial No.	*State*	*Additional Expenditure (Rs. crores)*	*Number of Employees Benefited (in lakhs)*
1.	Tamil Nadu	21	6
2.	Mysore	3	2.5
3.	West Bengal	9.25	2.75
4.	Rajasthan	3.25	2.25
5.	Gujarat	2.71	2.76
6.	Kerala	5	3.5
7.	Maharashtra	11	5
8.	Bihar	5.40	Not available
9.	Madhya Pradesh	7	4
	Total	67.61	28.75

Note: In Andhra Pradesh increase in Dearness Allowance, House Rent Allowance and City Compensatory Allowance was announced in June 1971. The number of employees benefited is about 5 lakhs and the burden an exchequer is 6 crores per annum.

The estimated burden on the state exchequers will amount to not less than Rs. 100 crores per year, if under pressure, other states revise the pay and allowances of their employees. This trend is a repetition of what had happened in 1967 before the Fourth General Elections, when some of the state governments because of agitations had increased the pay of their employees. Consequently, the rise in non-plan expenditure in 1967-68 was about Rs. 130 crores.

Because of the enhanced emoluments or ad hoc interim relief, the state governments are compelled to meet additional expenditure of crores of rupees. The position is paradoxical in the sense that the State Chief Ministers have agreed that their employees deserved a better deal but for the limited financial resources of their Governments. Unable to meet the extra burden, the state governments have accused the Central Government for its unilateral policy, and its utter disregard for the financial doledrums in which the states lost themselves. While the leaders of employees unions are better aware of the meagre financial resources of the states, they want positive efforts to be made to improve the states financial position They suggest that the arrears of taxes and loans be collected and recovered properly, and that Central Government make available additional resources to the states enabling them to meet the extra expenditure.

All these raise number of basic financial questions closely connected with the question of strikes. Firstly, for an effective solution of strikes by state employees Central-state financial relations need to be modified. Financial allocation to states are partly modified on the basis of the recommendations of Finance Commission. The Commissions do not seem to have paid much attention to the question of the states ability and liability to meet the increased expenditure. Secondly, the Central Pay Commissions do not take an overall picture of Centre and States employees as their terms of reference are naturally restricted to the Central employees. Therefore, the state governments appoint their own pay commissions. The existing dichotomy of the Centre and States appointing different pay commissions, leads to many anamolous situations, resulting in perpetual disparities. Thirdly, even if the states were to concede to all the demands of the employees, there is a limit to the percentage of the expenditure that could be incurred on the services in the total budget. Finally, the pattern of expenditure normally has to be decided by the legislature as recommended by the executive and the financial policies and budgetary freedom of governments cannot be prescribed or restricted to the extent, the governments are forced to pay as a result of strikes.

Planning and Social Justice

Progressive development in various sectors of national activity is an impossibility without unstinted loyalty of government employees and coveted peace.

It may be seen in any strike by government employees, that the government or the employees do not seem to lose much in the game. But it is the general public that is put to great inconvenience and dislocation in normal civic life. The government employees constitute only a negligible percentage of the total population. In a developing economy, where huge amounts are required to be spent on planning, defence and social welfare, disproportionally high expenditure on employees emoluments may be unwarranted and prone to invite public criticism.[3]

Grant of interim relief by the state governments to their employees roughly amounts to an extra expenditure of Rs. 100 crores per year. The future liabilities though bound to be high are not readily predictable. It must be noted that unforeseen expenditure upset the Centre and States annual budgets. In relation to planning and development there has been growth of non-plan expenditure.

Although strikes are based on genuine grievances, they have partially paralysed administration and disturbed the pace of planning and development. India can ill-afford such breaks and situations which retard the plan process and over-all development.

Governments must give serious thought to maintain social justice as between sectors of employees and between employees and public who are served by them. The Governments are faced with problem of solving unemployment. Future policies on full employment that the governments are required to follow and other welfare objectives to be achieved will be thwardted if governments neglect to maintain a sort of balance guaranteeing social justice. Governments should explore the possibility of fixing the reasonable percentage of expenditure on salaries of employees leaving enough margin for developmental and welfare activities.

A few inconsistencies in governmental policies in dealing with strike situations are now stated. The state governments have been lenient when employees went on mass casual leave. Further, the action of the employees never stopped with having availed mass casual leave. Actually in some instances, the manner of treating the mass casual leave itself became a subject matter of future dispute.

Governments passing ordinances prohibiting strikes in essential services is another instance. In many states such a ban proved to be quite ineffective as ordinances could not cover all the employees.

Yet another case is the way the governments handle the demands. Generally, in the beginning, the governments refuse to accept the demands. After protracted and delayed bargaining, they partially accept the demands. Finally, after cessation of strike, the action taken and the punishment imposed are usually withdrawn. Yielding to the demands before the elections, with usual indifference in normal conditions is undesirable and indicates the weakness of the governments in dealing with situations calling for firm action. It reflects also absence of clear policy in personnel matters. The hesitant approach is largely due to the governments stand on prestige rather than their willingness to solve the problems in a realistic manner.

Conclusion

Practical considerations require that in future strikes by state employees must be tackled on a national basis and not in an isolated manner as at present. Political parties of India must attempt to evolve clear cut policies on problems of personnel. Serious thought has to be bestowed on the pressing problem of evolving a national wage policy. Rethinking in Centre-State financial relations is absolutely necessary to improve States' financial position. Positive efforts must be made by the governments to secure and maintain social justice among various sectors of employees. It is desirable to set up a suitable machinery to review periodically Centre-State personnel problems. Unless an integrated policy is formulated and implemented by the States in dealing with the strikes there is imminent threat of their employees going on sporadic strikes particularly after the release of the Third Pay Commission's report.

References

1. *Patriot,* New Delhi, dated 24-11-1970, p. 1.
2. However, in Kerala the employees have accepted to work on second Saturdays for to strike period to avoid possible loss of pay.
3. For example, in Kerala, the employees constitute less than two per cent of the population Administrative expenditure of Rs. 92 crores is out of proportion to the States' own revenue ol Rs. 83 crores. The establishment charges are over 63 percent of the total revenue including the State's share of the Union taxes and duties and Central grants-in-aid. (*The Hindu*, Madras, dated 25-2-71, p. 8).

9

Panchayati Raj in India : Local Governance in Action

ABSTRACT

The Constitution (73rd Amendment) Act, 1992 brought into force a new form of Local Self-Government in India popularly called 'Panchayati Raj'. Earlier in 1991, the Government of India adopted a 'New Economic Policy' in pursuance of Liberalization, Privatization and Globalization forces. These economic and political reforms may not be complementary but appears to have some underlying goals. However, examination of the relations between the two is not undertaken by this study. Here in this paper, a brief history of Local Self-Government in India and the situation that led to the present reform of the new Panchayati Raj is narrated. The salient features, aims and objectives of the new Panchayati Raj are described. A decade of local governance in action in terms of its achievements and weaknesses is reviewed. In the light of experience gained by some state governments, it is found that the real decentralization reforms have not taken place. There are demands for further empowerment of the Panchayati Raj Institutions with genuine political will on the part of all the political parties. Further amendment to the Constitution with full devolution of the powers, functions and finances is not only felt the urgent need but also the Prime Minister of India has assured all the concerned to bring the amendment. However, with the present instability of political parties, the traditional reluctance for the local democracy, sharing of powers on democratic lines may not be immediately possible. Bureaucracy which has been enjoying the power all these decades may not yield the ground so easily but, if wisdom does not prevail and one does not want to learn the lessons of democracy and decentralization, the so-called economic reforms cannot be successful. The struggle for decentralized democracy is an unending process and we are only happy that the Journey is on.

Introduction

India's vast majority of people live in rural villages. They are largely dependent on remote and unresponsive government (the Central and the State) historically characterised as "centralised, bureaucratic, corrupt and non-transparent". In most parts of rural India there had been a continuous and deep rift between the people and the government(s). The people do not have proper access to the information regarding the developmental plans, schemes and actions of governments. Further, they have no effective means to influence the policies, programmes or resource allocations for their development. The people in general and the rural people in particular have lacked effective ways to participate in shaping of their future. The essential needs of the people in health, sanitation, clean water, education, family planning, employment and their total development could not be solved by the centralised administration, top-down bureaucratic interventions. Therefore, it is finally felt that the critical needs of the people can be provided only with the local initiation, responsibility, accountability and local governance in action.

Policy Reforms in India

The last decade of the 20th century witnessed several policy reforms in India, which have far-reaching implications for the local governance.

Policy Reforms

From	*To*
Centralised System	Decentralised System (73rd and 74th Constitution Amendment Act)
Command Economics	Market Economics (Privatisation) (New Economic Policy)
Low Environmental Awareness	High Environmental Awareness
High Deficit Spending	Structural Adjustment Programme
High Subsidy	Low Subsidy (User payments)

To meet the emerging challenges of globalization, liberalisation and decentralization of development, it is felt necessary to enhance the capacity of local government authorities (Panchayats in rural areas and Nagara Palikas in urban) to assume responsibilities for delivery of basic services to the local people and mobilize local resources. It is also felt necessary to enhance the capacity of the citizens through education, information and access to technology, empowerment of women and the disadvantaged groups and strengthening the efforts to build self-reliance and developing participatory institutions such as Panchayati Raj Institutions (PRIs). To achieve these objectives, strategies are outlined in the ninth and tenth Five-Year-Plans of India.

Brief Historical Background of Panchayati Raj

The Sovereign, Socialist, Secular and Democratic Republic of India came into existence on January 26,1950 after achieving Independence on 15th August 1947 from the British Colonial Rule for over 200 years. At present (2003) India has a population of a little over billion (Census 2001)[1]. The country has adopted a federal constitution with unitary features. It is governed by a Union Government and 28 State Governments, seven Union Territories and over two million Panchayati Raj Institutions at the village and about 3,600 Town and City councils in urban areas. (95 City Corporations, 1,436 Town Municipalities and 2,055 Nagar Panchayats)

The peculiar feature of the Indian society is its kaleidoscopic diversity with an ancient and rich civilization of about five-thousand years. At the moment the traditional social norms co-exist with modern liberal democratic institutions in the form of parliamentary democracy which is centralised in nature. The "uneasy, ambiguous and contradictory relationship" between the tradition and the modernity is the order of the present society.

Brief History of Local Governance in India (1800 - 2000)

Period	*The Nature of the governance*
1800–1820s	Village republics managed village affairs independently
1830–1850s	To expand territory, the Britishers diluted power of village republics
1860–1900s	Centralised Forest and Land Acts alienated villagers from their natural resources

1900–1920s	Royal Commission on Decentralisation favoured Government imposed panchayats
1930–1940s	"Gram Swaraj" featured in freedom struggle. But the Government of India Act, 1935, formalised bureaucratic control over villages
1950–1960s	Vinoba Bhave started Bhoodan Movement. Balwant Rai Mehta Committee suggested three-tier panchayat system
1970–1980s	Asok Mehta Committee criticised the working of panchayats
1990–2000s	Government adopted three-tier Panchayati Raj system without effective transfer of powers

Mahatma Gandhi[2], the father of the nation, during the freedom struggle in 1940s explained his idea of Village *Swaraj* (Self-Rule) as it is a complete republic, which will be conducted by a panchayat of five persons annually elected by the adult villagers. This panchayat would combine the legislature, Judiciary and executive and there perfect democracy prevails based on individual freedom.

By 1947, there were the government created panchayats as units of local government with government defined judicial and administrative powers based on the recommendations of the Royal Commission on Decentralization in 1907. India's freedom fighters opposed this and proposed the agenda of *Gram Swaraj* (village republic) as nationalist struggle. During 1940s under Quit-India Movement village-based parallel governments were adopted in some parts of the country opposing the government panchayats. Many of such villages are now declaring self-rule[3]. About 1500 villages in seven states have already declared themselves village republics[4].

Even after India's Independence, despite all the commitment of nationalist leaders of *Gram Swaraj* (Village self-government), the constitution framers (-B.R. Ambedkar, the architect of the Indian

Constitution, Jawaharlal Nehru, the Prime Minister and others) decided the final draft of the constitution to continue the British policy rather more aggressively. The constitution failed to adopt the traditional village institutions as units of governance. Thus the village self-rule was not emphasised. The decentralised framework of rural local government was confined in the constitution to Article 40 of the Directive Principles of State Policy, which directed the state governments "to take steps to organise village panchayats and endow them with such powers and authority as may be necessary to enable them to function as the units of self-government".

Community Development Programme

In order to implement the rural development programmes of the First Five-Year-Plan in 1951, in the absence of any measures to organise village panchayats, the government of India divided the whole country into Community Developmental Blocks and decided to spend the developmental funds through these Blocks. The Community Development Programme was launched on October 2, 1952, (the birthday of Mahatma Gandhi). The Community Development Programme aimed at the socio-economic upliftment of rural people with several government schemes. In 1953 under the scheme of National Extension Service, 35,000 blocks were created each comprising about 300 villages to function under the supervision of a Block Development Officer (a bureaucrat). Despite good intentions, the 'governmentalised' development programmes could hardly evoke any people's participation and as such they could not create a real decentralised system of elected representatives.

To evaluate the failure of Community Development Programme, a committee was set up on 16 January, 1957 under the chairmanship of Balwantrai Mehta, an eminent social worker. The committee attributed the failure of Community Development Programme to the collapse of the village level traditional institutions or the collapse of the village republics. The committee submitted its report in November 1957.

The Balwantrai Mehta Committee recommended to create:

(1) A three-tier system of Panchayati Raj from the village to the district level with multi-level linkages *Zilla Parishad* at the district level, *Panchayat Samiti* at the block level and *Gram Panchayat* at the village level.

(2) Genuine transfer of powers to these Panchayati Raj bodies.

(3) Adequate transfer of resources to these institutions.

(4) All the developmental schemes at these levels must be chanelled through these institutions.

Panchayati Raj

Based on the recommendations of the Balwantrai Mehta Committee, Panchayati Raj was launched on October2,1959, (Mahatma Gandhi's birthday) in Nagaur district in Rajasthan State. In the same year Andhra Pradesh State also introduced the system. Soon after, many states established Panchayati Raj Institutions (PRIs). However, the enthusiasm with which these institutions were created could not be sustained. In the mid 1960s the Union Government at New Delhi almost setting aside the local bodies created a district programme, namely Integrated Rural Development Programme (IRDP). To meet the crisis in the agriculture, national level programmes like Small Farmers Development Agency (SFDA), Drought Prone Areas Programme (DPAP) and Integrated Tribal Development Agency (ITDA) were introduced. Gradually the concept of local development was withdrawn from the official agenda. Instead programmes for providing employment and for eradication of poverty were implemented throughout the country by the bureaucracy. Due to the increasing tendency towards centralisation in the state and central governments, and not providing finances which are due to the local bodies, the Panchayati Raj institutions could not participate in the developmental activities. The political leaders at the state level also lacked political will to transfer powers and finances to these bodies. Further, repeated postponement of elections of these bodies led to inefficiency and ineffectiveness of this first generation Panchayati Raj system.

With a view to explore, the possibilities of strengthening Panchayati Raj in 1977, the Janata Government (the first non-Congress government after 30 years) appointed Asoka Mehta Committee which reported in 1978. The main recommendations of the committee were:

(1) Regular and periodical elections to the Panchayati Raj bodies by the constitutional authority

(2) Elections through participation of political parties

(3) Powers of Taxation to the Panchayati Raj bodies

(4) Transfer of developmental functions to the Zilla Parishads

The recommendations could not be implemented due to the downfall of the Janata Government in 1980. In 1984 and in 1985 also, there were reports on the District Planning and Rural Development Administration. They pleaded greater powers to the Panchayati Raj bodies and advocated decentralized planning. L.M. Singhvi Committee in 1986 recommended constitutional status for Panchayati Raj, giving importance to *Gram Sabha* and *Nyaya Panchayats* (Judicial Panchayats)

On the basis of these recommendations, the Government of India under the Prime Ministership of Rajiv Gandhi of Congress Party introduced in July 1989, 64th and 65th Constitution Amendment Bills in the Parliament. The bills could not be passed in the Rajya Sabha. The bills were opposed initially alleging that the Central Government neglecting the State Governments, and likes to establish direct relations with the local bodies. After prolonged negotiations and consultations with different parties and state governments, the Janata Dal Government and Prime Minister V.P. Singh introduced another Amendment Bill in September 1990 in the Lok Sabha. The Amendment could not get through due to collapse of Janata Dal Government.

The Congress Party which came into power back in June 1991 under the Prime Ministership of P.V. Narasimha Rao, re-introduced the 73rd and 74th Amendment Bills which were passed by Lok Sabha and Rajya Sabha in December 1992. The Amendment Act, 1992 came into force on 24th April, 1993. The Act is to provide constitutional guarantees to safeguard the interests of Rural (73rd) and Urban (74th) local governments to empower them as effective democratic and self-governing institutions at gross-root level. The Act provides a constitutional form to structure mandate to these institutions. The objectives of the Act include decentralization of power and ensuring popular participation in planning, management and delivery of civic services.

New Panchayati Raj

Prime Minister P.V. Narasimha Rao described the emergence of the new Panchayati Raj as against the unjust and exploitative society, stands a bridge for development, symbolizes social harmony and future equity and a training school for autonomous political process. It provides, he hoped, an opportunity to transform the face of rural India having potential to create genuine democracy at the village level.

The 73rd amendment to the Constitution promoted decentralized democracy in the country, recognized the Panchayat as the local level of government and opened up possibilities for strengthening people's participation in decision making regarding their own development. It also setforth a process of providing and building up new leadership among women and weaker sections of the rural community. The 1992 Act specifically and explicitly made certain provisions mandatory and few others were left to the discretion of the State Governments.

The 73rd amendment was further extended on December 24, 1996 to the tribal population areas designed in the Constitution as Schedule V areas[5] with provision for stronger representation of tribal community and their access and control over community resources, institutions and instruments of governance. This extension gave absolute power to the *Gram Sabha* (Village Assembly) over resources and its management. Extension to the Scheduled Areas Act, (PESA) 1996, came into existence on the recommendations of the Bhuria Committee. It is applicable to eight states and 60 districts where the scheduled areas are there.

The salient features of the new Panchayati Raj:

(1) Establishment of *Gram Sabha* and three tiers of panchayats (*Panchayat, Panchayat Samities* and *Zilla Parishads*) at the village, block and district levels.

(2) Regular electrons every five years.

(3) Reservation of not less than one-third seats for women as members and chairpersons at all the three levels.

(4) Reservation of seats for Scheduled Castes, Scheduled Tribes and other backward communities.

(5) Constitution of State Election Commission.

(6) Constitution of State Finance Commission.

(7) The PRIs are to function as institutions of self-governance and they have been endowed with powers and authority to formulate and implement their own plans for economic development and social justice.

The number Panchayati Raj Institutions in 24 States and 3 Union Territories and the number of democratically elected representatives at different levels may be seen in the following table:

Level	*Tiers of local Govt.*	*Number*	*Number of Reps.*
Village (out of 5,79,000 villages)	Village Panchayats	227,698	3,198,554
Intermediate	Panchayat Samities	6000	151,412
District	Zilla Parishads	500	15,935
	Total	234,198	3,365,901

Gram Sabha: (Village Assembly)

"Gram Sabha" consists of all persons registered in the electoral rolls relating to a village panchayat. It provides an opportunity to all the adult members of the village panchayat to participate in the village affairs. Gram Sabha has to meet at least twice a year. Gram Sabha exercises such powers and performs such functions at the village level as provided by the legislature of a State. Except a few states like West Bengal, Madhya Pradesh and Kerala, the Gram Sabhas are not given any overriding power over gram panchayats. The Gram Sabha's recommendations are not binding on gram panchayat. The empowered gram sabhas in some of the states proved better in providing water and housing etc. The experience of participation of people in gram sabha meetings is not that encouraging due to different social, political and economic factors.

Panchayats

There are three institutions, i.e., Gram Panchayat at Village Level, Mandal Panchayat at Intermediate Level & (Cluster of some villages) and *Zilla* (District) *Parishad* (Council) at District Level are elected (Directly and Indirectly) once in five years by the people and their elected representatives. The *Sarpanch* (Chief of the Gram Panchayat) is directly elected by all the voters of the village. The chiefs of the Mandal Parishad and Zilla Parishads (President/Chairman/Pradhan differently named) are elected by the members elected to those bodies. The positions of the members and the chiefs are reserved to the women (at least 30%) and to Scheduled Castes, Scheuled Tribes and Backward Communities in proportion of their population in the area on rotation basis.

In the past, prior to the Amendment (1993), the Panchayati Raj was not successful mainly for not conducting regular elections to the PRI's bodies by the State Governments. Therefore, the Amendment made a provision for the constitution of autonomous Election Commission at the State Level to hold the elections regularly once in five years on democratic lines. Despite this compulsive provision many state governments put spokes in the democratic wheels and stalled the elections to the extent possible even against the Judicial Pronouncements.

The Panchayati Raj Institutions are required to constitute a number functional communities for Agriculture, Public health, Water supply, Family planning etc., and Beneficiaries Committee to execute public works at Gram Panchayat level. The Zilla Parishad is required to constitute a number of Standing Committees for Planning and Finance, Rural Development, Agriculture, Education and Medical Services, Women Welfare, Social Welfare and Public Works. At every level Chief Executive officers and other administrative staff assist the elected representatives and the chiefs of the PRIs.

Third Stratum?

Some supporters of local self-government and democratic decentralization are considering that the 73rd Amendment has created a third tier of the Indian State. They also plead that all the rural development agencies like District Rural Development Agency and Integrated Tribal Development Agency and other state government departments working at the district level must be transferred to the district to work under the control of PRIs. In a way all the bureaucrats and their agencies along with their budgetary allocations must be under the supervision and the direction of the democratic government at the district level under the control of the Zilla Parishad and its chief. This kind of experiment is initiated to some extent in Madhya Pradesh, Kerala and West Bengal. However, the Governments at the Centre and the States have not initiated any steps in this direction and do not have any intentions to establish a third stratum.

Panchayat Responsibilities

The Schedule XI of the Constitution specifies 29 "subjects" of responsibility that state government *may* devolve to the Panchayati Raj Institutions. They are:

(1) Agriculture, including agricultural extension

(2) Land improvement, implementation of land reforms, land consolidation and soil conservation

(3) Minor irrigation, water management and watershed development

(4) Animal husbandry, dairy and poultry

(5) Fisheries

(6) Social forestry and farm forestry

(7) Minor forest produce

(8) Small-scale industries, including food processing industries

(8) Khadi (homespun cloth) village and cottage industries

(10) Rural housing

(11) Drinking water

(12) Fuel and fodder

(13) Roads, culverts, bridges, ferries, waterways and other means of communication

(14) Rural electrification, including distribution of electricity

(15) Non-conventional energy sources

(16) Poverty alleviation programmes

(17) Education including primary and secondary schools

(18) Technical training and vocational education

(19) Adult and non-formal education

(20) Libraries

(21) Cultural activities

(22) Market and fairs

(23) Health and sanitation, including hospitals, primary health centres and dispensaries

(24) Family welfare

(25) Women and child development

(26) Social welfare, including welfare of the handicapped and mentally retarded

(27) Welfare of the weaker sections, and in particular of the Scheduled Castes and the Scheduled Tribes

(28) Public distribution system

(29) Maintenance of community assets

Reservations

One of the outstanding features of the Amendment is reserving almost one-third of the seats (membership, chairpersons and institutions) to the women, and scheduled castes (SCs), scheduled tribes (STs) and backward classes (BCs) in proportion to their population. The Amendment gave more powers to the rural political elite, and as a check over them empowered the marginalized groups, weaker sections and disadvantaged by providing reservations. This counter balancing of the local elites is of strategic significance to maintain the over balance of power in the hands of the centralized Indian State and the ruling groups behind.

Provision of reservations indeed widened the democratic base. It brought about one million women and 0.7 million of SCs, STs and others, enabled to legitimately participate in the local democracy. A number of studies suggested a systemic change in the rural economic relations and power structure for their effective participation. These reserved candidates may not be very effective particularly women of deprived classes, SCs and STs in the initial years. But their very representation in such large number itself strengthen their voice. Their initial inability in participation is mainly due to their historical background, lack of past experience, exposure, illiteracy, economic weakness and less genuine interest on the part of the representatives to get empowered.

Finances of Panchayati Raj[6]

Financial paucity has been one of the main causes of failure of the Panchayati Raj in the past. Therefore, the Panchayats are empowered to levy and collect taxes, duties, tolls and fees. To improve their financial position, the 1992 Act made it mandatory on the part of State Government to constitute a Finance Commission at the expiration of every fifth year to review the financial position of the panchayats and to make recommendations to the Governor regarding formulae on distribution of revenue between the State and the Panchayats and also among the different levels of Panchayats. The Finance Commission also determines the rates of taxation, duties, tolls and fees. The principles on which the grants-in-aid to be paid to the panchayats from the consolidated fund of the state will be made by the Finance Commission.

Experiences of Some States in Implementing the New Panchayati Raj

West Bengal[7]: It is the first State under the leadership of Left Front Government led by the Communist Party (Marxist) for the last 25 years realized and proved the importance of Panchayati Raj for sustaining political power. Land reforms were implemented with the help of middle and rich peasantry which led to the effective implementation of panchayat system. Since 1984 it has given an access to power and resources. For the first time in India local elected bodies became more powerful than the bureaucracy at local level. Under the new Panchayati Raj Act, elections are held regularly, all the 29 subjects are transferred to Panchayats, funds were transferred on 12 items. All the development officials are brought under the control of District Panchayat and administrative staff pertaining to 12 items are transferred.

Madhya Pradesh[8]: The State under the Congress Party passed the Panchayati Raj Law as per the constitutional requirements, held panchayat elections, transferred funds, functions and functionaries. Each village now has a *'Gram Kosh'* (village treasury) having Rs. 60,000 to Rs. 70,000 for development. The villagers are taking decisions on their own with the help of the *Gram Sabha.* The Government's positive policy towards 'Power to the People', the social welfare reforms and eradication of poverty enabled a 'rule by the people' in place of 'ruling the people'. It is the vision of the state leadership that made a difference and people's participation in solving their own problems with local governance.

Kerala[9]: In the Panchayat elections held in 1995 the Left Democratic Front, CPI(M) led alliance won the majority of local bodies in Kerala. The government devolved powers to the panchayats and "People's Participation in Planning". It is the first state which transferred several government departments and all the 29 subjects and diverted 35 to 40 per cent of the state budget outlay to Panchayati Raj Institutions. The Government asked local self-government institutions to prepare and implement "Local-level need-based Plan Programmes". Kerala launched "People's Campaign for Decentralized Planning" on August 17, 1996 to empower the PRIs. It is reported that the concept of People's Planning was flushed out through a six-phase campaign in which tens of thousand of officials and experts and about three million people participated. The *Gram Sabha* is activised in identifying the people's felt needs. Inspite of initial setbacks, the concept of people's planning and decentralization demystified the planning process. The financial position was improved after the launch of the People's Planning process.

Gujarat[10]: Gujarat State, home of legendary figures of panchayati raj like Mahatma Gandhi, Balvantrai Mehta, Asok Mehta is not acting in the recent years in the letter and spirit of the Constitution, because of the present ruling party's antipathy to grass roots democracy. It was one of the states known for the activities of the Panchayati *Raj* in the past during the early period of 1960s.

Rajasthan[11]: Rajasthan was the first state to introduce Panchayati Raj in 1959. Under the Amendment Act, it has only recently (2003) decided to transfer all the 29 subjects to the PRIs with funds, functions and functionaries in true spirit. This long awaited step will strengthen the position of Panchayats and empower PRIs to ensure sustainable rural development. In the new pattern of governance, the Zilla Parishads have been made the premier agencies for rural development and the District Rural Development Agencies have been merged with them. The rural development department of the state government has also been merged into the Panchayati Raj Department. The administrative staff are brought under the control of the Zilla Parishads and their Chiefs *(Pradhans)*. Panchayat will now have full rights to utilize their income at the local level[12].

Andhra Pradesh[13]: Andhra Pradesh was the second state which introduced Panchayati Raj in 1959. It is one of the few states, under the leadership of Telugu Desam Party, a regional party revived the dormant first generation Panchayati Raj. It sustained continuous political will and took steps to bring administration to the doorstep of the people *(Prajala Vaddaku Polana)*. It provided reservations to the women and weaker sections and disadvantaged groups in the

Panchayati Raj Institutions on rotation basis. The new Panchayati Raj Institutions came into existence in 1994 and elections were held. Election Commission, Finance Commission were constituted. But so far only 20 subjects are transferred to the Panchayats, did not transfer the administrative staff and the funds are not fully transferred. District Planning Committee is not constituted. Over and above the amendment, the state government constituted a number of committees[14] by special Act. There is no co-ordination between the committees of Panchayati Raj Institutions and the special committees. The funds of the PRIs are diverted to the activities of these committees without any participation of the elected representatives.

It is important to note that a massive rural development programme was launched on 1st January 1997 in the name of *Janma Bhoomi* (Native Land) wherein the leaders and the workers of the ruling Telugu Desam Party campaigned about 18 times meeting the people directly and undertaking developmental programmes involving state administrative staff and PRIs funds. A kind of decentralization has been taking place without local democracy.

The struggle for empowerment is on by the representatives of Panchayats and Zilla Parishad chiefs wherein they formed in 2003 a Federation for the Empowerment of Local Self-Government with the help of an organization known as *Lok Satta* (People Power) for the establishment of "little republics". Peoples campaign is on vigorously for collecting one million signatures to bring pressure on the state government to devolve all the powers to the PRIs as per the 1992 Act.

In Orissa State the new panchayats were elected only in January 1997. Though the Act was passed in 1995, not much progress is made so far. In Bihar State, state elections were not held till 2001 and the Government has been reluctant to transfer powers inspite of the judicial directives. Karnataka is one of the states which transferred all the 29 subjects and much progress is reported due to its earlier history. In Tamil Nadu, the two ruling parties, the Dravidra Munnetra Kazagam (DMK) and All India Anna Dravida Munnetra

Kazagam (AIADMK) are not in favour of sharing power with the Panchayati Raj Institutions. The state is not having much progress of PRIs. The Assam state transferred 11 subjects to PRIs. The Punjab state initiated to transfer the subjects. Not much advance is made in the smaller states like Goa, Pondicherry, Tripura, Meghalaya, Mizoram and Nagaland.

A Decade of Progress

No celebrations are held anywhere marking the tenth anniversary of the world's largest experiment in decentralized governance. The Prime Minister assured further empowerment and another constitutional amendment to enable the direct flow of funds to the panchayats as the devolutionary process remained static. Various studies confirm the PRIs remained ineffective due to the lack of commitment of successive governments. Simply stated panchayats have no funds, functions and functionaries. A study of panchayats in 19 states by the National Institute of Rural Development reveals that the parties across the political spectrum are unwilling to devolve powers to the Panchayati Raj Institutions, in brief there is power shortage[15] because:

(1) Elections to panchayats are yet to be held in four states

(2) 24 states have not transferred administrative powers to panchayats

(3) Panchayats do not have financial autonomy

(4) 12 states have yet to constitute District Planning Committees for decentralized planning

(5) Some state governments (Andhra Pradesh, Karnataka and Kerala) promoted parallel or variant structures to PRIs.

To review the progress of states regarding devolution of powers to the PRIs, the union government constituted in December 2002 an Empowered Sub-Committee on Financial and Administrative Powers of PRIs. The committee felt significance of the District Planning Committees (DPC) which have to be constituted in every state for feeding of district plans finalized by the DPCs into state and national level planning.

Parallel Bodies

While the powers are not completely devolved to the panchayats, the problem is further worsened by the creation of a large number of village level user groups formed under developmental programmes of state governments, all of which function independently of the PRIs but on the 'subjects' assigned to them in Schedule XI of the constitution. These user-groups include the Village Forest Committees, Self-Help Groups, Water Users Associations, Watershed Development Committees, Education Committees and programmes like *'Janma-Bhoomi'* in Andhra Pradesh, *'SwaJala Dhara'* in Karnataka and 'Peoples Planning' in Kerala, *'Gram Vikas Samity'* in Haryana, Vigilance Committee in Himachal Pradesh, Joint Forest Management in Gujarat and water user groups in Uttar Pradesh and Rajasthan.

It is alleged that these user-groups are utilizing the funds of the panchayats without involvement of the representatives elected to the panchayats. It is a phenomena spreading and running parallel to the growth of PRIs scuttling the democratic initiation of the panchayats and imposing bureaucratic domination over the panchayats like the Nodal Officer system in Andhra Pradesh.

Campaign for Empowerment

The heads of panchayats from all over India assembled in New Delhi in March 2002 to express their discontent and demanded the government a deadline to give effect to 73rd Amendment. They demanded that State Governments devolve funds, functions and functionaries to the Panchayats Raj Institutions as per the spirit of the Amendment. In August 2002 the Bihar High Court, Patna castigated the State Government for not transferring due powers to the panchayats. In September 2002 the Zilla Parishad Chiefs in Andhra Pradesh filed a case in the High Court forcing the State Government to implement the Amendment. They demanded changes in the Panchayati Raj Laws through a new constitution amendment to enable the PRIs to collect revenues and augment financial resources.

Politics of Panchayati Raj

Decentralization became important from the point of the twin objectives of the Indian polity viz. democracy and development.

However from the beginning, the Panchayat Raj Institutions were not regarded either as a "political means" to bring about a change in rural India or as part of the overall political process in the country. It was felt that as 'politics' is divisive, the Panchayati Raj Institutions should be 'non-political'. The Asoka Mehta Committee (1978) treated the Panchayati Raj as an 'extension of democracy' and recommended establishment of PR bodies below the state level as democratic bodies, with constitutional sanction of transfer of substantial powers to local bodies from the state governments. The report of the Sarkaria Commission on the Centre—State Relations (1983) also placed importance of democratic decentralization.

During 1959-64 under the leadership of Jawaharlal Nehru, the first Prime Minister, the first generation of Panchayati Raj was conceived as local bodies meant to ensure people's participation in development. After Nehru from 1964-77 panchayati raj remained the whipping boy of all those who wanted to discredit the decentralization of power[16].

The second generation of panchayati raj started when West Bengal state initiated new life to panchayati raj in 1978 on the lines of Asoka Mehta Committee recommendations to make panchayats an "organic, integral part of democratic process". The second generation panchayats in West Bengal[17], Karnataka[18], Andhra Pradesh[19], Kerala[20] and Jammu Kashmir[21] under non-Congress, left parties and regional parties attempted to make the panchayats the genuine political institutions, self-government institutions and microcosm of the state itself, the emphasis shifted from the bureaucracy to the political elements[22]. Local elections were fought in West Bengal (1978-2003), Karnataka (1987), Andhra Pradesh (1986-2000) on party lines despite opposition from other parties to the participation of political parties. These states inspired the rural people and created self-confidence in them. They introduced an element of reservations for the weaker sections and women. The second generation panchayats disturbed the earlier "balance" between the role of government officials and non-officials (peoples representatives).

The states ruled by non-Congress(I) and non-BJP Governments[23] are revitalising the panchayats and developed a pattern of politicization of the rural masses taking the administration to the doorstep of the poor people. They are building local political leadership. This will ultimately lead to build an organic link between *Gram Sabha* at the village level to *Lok Sabha* at the national capital.

Almost all political parties except the Congress(I) welcomed the politicization of the people in Panchayati Raj. The party's attitude is not helpful for genuine devolution of powers at the grass root level. The very great idea and the historical step taken to amend the constitution by the Congress (I) to establish the "Third Stratum"[24] will not be a success unless it sets aside its fears about local democracy and peoples participation in governance and development.

Achievements of Panchayati Raj

Ashok Mehta Committee (1978) reported that Panchayati Raj has many achievements to its credit. Politically it became a process of democratic seed drilling in the Indian soil, making an average citizen more conscious of his rights than before. Administratively, it bridged the gulf between bureaucratic elite and the People. Social-Culturally it generated a new leadership whict was not merely relatively young in age, but also modernistic and pro-social change in outlook. From the development angle, it helped rural people cultivate a developmental psyche[25].

It is observed that constitutional amendments will alone can not usher in meaningful devolution of power or vibrant panchayats except with strong political will. For that a strong people's movement[26] is felt necessary to oversee that regular elections are held, democratically elected strong local government institutions are formed, powers over bureaucracy are given to the elected representatives to prompt them to action and to maintain the presence of strong opposition.

To sum up, despite many teething problems, political reluctance, in a short period of about 10 years, the new Panchayati Raj created much impact on the Indian polity in general and on PRIs in particular. Reservations in PRIs provided opportunities for active participation and representation of reserved categories which paved way for the emergence of new leadership among women, SCs, STs and other backward classes[27]. Further, where the national political parties, the state governments and the political leaders encouraged and empowered the PRIs, the representation and participation of the people has been very effective. The current political struggles, legal battles, the pressures of the intelligentia, the media, the activism of many NGOs, the advocacy of the global forces certainly made the ruling parties at the Central government to realize the need for the genuine political interest in the democratic decentralization. In this direction necessary steps are being taken to amend the constitution once again to empower the Panchayati Raj Institutions to act as the third tier of the government in India.

References

1. 72% of population of India lives in more than half-a-million villages. The rest 28% dwells in about four-thousand urban settlements (Towns and Cities).
2. 'Question Box', *Harijan,* July 26,1942.
3. For details, Mahapatra Richard with others, (August 31,2002) The Second Independence, *Down to Earth,* pp. 22-36.
4. *Ibid.,* p. 23.
5. For details, Singh, S.K., (1997), Self-governance for the Scheduled Areas, *Journal of Rural Development,* Vol. 16, No. 4.
6. For details, Ananth S. Pathi and Om Prakash Bohra, (Jan-March 1995) Finances of Panchayati Raj Institutions, *Indian Journal of Public Admn,* Vol XLI, No. 1, PP. 68-77 and John, Oommen (2000), Strengthening of Panchayat Raj Finances in Kerala: A New Phase, *The Indian Journal of Public Administration..*
7. For details, Ghosh D.K., Transparancy in Panchayats: West Bengal Scenario, (2001) *Administrative Change,* Vol. XXVIII, No. 2, pp. 69-80, and Mukherjee, Nirmal. (1 May 1993) The Third Stratum, *Economic and Political Weekly.*
8. For details, Singh SS, and Suresh Mishra, (1991), Panchayati Raj Experiment in Madhya Pradesh, *Indian Journal of Public Administration,* Vol. XXXVII, No. 4, pp. 687-697 and Subramanayam C.N., Observations on the New Panchayati Raj:

Experiences in Madhya Pradesh, and, Power to the People, (March 17, 2003) *Outlook,* pp. 32-34.

9. For details, Isaac T.M. Thomas with Richard W. Franke, *Local Democracy and Development,* LeftWord Books, New Delhi, and Mathew George, (July-December, 1997), Institutions of Self-Government in India: Towards Multi-level Federalism, *Review of Development and Change,* Vol. II, No. 2, and K.P. Kannan, *People's Planning: Kerala's Dilemma.*
10. For details, Mathew George, Gujarat: Where are the Panchayats? *The Hindu.*
11. For details, Hooja, Rakesh and Meenakshi Hooja, (2001), The Status of Panchayati Raj in Rajasthan - Reflections on Some Select Indicators in the Context of the 1994 Act, *Administrative Change,* Vol. XXVIII, No. 2, pp. 81-104.
12. *The Hindu,* dated 17 August, 2003, p. 13.
13. For details, Reddy G. Sreenivas and M Vidyasagar Reddy (1996), Panchayati Raj in Andhra Pradesh: Pre and Post 73rd Constitution Amendment Position, *Dynamics of Public Administration,* Vol. 1, No. 1, pp. 129-152.
14. Watershed committee, forest protection committee, Irrigation committee, education committee, mothers committee, water and sanitation committee family welfare committee, youth associations, self-help groups, farmers clubs, Janma Bhoomi habitation committee.
15. For details, Mahapatra Richard, Toothless at 10, January 15, 2000, *Down to Earth,* pp. 13-14, and Kulkarni Manu, (May 15, 2003) Still Born Devolution, *Down to Earth,* p. 2, and *The Hindu,* dated August 19, 2003, p. 13.
16. Mathew George, *Panchayati Raj: From Legislation to Movement,* (1997) Concept Pulishing Company, New Delhi, p. 15.
17. Left Front Government, under CPI(M) 1978-2003.
18. Janata Dal Government, 1986-90.
19. Telugu Desam Party (TDP) 1983 - 88 and 1994-2003.
20. Left Democratic Front under CPI(M) 1997-2001
21. National Conference 1988-2003.
22. Mathew George , *Op.cit.,* pp. 17-18.
23. Left Parties in West Bengal and Kerala, Janata Party in Karnataka, Lok Dal in Haryana, Telugu Desam Party in Andhra Pradesh, Janata

in Orissa, National Conference in Jammu & Kashmir and DMK and AIADMK in Tamilnadu.

24. Mukarji, Nirmal, The Third Stratum, (1 May, 1993) *Economic and Political Weekly.*

25. Asoka Mehta Report 1978.

26. Mathew, George, (1994), Panchayati Raj: From Legislation to Movement, Concept Publishing Company, New Delhi, p. 41.

27. For details, Buch, Nirmala, Panchayats in India—Forum for citizens' participation in local governance: Representation and Participation of Rural Women - Experience and Challenge, paper presented to International Forum on Federation in Mexico, Veracruz, 15-17 November 1991, and Palaniturai, G. (2001), The Genre of Women Leaders in Local Bodies Experience from Tamil Nadu, *The Indian Journal of Public Administration,* Vol. XLVII, No. 1, pp. 38-50, and Panda, Snehalata, (1999), Political Empowerment of Women: Case of Orissa PRIs, *The Indian Journal of Public Administration,* Vol. XLV, No. 1, pp. 86-94.

10

The Status of Public Administration Education in India

The term 'Public Administration' is usually understood as an instrument of action, as a profession and as an academic discipline. In the context of independence, democracy, constitution, planning and development, Public Administration in India as an academic discipline, an instrument of action and as a profession is only about four decades old. Therefore, all teething problems are natural in its infancy.

The focus of this paper is on the present status of the discipline of Public Administration in India in respect of teaching and research and as an instrument of action.

Post-Independence Development

The most important change in the public administrative system of India after independence is the continuously expanding scope of public administration. The academic discipline of public administration in the universities, research and training institutes and the profession of public administration as a practising civil service have been enlarging their extent and scope due to the constitutional guarantees and political developments. But it is important to note that both the academic discipline of public administration and the profession of public administration have not been growing in mutual cooperation in one direction with one purpose and one ideology. They appear to be enlarging and extending their areas in different directions with an implicit common understanding. For, on the professional side India inherited the British civil service with parliamentary democratic institutions and administrative set-up. But on the academic side much of our knowledge and curricula of public administration and public management is imported from the US. Even on the administrative side, soon after independence, India sought administrative expertise and advice from the US experts. India attempted to introduce managerialism in the traditional administration and civil service.

Though the academic bodies in India attempted to study something about Indian situation like the urban and rural governments and the state administration, their approach of study, research and solutions offered are either influenced by the US administrative theorists and management experts and academics, or by the US-educated Indian scholars in our universities. It appears they are caught up in a web of circumstances and did not attempt to come out of it. To many scholars and administrators, everything seems to be going on the right lines in India, though they are not satisfied with the happenings, events and results. For, they desire 'change' within the 'stability', they dream of 'welfare state' retaining 'inequalities', they conceive of 'democracy' without 'decentralisation', they imagine 'secularism' in 'Jai Hind', they demand 'unity' and 'integrity' in 'diversity' and they visualise 'sovereignty' without 'political development' and 'nation-building'.

Teaching of Public Administration in Universities

The universities in India have adopted different approaches about the 'core' of the discipline of Public Administration. It is high time to clearly lay down the objectives of teaching of public administration at various levels according to the emerging needs of a changing society.

In a country like India, the purpose of teaching public administration must be directed towards the social goals, and to create a generation of conscious and responsible citizens equipped with the necessary skills to effectively perform their roles as 'change agents'. To achieve this purpose what is required is, first, the modernisation of the syllabus in the 'core' of public administration and, second, training of the teachers to equip themselves to attain the desired goals.

Public Administration may be a 'chance-erected and chance-directed subject' in Indian universities. But over the last four decades the discipline has been growing. Having recognised this fact, one should think about the direction in which it should develop in future. It has been realised that the study of institutions and the systematisation of knowledge and 'public problem-solving' as important in the light of planned development and socio-economic reconstruction. But at present only the descriptive aspects of government machinery and procedure and evolution of the Constitution of India are taught. It means that much importance was attached to the historical and structural aspects rather than to the processes and functional aspects. It may be due to three factors:

First, the emergence of new institutions and opening up of the old institutions for the study.

Second, the secretive nature of the official work due to the colonial and anti-public attitude of the governmental machinery. Third, lack of training, probing aptitude and skills of analysis on the part of the Indian social scientists in general and their prohibitive social background in particular.

As such the prohibitive and inhibitive social and psychological attitudes of the government and the researchers did not permit the study of the functional aspects of the governmental administrative machineries. For this many persons, personalities, and institutions also played a key role in such kind of development, like Paul H. Appleby, A.D. Gorwala, Jawaharlal Nehru, Vallabhbhai Patel, Fred Riggs, the Indian Institute of Public Administration, and others who advised the Indian Government and experts. Accordingly, the discipline, the profession and the instrument of action developed to the present status. There lies the strengths and weaknesses of the subject. The UGC, UPSC and the IIPA have failed to realise the importance, recognise the role and enforce the recommendations of expert bodies and, as the universities in India are autonomous, they are left to develop on their own without any direction from any recognised quarters. In brief, Indian universities do not claim a clear public administration education and training policy and programme.

If planned socio-economic reconstruction is our motto, the concerned agencies, such as the UPSC, the IIPA, the UGC, the ICSSR, the Universities and, finally, the education departments of different governments might have realised the necessity of public administrators/managers and other human resources and directed the type of social sciences knowledge to be developed and imparted. In the absence of clear thinking and direction, alongwilh the science and technology, social sciences, particularly Public Administration, was imported in its crude form leaving the study of its essence like 'government and politics', 'public policy' and 'public affairs' in the exporting countries.

Public Administration as a Discipline

Planned socio-economic reconstruction of a nation means it is necessarily concerned with Politics, Sociology, Economics, Law, Management and other allied subjects including Science and Technology. Therefore, Public Administration as a discipline should have strong linkages with a number of other disciplines and should be approached as an inter-discipline; nothing much can be done by separate autonomous departments. Public Administration may be born in the family of Political Science, but its marriage with other disciplines enriches the subject and it need not be the sub-field of Political Science alone.

It is true that in the absence of recognition of the 'core' of the discipline of Public Administration in diverse, autonomous universities, as in India, there are considerable variations between one department and another, depending upon the nature of the birth of the department, the type of the faculty and other local requirements. The Iqbal Narain Mathur survey report of the UGC, 1981, has not been taken up for discussion for so many years. The two surveys of research on Public Administration of ICSSR also were not much discussed. A concerted effort on everyone's part is lacking.

The Indian Public Administration Association, the UGC, and the IIPA, could think of these issues but could not arrive at any conclusion or influence anybody.

It may also be a fact that there is not much difference, in many universities, between the undergraduate syllabi and the post-graduate syllabi. But one must recognise the number of papers taught at undergraduate level (3) and post-graduate level (9). Therefore, the nature, the quantum of syllabi and the quality of teaching are not the same al the undergraduate and post-graduate levels.

There is nothing wrong if a subject could not attain intellectual autonomy in the historical process and continues to depend upon the inter-disciplinary patrimony. Public Administration, therefore, should preserve and foster its backward linkages with Political Science, Law and Sociology and develop new forward linkages with Economics and Management.

One should agree with the Iqbal Narain-Mathur survey report in many respects:

First, Indiscriminate borrowings by Public Administration from allied disciplines should be streamlined.

Second, Over-emphasis on descriptive teaching of organisations and formal legal institutions should be avoided. Third, Its backward and forward linkages have to be strengthened.

Fourth, A clear-cut difference between undergraduate and PG syllabi must be maintained.

Fifth, It must be compulsory to introduce courses in Government and politics in India.

Text Books, Teaching Material and Journals

As regards the dearth of teaching material and high quality textbooks on Public Administration, neither the universities nor the UGC, have taken any steps. It is interesting to note that many universities (Punjab, Rajasthan, Madras, Utkal, Kakatiya, Andhra, Open Universities, etc.) are conducting correspondencc-cum-contact courses providing printed matter to the private students. But the same kind of effort is not made to provide textbooks and other reading material to the regular PG students.

However, the language academies in different states and the Open Universities have been doing a good job in this respect. The universities have to take special steps to encourage production of high grade textbooks on Public Administration. This Seminar should recommend to the UGC to provide liberal grants to the universities for this purpose. Meanwhile, some efforts may be made by the universities to bring out edited works as readings on different areas of Public Administration as it is done by the IIPA on the occasion of its silver jubilee celebrations.

At present the *Indian Journal of Public Administration, Nagarlok, Management in Government,* and *The Administrator* are the main journals on the subject, which are published regularly with governmental patronage. However, there are no independent journals except *Administrative Change;* a bi-annual. The *Indian Journal of Political Science* and other Political Science journals may now and then also publish some research papers pertaining to Public Administration. The Indian Public Administration Association has been contemplating to bring out an independent journal of its own, but could not do so for want of funds. The UGC and the ICSSR should provide liberal initial grants to support the efforts of such kind of academic and recognised bodies.

Course Content

The Public Administration syllabi in almost all universities generally tend to avoid teaching of theories of the state, political analysis and Indian Government and politics. These papers are considered as part of Political Science. This view is influenced by Woodrow Wilson and Max Weber who believe that Political Science is different from Public Administration and Public Administration means the study of bureaucracy and organisations. This kind of avoidence of courses is very much useful to the government and the state. The teachers and the taught and the professionals in civil service would not only believe in the 'political neutrality' and safely serve the state with all the loyalty to the government. The teachers and the students along with the bureaucracy would work together to propagate the 'service nature' of the state and to extend necessary publicity that the government is for social service, economic development and public welfare. If theories of the state, political analysis, public policy and Indian Government and politics are taught, the anatomy, physiology and pathology of the state and government would be exposed to the young students, and this may create law and order problems in the universities and colleges.

Similarly a paper on state-level administration is also not included in the syllabi of many universities. But they attempted to teach state administration in parts or in a disintegrated manner in water-tight compartments as optionals. As such, students cannot have a comprehensive knowledge of the whole. For example, there are papers on Panchayati Raj, Urban Administration, Police Administration, Labour and Welfare Administration, Tribal and Rural Development, but there is no full-fledged paper on 'State Government and Politics'. It seems, such omission is the result of a certain sub-conscious effort on the part of the authorities concerned and as such the Indian administrative problems are not emphasised in the syllabi.

Another tendency on the part of some university departments is to sell the subject to the students through correspondence and regular admissions, announcing the courses as 'job-oriented', 'specialised', like Diplomas in 'Office Management', 'Personnel Management' and 'Industrial Relations', 'Rural Development Administration', Master's Degree in 'Public Personnel Management', etc., and including papers on Advanced Management Techniques, Business Administration, Public Accounting, Public Relations, Statistics, Public Sector Management, Labour Welfare, Office Management, etc. The youth are made to run from pillar to post and acquire all sorts of degrees and diplomas in order to get some employment in some sector/organisation. Interestingly, none of the universities have made any effort to prepare the students for civil service examinations or to evolve a syllabus, which may help the students to compete in the civil service examinations. Of course, the UPSC and some State Public Service Commissions have only recently recognised Public Administration also as one of the subjects.

> Mohit Bhattacharya in his paper raised a few salient questions. Perhaps, the following excerpts may throw some light:
>
> First, Public Administration should be developed as a Social Science Discipline with inter-disciplinary linkages.

Second, A proper blend of all sciences (including Social, Biological, Physical, Behavioural, Management and Policy Sciences) should develop a common perspective.

Third, Public Administration adopting the management orientation as Applied Science and 'problem-solving discipline' may be more useful.

Fourth, Public Administration programme should in a big way bring in the National (Indian) administrative perspective.

Fifth, The future Public Administration should develop in close collaboration with other Social Science departments (particularly Political Science and Economics) either under the overall umbrella of a composite department or independent departments as per the local requirements and the faculty position.

Research in Public Administration

The strength of the discipline of Public Administration depends as much on teaching as on research. It is for the community of the scholars in Public Administration to engage themselves in fruitful and imaginative research in order to develop the discipline in its width and depth. But it depends on the socio-economic and political background of the scholars in Public Administration. Most of the scholars hail from forward and middle class background. They generally prefer to be part of the 'Public Administration' of India due to their earlier education and training in liberal democracy and elitism. Therefore, their studies/research mostly deal with institutions and their functioning. Their research is mostly descriptive, seldom prescriptive and recommends half-hearted reforms in the administrative set-up. Their diagnoses of the problems are symptomatic, rarely clinical and generally shun any radical prescription. They remain indifferent to the problems of social change and inequalities, and keep themselves busy tightening the loose nuts and bolts of public administrative machinery and discipline. Therefore, the syllabi of M.A., M.Phil, and the Ph.D. research topics still do not display any change. They patternise the public bureaucracy, advocating suitability of the Weberian theory of bureaucracy to the 'Development Administration' of India. Thus, the university departments neither engaged in prioritisation nor theoretisation of Public Administration.

Conclusion

To conclude, the discipline of Public Administration has to be urgently geared to the study of the problems of the masses in the society. For this purpose, it must go beyond the forms of organisations and processes of administration and explore the social structure, social problems, character of administration and the State. A 'new' and 'radical' Public Administration should be developed keeping in view the social, economic and political realities of India.

Reference

1. S.R. Maheshwari (Ed.), Education in Public Administration in India, Indian Institute of Public Administration, New Delhi, 1992.

11

Strategies of Successful Administrative Reforms

Introduction

Most of the countries in the world, irrespective of their ideologies and levels of development, have been under a reform process during the last three decades. The role of the state in these countries came under attack, to a large extent due to certain historical situations that emerged during this period. In the context of liberalization and globalization, governments in most countries are called upon to reform and re-engineer their administrative apparatus in pursuit of good governance. There have been periodic efforts for administrative reform, based upon the recommendations of autonomous Administrative Reforms Commissions consisting of quasi-political and non-bureaucrat members. This chapter does not attempt to discuss the success or failure of past reforms. Instead, it traces the strategies adopted in recent reforms.

Administrative Reforms

Administrative reforms enjoyed significant support in Europe, the USA, Australia and New Zealand during the 1990s. They permeated Latin America, entered Asia and have very recently penetrated Africa. These reforms are aimed at a major transformation of the ideals and practices of traditional civil services. These efforts have been deliberate, and designed towards a desired change. However, devising strategies for successful implementation of major administrative reforms is not an easy task for bringing wide-ranging changes in well entrenched and tradition-bound public administration, particularly in the developing countries.

It is observed that two institutions, namely unaccountable Big Business and indifferent Big Government, caused most concern to society. There has been universal unhappiness with the prevailing administrative systems in general. Public institutions created during colonial regimes failed to keep abreast with the changing times. In response to this fall from public grace, since the mid-1980s there has been a common trend in many of the industrialized countries to redefine the role of the state and public administration. Several aid-giving bodies like the International Monetary Fund, the World Bank, the Commonwealth and the United Nations commissioned studies and recommended a number of strategies for administrative reforms. They include: "liberalization, deregulation, downsizing the public sector, shrinking bloated public organizations, privatization, debureaucratisation, civil services reform, budget reform, performance measures, business like management, long-term transparency, computerization, and mechanization, and greater productivity, efficiency and accountability".

Their agenda had many targets, including government as an economic manager and the role of the state in society. The civil service was singled out and accused of many shortcomings, such as being bloated, expensive, unresponsive, deliberately resistant to changes and incapable of dealing with new challenges. In short, the civil service lacked the ability to focus on clients and manage operations efficiently, and to provide sound and unbiased policy advice. It was thought to sabotage new programs, and undermine attempts at major policy choices and administrative reforms in general. Thus, the fundamental task of a reformer is to regain control over the public sector and exercise greater control over the broad public policy agenda. The politicians made it clear that they wanted doers not thinkers. They felt that they themselves had the policy answers. Officials understood the message and developed a tendency to recommend safe policy options and what "politicians would wear". As such, in effect the senior civil service has been the target of administrative reform.

Politics of Reform

"Failure to understand the political nature of administrative reform and to develop a political strategy to overcome resistance lies behind the failure of many reform attempts". The pre-requisites of reform include political will and a strategy of implementation. The politics of reform cannot be overlooked in any analysis of administrative reform.

One of the major differences between the administrative reforms of the past and the present is that in the past it was a specific task of a particular country. The reform in the past was generally to repair administrative machinery as recommended by expert bodies. These efforts were resisted initially by the bureaucracy and the organized unions, but later accepted after consultation and negotiation. However, such reforms were only successful in tinkering with the structure of administrative organizations. They were half-hearted, and the governing elite, particularly the ruling political parties, never seriously insisted on the successful implementation of reforms. But present reforms are completely different, and appear to be "episodic", aiming at "reorganization" and "re-engineering" of public administration. These do not pertain to a simple administrative system of a single country. It is a world-wide phenomenon, mainly suggested by international organizations based on principles of new economics fully supported by almost all political parties and groups, including the trade unions. There is not much resistance from any particularly known quarter; it seems appreciated by the people at large.

Reforms of the 1980s and 1990s are essentially a deliberate attempt to use political power to influence the change of goals, structure and processes of state bureaucracy. At the outset, reforms seem to be wide-ranging, involving a major shakeup in administrative organizations to remedy the malfunctioning of traditional processes. But an in-depth analysis reveals the dominance of neo-liberal economics over politics. The intensity of change in fact, is indeed more political and economic than administrative. The strongest political impulse for every phase of administrative reform came from the "new right", while defenders of the old order had themselves been weakened and divided. The new right criticized the existing old order on at least six counts.

- The state, in dealing with the powerful interest groups (especially trade unions), contributed to higher public spending than the median voter would have supported.
- Public officials were mainly concerned with the maximization of their own budgets and status.
- The professions were regarded as self-interested monopolists, restricting the supply of their services, demanding higher salaries and pursuing their own professional ends, rather than responding to users of their services.
- The growth of government undermined the freedom of the individual, "Big Government" sapped the entrepreneurial spirit of the citizen and the sense of self-reliance.
- Center-Left governments mistakenly pursued artificially egalitarian notions of social justice, which undermined individual freedom and the fiscal self-discipline of the state.
- The expansion of the public sector had stunted private sector growth.

Conservative governments of the 1980s and 1990s repeatedly expressed their anti-state stand. Different anti-state theories were fed to the political masters in different countries through a variety of right wing "think-tanks" which influenced policy formulation. While there may not be any particular anti-state theory, dependence upon market forces and practices is clearly noticeable.

In the past, despite the intellectual attacks and public criticism against the maladies of public bureaucracy; ruling political parties and their leaders never seriously condemned bureaucracy. But now it is well known that the leading politicians in the United States, the United Kingdom, Canada, Australia, New Zealand and other countries have been openly hostile to state bureaucracy. "Bureaucratic bashing" by political leaders has become a common tactic to denigrate public employees and generate public support to win elections.

The present assault on the public services led to radical pro-market reforms in downsizing the public sector and transforming public services on the lines of business enterprise. It facilitated the expansion of political control over public bureaucracy, and enabled the introduction of reforms and re-engineering techniques used in the private sector.

Characteristics of Reforms

Administrative reform is classified into three categories:

- Those that turn out to be strictly tied to and shaped by a simultaneous constitutional revision;
- Those encouraged by economic models, promoted in particular by the desire to open up public service to the logic of the market or to connect the provision of public service to the financial needs of the state; and
- Those encouraged by renewed attention to the rights of each citizen, considered to be an aware and sovereign subject, who looks to the administration for the satisfaction of his or her individual needs.

Six essential challenges have been perceived in this context:

- The managerial challenge (process);
- The challenge of quality (3 E's: efficiency; economy and effectiveness);
- The democratic challenge (friendly with citizens);
- The challenges of professionalism (policy and operation expertise);
- The challenges of responsibility (limit public spending, re-design the welfare state); and
- The challenges of decentralization (closer to citizens).

It is argued that two swings, one upward from national governments to international organizations, and the other downward from national governments to grass-roots non-governmental organizations, are the keys to understanding the challenges that confronted public administration in the 1990s.

Approaches to Reforms

Based on the solutions offered by the international bodies like the IMF, World Bank, United Nations and Commonwealth Secretariat and others, to the ills afflicting the civil service systems all over the world, a number of approaches are adopted to bring improvements in the efficiency, effectiveness and performance in the public sector: a citizen's charter, re-engineering, reinventing government, New Public Management, privatization, financial reforms, democratization, and decentralization.

Citizen's Charter

The British Government, which launched its Citizen's Charter in July 1991, is a good example. The Charter is meant to raise the standard of public services by making them more responsive to the wishes and needs of the users. It treats the citizens as customers. To realize its objectives, the Charter lays down certain principles to be observed in the daily management and operation of public services. In brief, these principles are:

- Establishing and monitoring explicit and measurable standards for the civil service. The actual performance against set standards needs to be published.
- Providing readily available, easily accessible information about each service, how it runs, at what cost, how well it performs and who is in charge at what point. This openness builds rapport and trust between civil servants and citizens.
- Providing citizens the maximum opportunity to choose among competing services. Regular and systematic consultation must take place between civil servants and users of services. Users' suggestions are important in finalizing the standards.
- Public service should be provided equally to all, without any discrimination and bias; the public are entitled to have the administration run in a manner that suits their convenience.

- Awareness on the part of civil servants as to what to do when things go wrong. It makes them more responsible and accountable. Procedures of work should be reviewed to suit the needs of the users.
- Tax payers should be assured of efficient and economic delivery of services (Value For Money). Independent validation of performance standards must be undertaken on a continuous basis.

In short, the Citizen's Charter is about:

"Outcomes and outputs, rather than inputs, needs of users, not the interests of the producers, Government sticking to essentials and doing those well, using markets, improve choice, using competition, achieve better value for money, addressing the particular service, designing the shape of the organization which best meets it, and delegating responsibility for delivery for that organization, raising the performance of individual public servants through effective recruitment, training, appraisal and incentives".

Re-engineering the Government

The concept of re-engineering the institutional structure emerged out of fascination with new management philosophies. It acquired increased significance in recent years with the publication of M. Hammer and R. Champy's *Re-engineering the Corporation* in 1993, and the 1992 book of David Osborne and Ted Gaeblers' *Reinventing Government: How the Entrepreneurial Spirit is Transforming the Public Sector.* Both works generated a set of propositions for dealing with reforms in management. Re-inventing government attempts to transfer a part of the reformist agenda of the private sector to the public sector. Thus, issues like competition and the empowerment of citizens by means of a customer-oriented approach have become the criteria by which "good governance" is measured. According to the National Performance Review Team in the United States, re-engineering in the public sector calls on reformers to forget how agencies were organized, and decide what they have to do and then design the best structure to do so.

Re-engineering, with its origins in American big business, is considered equally applicable to the public sector. It is considered to be a comprehensive and effective way for organizations to reduce cycle times, surpass customer expectations, enhance productivity, increase sales and reap higher profits.

The concept of re-engineering, however, is yet to be defined precisely. Nonetheless, some major attributes to be mentioned are:

- Developing processes and outcomes. Preference is given to individual performance;
- Focus on the customer or client within a results-oriented and team-based approach. This requires rigorous measurement of performance, and close analysis of change and the rate of change for assessing performance. It is only possible with the total commitment of all the employees and a substantive involvement of top management at all levels; and
- Undertaking systematic searches to bring radical change, for improvements and breakthroughs, whenever an incremental approach fails.

However, it is proved beyond doubt that re-engineering has been more successful in the private than in the public sector. Therefore, the reformers are more cautious in their recommendations for re-engineering the latter, confining themselves largely to the reform of selected processes, the introduction of cost-benefit analysis and performance measurement. It is also now being recognized that the two critical obstacles to the re-engineering efforts in public service organizations are structure and culture.

Re-inventing Government

Osborne and Gaebler popularized the term "Reinventing Government". They raised issues that confront state administration, and developed an "entrepreneurial government" based on the following ten point program:

"Empowering citizens, promoting competition between providers of goods and services, promoting a mission driven leadership in order to 'steer rather than row', decentralizing authority, measuring outcomes, earning money, deregulation, preferring market mechanisms, performance budgeting, support for civil service reform and catalyzing all sectors—public, private, voluntary."

Their work caught the attention of anti-bureaucracy campaigners who welcomed them as advocates of a new form of public management. Re-inventing government was predicted to provide a saving of $108 billion for the United States government over a five year period and the reduction of as many as 252000 jobs. The intention of this reform, however, is to invent a government that "puts people first" by serving its customers, empowering employees and fostering excellence. It is expected to caste aside red tape, achieve results to satisfy customers, transform government's culture by decentralizing authority, and make government work better and cost less.

By the mid-1990s some states in the United States were actively implementing "re-invention", focusing particularly on total quality management. Though reinventing government has received wide publicity and prestigious political endorsement, it is not widely and quickly adopted across states. It has only a modest impact because there is no substantial conceptual power and clarity in the stated objectives of reinventing government. It also suffered from an extremely diffuse implementation strategy. The creation of about 340 re-invention laboratories in 1998 in various United States federal agencies, and a very modest legislative reform effort, made some changes in the Federal Personnel Manual. But there were no fundamental changes in financial management, budgeting or management systems, as such.

New Public Management (NPM)

The core public service reform principles included in most national efforts are frequently lumped under the term managerialism. In general terms, these new set of practices—calculation and control, reliance on competition to ensure quality, customer orientation, etc.—collectively represent what is better known as New Public Management (NPM). Its main aim is to provide cheaper services to citizens by responding to their demands, and by supplying more value for money, freedom of choice, flexibility and transparency. The focus is on performance and the ability of managers to accept responsibility for the whole system. Terms such as "search for excellence", "quality management", "public sector productivity", "organizational well-performing", and "entrepreneurial government" are also used alongside the dominating label of NPM.

That the concept of NPM is derived from the ideas of New Institutional Economics (NIE), i.e. the theory of public choice, makes it an ideological movement. It is, however, important to note that not only conservative governments in the United Kingdom and the United States, but also Labour Governments in Australia, and New Zealand also have implemented the NPM reforms. Thus, it appears to offer a framework to suit the needs of every one. It in fact claims to be politically neutral and provide an apolitical framework, making it possible to pursue different values and functions within multiple political priorities. It is presented as a remedy to cure management ills in various organizational contexts. It has several interrelated components:

- High quality of services that citizens value, and expect as customers. (The United Kingdom's Citizens' Charter 1991, launched by John Major, the Prime Minister).
- Increased autonomy to managers: more powers in financial and personnel management are devolved to the local managers. Organizational structures are simplified and hierarchies flattened to create conditions for development of more positive and productive managerial leadership.
- Rigorous performance measurement of individuals and organizations is periodically reviewed. Pay structures are based on fulfillment of performance targets. Tenure system is replaced by fixed term contracts. Public agencies are asked to be more cost-conscious and resource-saving.
- To achieve pre-set performance targets, managerial support services such as human and technological (IT) are facilitated.
- Receptiveness to competition and an open-minded attitude by the public sector are envisaged. Private sector and non-

governmental organizations are invited to involve themselves in social and economic activities that were formerly reserved for the public sector. Privatization has been adopted as an official policy in most of the nations, just as public-private joint-ventures are also encouraged.

While the new role of the government is considered as a move "from a concern to do towards a concern to ensure that things are done", simultaneous policies supporting the private sector activities, such as dismantling price controls, deregulation and downsizing the public sector, are adopted. All this leads to the fear that the state may be hijacked by private and powerful interests.

Privatization/contracting Out

Over the past two decades, many services previously provided by government agencies have been handed over to the private sector. In many countries government business enterprises have been privatized and government funding of services either has been maintained or reduced (disinvestment), or the provision of services has been contracted out. It is assumed that this experiment is taking place on the basis of division of the several functions into "core" and "non-core," thus raising the key question about the proper role of the state.

The "core" functions that the government needs to undertake are assumed to be policy making, coordinating the functions of other actors, regulating, facilitating and providing information. In the "non-core" sector, privatization and encouragement to autonomous non-governmental organizations, including contracting out, are advocated. These assumptions implied development of a "capable state" but a "minimal" role for government.

Privatizing and down sizing government institutions began in the United Kingdom for "Improving Management in Government; The Next Steps" in 1988. The purpose of "Next Steps" was to transform the delivery of the vast majority of central government services by establishing departmental executive agencies, where productivity and effectiveness could be more easily measured and monitored. The Chief Executives of these agencies were brought from outside the government to create a new management culture. They report directly to the ministers concerned. Such an arrangement is considered to be a compromise between the market and traditional forms of organization. By 1995, over one hundred Next Steps agencies were created and nearly two-thirds of the British Civil Service was employed in those agencies. Yet the United Kingdom experience appears to be relatively modest and restrained when compared to the radical and comprehensive reforms in New Zealand.

Reforms in New Zealand were first initiated by the Labour government (1984-1990) and have subsequently been pursued by Conservative governments since 1990. Several pieces of legislation, such as the State Sector Act (1988), The Employment Contracts Act (1991), and Public Finance Act (1991), have ensued. A number of state owned enterprises were privatized and most others corporatized. A systematic program of competitive tendering and contracting was introduced. Even a large part of the policy advising function, traditionally the purview of the higher Civil Service, was contracted out. The Chief Executives of the new agencies were placed on fixed-term performance contracts with full financial and personnel authority. A Senior Executive Service was created to facilitate the new management system with a provision to recruit outside of government. The government claims that reforms are meeting most expectations, and reform literature showers praise, holding up the New Zealand reforms as a leading model.

The contraction of government in Australia began in 1975, but proceeded until the mid-1980s. Australia relied heavily on the commercialization (contracting out) of many services. To better manage the new systems and to improve the leadership for the public service, Australia too established a Senior Executive Service enabling recruitment through public advertisement and competition.

It is claimed that contraction of the role of government is an inevitable reaction to the developments in the global economy. But such a diminished role of the state is attained by dismantling policies of the mixed economy and welfare state. It may even lead to the restoration of the situation prevailing one hundred years back in a *laissez faire* state.

Financial Reforms

The fiscal reforms agenda advocates consolidating and tightening financial discipline, reducing government budget deficits, improving tax administration, clearing government arrears, reducing subsidies through improved cost recovery, and raising funds for modest public investment and the maintenance of existing public works.

In developing countries, as in industrial countries, governments have undertaken to reduce public spending. They introduced cut backs in socio-economic programs, and resorted to improving the efficiency and effectiveness of public spending, by privatizing public services or by imposing user fees. However, reduction in public spending entails political costs, favoring the wealthy at the expense of the poor and disadvantaged groups.

As a part of overall reforms, several countries adopted different measures of financial management: the Financial Management Initiative (FMI) of the British Government, for example, simplified financial reporting and accounting systems. It strongly emphasized cost consciousness, and clearer and stronger controls over public spending responsibility and budgets in each minister's portfolio. But its impact was stronger on the control of administrative costs than on program expenditure, as political considerations continued to overrule managerial rationality.

In Australia, the Financial Management Improvement Program, and Program Management and Budgeting, emphasized the quality of service delivery as well as a more simple and transparent process. There was strong emphasis on controlling the cost of government operations and eliminating the traditional bureaucratic "inching up" of annual costs. From 1987 onwards, an efficiency dividend was exacted from Departments by reducing their administrative expenditure allocation by 1.25%. Departments were allowed to negotiate "borrowings." However, the government continued to be involved in wage setting and borrowing by public enterprises.

In New Zealand the Public Finance Act of 1989 required Departments to move to a new accounting system which reflected the full cost of resources and enabled better monitoring of efficiency.

In Norway, budget reform was initiated in 1986 and gradually extended in recent years for a more efficient governmental budget system. Whether all this resulted in improving performance and political control is yet another matter.

Three aspects of modernity—industrialism, democracy and nationalism—have impinged on bureaucracy in the world today. Bureaucracies are not democratic; they are hierarchic. Modern bureaucracies have been functioning as organs of domination and exploitation. Therefore, responsible political institutions are needed that can effectively impose accountability on all the appointed officials of government. To do this, it is necessary to understand how the institutions of representative governance can most effectively be organized and used to impose accountability on public bureaucracies. The basic principle of democracy insists that the citizens be able to participate in governance and choose their political representatives. But in the so-called "democracies" (oligarchies) all people are not allowed participation.

The reform movement sought to democratize bureaucracy, to make it more responsive to the citizens. The fundamental problem here is how to transform domineering bureaucrats into responsible servants, particularly in the newly liberated countries of Asia, Africa and Latin America, Central and East European countries. The question, therefore, is not how to re-design or modernize bureaucracy, but how to enhance political control over bureaucracy. This is expected to be accomplished by democratizing the institutions of governance at various levels of government. However, the capacity of representatives and the institutions to monitor and inspire the highly professional and competent public administrators is becoming increasingly problematic. Thus, administrative reform in a way also calls for political reforms, i.e. through popular elections, political parties, elected assemblies, responsible heads of government, and the rule of law. Some action to offset "the democratic deficit" must be taken.

Decentralization

Decentralization is defined as the outcome of a contextual process of decentralization of functions and the development of political autonomy in the community. The difference between administrative and political decentralization needs to be clearly noted. Decentralization of functions, plus increased powers granted to politically autonomous bodies (local self-government etc.), denotes decentralizing. Decentralization of functions within the state is deemed to be bureaucratic decentralization. Decentralization reduces the distance between citizens and public administration. The decentralizing exercise of administrative action need not be considered an indirect form of administration by the state, but a direct expression of the will of the community it represents. Decentralization affects the distribution of powers between the center and the local authorities. There should be a shift not only from state to local authorities, but also from a bureaucratic to functional state.

Decentralization needs a coherent set of rules to replace the hierarchical system of governance which is characteristic of centralized systems. As such, the major challenge of decentralization is to institutionalize the balance of power between the national and local governments. The rules of decentralization must be explicit, stable and self-enforcing, providing common ground to all the players in the political process.

The experience of the last fifteen years shows that devolution of powers affects political stability, public service performance, equity and macro-economic stability. However, governments responded to demands for increased self-government by devolving power and authority to lower-tiers of government. By 1998, out of the forty-eight largest countries, thirty-four had held elections at both the national and local levels. Half of them not only decentralized politically but also decentralized major functional responsibilities. Due to decentralization there has been substantial increase in the division of public expenditure. Now local governments account for 20% of government expenditure in many countries. About 95% of democracies have erected sub-national governments. The implementation of decentralization, however, is haphazard. The pace of decentralization and the kinds of reforms implemented varied from country to country. Many countries gave priority to economic growth and administrative efficiency rather than political decentralization.

In many countries decentralization has not resulted in the center relinquishing much control to the periphery.

Regarding the structure, functions and resources, traditional "fiscal federalism" is advocated. This meant that the central government should continue funding and redesigning redistribution efforts. Emphasis is placed on synchronization of all elements of reform, such as holding local elections rapidly, creating new regulatory relationships between central and local governments, transfer of assets and staff to local levels, and replacing annual budgetary transfers with a system of tax assignment and intergovernmental transfers.

The Indian Experience

While administrative reforms were in full swing all over the world for many years, the Government of India held top level conferences only at the end of 1996 and in May 1997 to discuss the crisis in Indian administration. It was recognized that governance has to be extended beyond traditional bureaucracies, and to involve citizens and consumer groups actively, to empower and inform the public, and to ensure service delivery and program execution through autonomous elected local governments.

There was consensus for ensuring responsive, accountable, transparent, decentralized and people-friendly administration at all levels. An action plan for an Effective and Responsive Government was prepared by the government, which included:

- A Citizen's Charter and an accountable administration;
- An effective and speedy public grievance redress system;
- Empowering elected local bodies, and a decentralized delivery of services;
- A review of laws, regulations and procedures;
- Transparency and the right to Information;
- A code of ethics for the Public Service, and
- Tackling corruption and cleansing administration.

Prime Minister Atal Bihari Vajpayee emphasized the need to make the administration responsive, efficient and compassionate. He blamed largely the political class for the ills of administration. He wanted the administration to work with a sense of mission and a results-oriented approach. Along with the Prime Minister at the Centre (as the federal government is known), a few Chief Ministers at the states level are also struggling to tune the administration.

Though not much can be expected in a short span of four years, as parts of the overall reform process many Departments have announced some sort of citizen's charter and citizen-friendly initiatives. In bigger states elected local bodies have been empowered. But in many other states a power struggle between the state governments and their local bodies is going on. Some Bills, like the Freedom of Information Bill and the Bill on Electronic Data Transfer and Transaction, are pending approval of the Parliament. As a part of this reform agenda, the Government of India constituted a Constitutional Review Committee, whose report in 2002 ran into nearly 2000 pages. While a lot of debate and discussion has been initiated throughout the nation, particularly about the eradication of political and administrative corruption, not much has been accomplished, mainly because of political instability and administrative disinterest.

Evaluation of Reforms

The reform process is on in virtually all countries. In the light of the experience of the three general models — the incremental model of the United States; the stages model in Australia, and the British "Fresh Start" model—the following observations can be made:

(1) All reforms created new expectations for governments. But the fulfillment of expectations depended on the political commitment for change, the reform model opted, and the need and desire for reform. (2) In most cases public organizations became smaller and slimmer. To a great extent the reforms restructured the public service. (3) There is considerable improvement in the leadership roles of public managers at different levels, helped by innovations such as the NPM, and Human Resource Management (HRM). (4) Also noted

are simplification of financial management, budget coordination, and increased transparency. (5) Efforts at redesigning public service culture (towards a new, output oriented, cost-conscious, decentralized, customer-focused culture) are not very visible. (6) Public service users are empowered to an extent (e.g. the Citizens Charter in the United Kingdom). (7) Business interests and the world of finance liked the sound of less government, and are benefited by reduction in public expenditure, deregulation and low taxation, purchasing/privatizing government assets at cheaper rates, acquiring government contracts to produce and deliver goods and services, and expanding the volume of imports and exports under the liberalized trade system. (8) It is believed that the market-oriented restructuring of public policies and organizations are not favored by the majority of population, particularly the poor, the peasants, and minorities due to the withdrawal of subsidies, and by the working class due to reduction in the work force and cutback of welfare programs (health, housing and education). To this extent, the public who have missed the gains of public service have lost confidence in the new reforms. (9) The public may further lose their faith in public service if deregulation is ineffective in containing vested and business interests. The situation may be worsened with the introduction of a pro-market government bureaucracy (hiring outsiders, party advisors, former politicians and bureaucrats etc.) to carry out disinvestment programs, make deals with private contractors, and finalize joint ventures. For the mission of the newly emerging public service is not to play an active role in production, distribution, welfare and socio-economic development, but to design, facilitate, regulate, monitor and evaluate the restructuring of the public sector itself. Thus, the state may weaken its legitimacy. (10) The basic norms of public service (impartiality, representativeness, equality, justice, accountability) are being replaced by commercial and market values (competitiveness, efficiency, productivity and profitability). This may weaken the credibility of public interest and further challenge the legitimacy of public service. (11) Reforms might have resulted in efficiency gains, but they have threatened the social capital of public service as a community of trust, committed to pursue the public good. It raises the issues of ethics, morale, motivation, commitment, and the price of public service.(12) Downsizing, freezing recruitment, an inability to attract and retain the meritorious and competent in the public service, and imposing private/political consultants/advisors over the permanent policy advisors, may undermine the performance of the public service in meeting the emerging complex socio-economic problems. (13) Politicization of the civil service is reported to have increased in France, Australia, the United Kingdom, the United States and other countries, due to the emergence of managerialism in the public sector. (14) It is pertinent to note that administrative re-organization or structural adjustment programs are well publicized on a global scale. The advantages and disadvantages of changes are known to the public. Yet the public is divided, administration is weakened, and the political masters have surrendered to the onslaught of the global forces for a "New World Order" and global public administration. (15) The implications of the New World Order and the emerging global public administration will likely be more negative for developing countries in particular, insofar as all this might further empower the ruling elite (the big capitalists, large land owners, big corporate powers, corrupt regimes, and undemocratic and repressive forces). (16) Reforms in Australia, Britain and New Zealand gave total autonomy and responsibility to Departmental heads, and they moved to a system of managerial incentives based on output as a basis for performance measurement. Administrative reforms, it is alleged, reduced the public accountability aspect to a technical question of designing control procedures and institutions.

In spite of the political will and commitment in policy changes, legislative enactments and executive decisions, the implementation of reform programs is frequently restrained due to the absence of political consensus. While in most countries someone, or a group near to the chief executive, has been entrusted with the responsibility of reform implementation, the allocation of responsibilities among the politicians and the managers is not particularly clear. As such, there are deficiencies in political decision making goals, of reform programs and management change.

It is argued that "political leadership not only mis-diagnosed the patient but also applied the wrong remedy". It requires a strong capacity to adapt and to deal with a better informed media, policy communities, interest groups and the public. Therefore governments, it is suggested, now require a "strong policy advisory capacity". Political leadership of the 1980s ignored this aspect, or even downplayed it.

BIBLIOGRAPHY

Bissessar, A.M. (1998). "Re-engineering the Public Services of the commonwealth Caribbean," *International Review of Administrative Sciences* 64: 305-326. [This article elucidates the changing dimensions of human resources management in the public sectors of the commonwealth Caribbean. It looks at the foundation of personnel systems set up under the crown colony government and its legacy.]

Brudney, J.L., Ted H.F. and Wright, D.S. (1999). "Reinventing Government in the American States: Measuring and Explaining Administrative Reform," *Public Administration Review* 99(1): 19-30. [This study examines whether reinventing government is the state reform wave of the 1990s, and the extent of implementation of 11 reinvention reforms.]

Caiden, G.E. (1991). *Administrative Reform Comes of Age,* Berlin: Walter de Gruyter.

———(1994). "Administrative Reform - American Style," *Public Administrative Review* 54(2): 123. [This describes different phases of American reforms in a comparative perspective.]

Duggett, M. (1998). "Citizen's Charter: People's Charter in the U.K.," *International Review of Administrative Sciences* 64: 327-330. [This articles reviews the success of Citizen's Charter as a people's charter in UK irrespective of the political party in power.]

Farazmand, A. (1999). "Privatization of reform? Public Enterprise Management in Transition," *International Review of Administrative Sciences* 65: 51-567. XXXX [This article addresses the pervasiveness of the goodness, the limit, and the alternatives to privatization. It examines the current status of public enterprises and their reforms for high performance and accountability.]

Gaincarlo, R. (1998). "Autonomy: A Guiding Criterion for Decentralizing Public Administration," *International Review of Administrative Sciences* 64: 27-39. [This article is a thoughtful discussion of the general principles involved in implementing decentralised administration within a framework of tradition and law.]

Gregory, R.J. (1999). "Social Capital Theory and Administrative Reform, Maintaining Ethical Probity in Public Service," *Public Administration Review* 59 (1): 63-71. [This paper points out the administrative reforms with particular context of the recent social capital theory.]

Guy, P.B. and Saroje, D.J. (1994). "Civil Service Reform, Misdiagnosing the Patient," *Public Administration Review* 54(5): 418-425. [This article looks at the measures to reform the bureaucracies of Anglo-American style democracies. The authors argue that the reforms attempted to address largely non-existent problem and overlooked problems that now need urgent attention.]

Halachmi, A. (1995). "Reengineering and Public Management: Some Issues and Considerations," *International Review of Administrative Sciences* 62(3): 329-341. [This article reviews the basic tenets of re-engineering. It examines the relationships between re-engineering, information technology, innovation and the reinvention of government.]

Hammer, M. and Champy, R. (1993). Re-engineering the Corporation, Sydney, Alien & Unwin. And Hammer, M. (1990) "Reengineering Work: Don't Automate, Obliterate," *Harvard Business Review* 68(4): 104-112. [This paper suggests using the power of modern information technology to radically redesign business processes to achieve dramatic improvements in their performance.]

Haque, S.M. (1998). "Legitimation Crisis: A Challenge for Public Service in the Next Century," *International Review of*

Administration Sciences 64(1): 13-26. [This article contends that the critical challenge to the current and future public service is the erosion of its legitimacy or public confidence and recommends some alternative policies for revival and maintenance of legitimacy and strengthening public confidence.]

Indian Journal of Public Administration (July-Sept 19993). *Action Plan for an Effective and Responsive Government,* Department of Administrative Reforms and Public Grievances, Government of India, 1998, 626-660. [This document shares the concern of government of India for ensuring responsive, accountable, transparent, decentralised and people-friendly administration at all levels.]

Ingraham, P.W. (1997). "Play it Again, Sam; It is Still not Right; Searching for the Right Notes in Administrative Reform," *Public Administration Review* 57(4): 325-331. [This article examines administrative reform in the comparative context of the United Kingdom, Australia, New Zealand and United States.]

Jha, N. (1999). "Effective and Responsive Govt. Regulatory Reform Initiatives of Union Government," *Indian Journal of Public Administration* XLV (2): 240-249. [It presents details of regulatory reform measures at the government of India level initiated as a follow up of an Action Plan endorsed in 1997 by the conference of Chief Ministers.]

Kaul, M. (1997). "The New Public Administration: Management Innovations in Government," *Public Administration and Development* 17: 13-26. [This article discusses the issues arising out of the innovations in the new public management reforms.]

Khator, R. (1995). "Managing the Environment in an Interdependent World," in Jean-Clause Garcia - Zamor and Renu Khator (Eds). *Public Administration in the Global Village,* West Port: Praeger: 83-98. [This study argues that the environmental crisis, along with other globalizing forces has changed the role of the nation-state which in turn has changed the nature of public administration as field of study.]

Moe, R.C. "The Reinventing Government Exercise: Misinterpreting Problem, Misjudging the Consequences," *Public Administration Review* 54(2): 111-122. [This long commentary cautions the "Reinventing Government; exercise and asks us to rethink what we really expect from the government.]

O. Toole, B.J. and Jordan, G. (Eds). (1995). *Next Steps: Improving Management in Government?* Dartmouth, Aldershot. [This book catalogues and analyzes the changes set in motion by the *Next Steps* report and address their implications for the government of the United Kingdom.]

Olowu, B. (1998). "Strategies for Improving Administrative efficiency in the democratizing States of Africa," *International Review of Administrative Sciences* 64: 611-623. [This article highlights the changes taking place in Africa and the inadequacy of present public administration systems and current administrative reforms. It also discusses the public administration systems transformations necessitated by the environmental changes and a strategy for actualizing such reforms.]

Osborne, D. and Gaebler T. (1992). *Reinventing Government: How the Entrepreneurial Spirit is Transforming the Public Sector,* Reading, Ms: Addison-Wesley. [This book contains a number of rationales for the reinvention movement. This is about the pioneers of a new form of governance.]

Peri, A.E. (1995). "Reform's Changing Role," *Public Administration Review* 55(5): 413-417. [This article, questions the purpose of administrative reform of the President Clinton and how does it compare to those of predessor initiatives. It examined the national performance review with in the historical setting of predecessor efforts at comprehensive executive reorganization.]

Politt, C. (1996). "Antistatist Administrative Reforms and New Administrative Directions: Public Administration in the United Kingdom," *Public Administration Review* 51(1): 82-84. [It outlines the three phases of anti-state administrative reforms in the British Public administrative system since 1979 and describes their sources of support, underlying rationales, basic institutional elements and limitations.]

Quiggin, J. (1999). "The Future of Government: Mixed Economy or Minimal State?" *Australian Journal of Public Administration* 58(4): 39-53. [It describes the expansion of government from 1870 to 1970 and the subsequent retreat from intervention. It assesses the costs and benefits of microeconomic reforms applied to the government sector. It discusses the issues relevant in drawing the boundaries between the public and private sectors.]

Riggs, F.W. (1997). "Modernity and Bureaucracy," *Public Administration Review* 57(4): 347-353. [This Article strongly recommends the need of strengthening democratic apparatus to control the bureaucracy.]

Romzek, B.S. (2000). "Dynamics of Public Sector Accountability in an Era of Reform," *International Review of Administrative Sciences* 66: 21-41. [This article examines the accountability implications of contemporary administrative reforms.]

Stowe, K. (1992). "Good Piano Won't Play Bad Music: Administrative Reforms and Good Governance", *Public Administration* 70 (autumn): 387-394 [This paper is about good governance; it explores the hypothesis which connects administrative reforms with better government.]

Thompson, J.R. (1999). "Devising Administrative Reform that Works: The Example of the Reinvention Lab Program," *Public Administration Review* 59(4): 283-292. [This article reviews the National Performance Review's reinvention lab program, and concludes substantial success has been achieved.]

Vajpayee, A.B. (1999). "Indian Administration To-day; Remedying its Weaknesses," *Indian Journal of Public Administration* XLV(1): 1-4. [This is concerned with Indian administration being ill-equipped to fulfill national objectives; the author calls upon the politicians and administrators for self introspection, and upholding of national and public interests above all.]

Wilenski, P. (Autumn 1986). "Administrative Reform—General Principles and the Australian Experience", *Public Administration* 64: 257. [This article addresses the factors critical to the translation of reform ideas into real change is administrative structures and processes.]

World Development Report, (1999/2000). *Entering the 21st Century,* New York: Oxford University Press, 2000: 4-50 and 107-124. [This report examines the unfolding dynamic changes at the supranational and subnational levels. It proposes new rules and structures to serve as a foundation for development policy in the twenty-first century.

12

India in Search of Good Governance

The first reference about the concept of good governance was made in 1989, in a World Bank report on Sub-Saharan Africa. It defined good governance as a 'public service that is efficient, a judicial system that is reliable and an administration that is accountable to the Public'. Kenneth Stowe, an experienced British administrator, has set out six characteristics for a better clarification of the meaning of good governance[1]:

1. political freedom, including free speech and a freely elected parliament, assembly or legislature;
2. constitutional and judicial protection for rights of the individual;
3. the maintenance of the rule of law by an independent judiciary;
4. the maintenance of a stable currency, the essential underpinning of economic and social development;
5. development of society as a whole by education and health care; and finally executive accountability to a freely elected legislature.

The World Bank has identified a number of aspects of good governance. One of them is a sound administrative system leading to efficiency and effectiveness in a democratic framework. The emphasis on these in public service is, reorienting public administration towards management philosophy. However, on efficient service cannot by itself, secure good governance, as also a good government.

The focus of "Governance" is basically on the process by which authority is exercised in the management of a country's economic and social resources and the capacity of government to design, formulate implement policies and discharge government functions.[2]

Globalization and Good Governance

The winds of change brought by economic globalization have made the state governments to redefine their roles and responsibilities. But, unfortunately, the academic departments of political science and public administration of the universities and colleges in India have not expressed much concern about globalization and its impact. They might have studied certain aspects of globalization in the name of good governance and new public management. Neither separate papers/courses, nor specific research projects are taken up for the teaching and research. The students in particular and the teachers in general are not very much aware of the current trends of globalization. Not that some seminars/workshops have not been held, but they did not evince keen interest. Infact, it appears, most of them have silently supported the ideology of LPG and kept quite for the operative part of the governmental activities. A few intellectuals/researchers particularly the leftist/Marxist oriented teachers/writers/activists might have raised their voice here and there and some serious minded scholars have written and organized some seminars. However, despite their little efforts not much deeper studies have been made by the states/governments and their well trained bureaucrats supporting the LPG policies have not seriously taken some projects in the name of NPM and good governance.

The theoretical literature presents conflicting expectations about the effect of economic globalization on national democratic governance. Some expect that globalizational promotes democracy. Quan Li and Rafael Reuveny[3] assessed empirically the effects of globalization on the level of democracy from 1970 to 1996 for 127 countries. Two questions were posed: Does economic globalization affect the level of democracy associated with a decline or rise of democratic governance?

Good governance represents a continuous quest for mass prosperity and endless effort for liberal democracy.[4] In the light of this general definition particularly after 1991 the efforts of good governance of governments in India are assessed. The slogans given and promises made to the people by the Congress party, the National Democratic Alliance (NDA) and the United Progressive Alliance (UPA) Governments at the Centre or different regional political party governments at state level[5] and their fulfillment in the shape of providing common minimum needs to the ordinary people must be examined in the light of the constitutional obligations and the moral responsibilities enshrined in the part IV of the Constitution, the Directive Principles of State Policy. If the policies of the government and their implementation benefit the majority of the people, then we can claim that the government is good and theirs is good governance.

To achieve the essential component of good governance i.e. the long term goal of transformation of mass poverty into mass prosperity, the government must feel responsible to achieve the enduring collaboration between the public, the civil and the private sectors. The government has to formulate appropriate public policies, stimulate the private sector and preserve the rule of law by a highly professional civil service and allow the operation of a free press. The government has to play the role of ensuring the good governance in all the sectors. Without Good Governance, the government cannot eradicate or even reduce the poverty levels. "Good governance is a necessity for development and poverty reduction, not a luxury".[6]

In India the possibility of good governance depends largely on the provisions of the Constitution, particularly, about the centre - state relations. For a longtime there was no harmony between the centre and the states due to centralization of powers at the Centre. But of late after the entry of coalition governments at the Centre and different regional, left and right political parties ruling many state governments started enjoying somewhat autonomous powers, some times leading to disharmony on ideological grounds.

Despite, the Centre is still having more powers and less autonomy to the states, which is not conducive to good governance. Good governance requires decentralization of powers not only to states and to the local governments. The constitutional amendment 73 and 74 during 1994 enabled to have a third tier of government at local level with stipulated powers and finances. But so far more than 90 per cent of state governments have not decentralized the powers to the local governments. What kind of democracy and good government can be ensured? Therefore, for the achievement of good governance constitutional obligations have to be fulfilled by all the governments at different levels. As long as political parties (National/Regional) with different uncompromisable ideologies do not arrive at a minimum consensus and as long as they do not realize that undisrupted public services must be allowed at the cost of political power, they will not allow the bureaucracy to function on a minimum scale. Then where is the scope for governance and good governance. Bureaucracy has become non-developmental and anti-public with rampant corruption and with political collaboration. This dirty story of civil service in India is known already to all the people. If this is the pitiable plight of the situation, what can anybody do for good governance? Neither the policies are very good, nor the implementation is good, how can the results will be good? Outcomes are poor and the poor have become much poorer.

In good governance the legislature particularly in the Indian context of parliamentary democracy must be more accountable to the people. But during last 20 years the legislature has become weak in its effectiveness of meetings, discussions and getting approval of the bills. The legislatures at the centre, state, municipality or at the panchayat level have not been living up to the mark of sustaining the democratic element. The powers of Legislature are being enjoyed by the cabinet or the ministry, in a way the executive has become powerful and its members are negotiating without much transparency in finalizing the public policies. The unofficial economic advisors are clinching the issues in many times keeping aside the regular higher bureaucracy. The decisions of the executive are often challenged in the high courts at the state level and the Supreme Court has struck down the executive decisions in a number of cases. On the one hand the amount of litigation increased many folds, on the other hand, the judgments of the courts either not respected or not implemented properly. The judiciary appears to be very active but its effectiveness either in the making of the laws or in their implementation is not spectacular. However, the people are looking towards the judiciary for justice against the arbitration of the executive.

Ruling parties/coalitions without much regard to the constitutional obligations and provisions are taking decisions, policies in the interest of groups/community to satisfy their supporters, much against the common good. This attitude cannot lead to good governance.

Budgeting in the government (passing and execution) has almost become a farce. The ministers make many public statements involving huge finances without any relevance to the budget. The people have been fooled by irresponsible slogans and statements. The budget allocations to the common needs of ordinary people i.e. in health and education, agriculture, housing etc have been cut to very low levels giving up the promised welfare by the state. The word 'public' today carries no meaning in the Indian welfare state. Public Administration by design serves the private interests. Since long, only 10-15 per cent of the budgeting benefits are reaching the expected. The rest is looted by the politicians, bureaucrats and the middle men. How can anybody call it as good governance? By any standards it cannot be called even as governance. Accounting and auditing in this kind of governance has no meaning. The dog stopped barking and biting its own bones.

The governments in India are not very seriously intended to bring any reforms in its governance to make it good. New policies and new laws like the New Economic and Industrial Policy 1991, The Environmental Protection Act, The New Educational Policy, The Human Rights Law, The New Panchayati Raj Act, The Right to Information Act, The Employment Guarantee Act, and a number of other positive laws might have been enacted for the benefit of the people. The budgetary outlays for education, health, housing also might have enhanced, a lot of interest might have evinced to provide better infrastructural facilities in road, rail and Air transport.

One has to accept that the people in general are benefited, but the fact is only a few people belonging to a class/community got the benefits at the cost of other general public who are poor and below poverty line (BPL). Good governance has to take special steps to arrest the BPL. The Employment Guarantee Act is expected to improve the situation. One important aspect is that policies are appeared to be good but at governance level they are not that good and some times very bad.

Good governance may be possible to some extent with specific and individual laws but the fruits of economic reforms of liberalization, privatization and globalization will not reach the general public without concomitant political and administrative reforms.

Certain electoral reforms for periodical and proper conduct of elections are introduced but the reforms could not deepen the democracy, particularly at the gross roots. At the moment democracy in India is not in a position to control the bureaucracy, despite downsizing and deregulation. There is a perfect understanding between the political executive and the bureaucracy at all levels of governance for the balanced share of public revenues. Globalization and privatization have played havoc with the sovereignty of the Indian Nation State, where the state lost its powers to multinationals and the financial institutions of the world governance. In this regard, India may be better compared to other countries. Democracy, rule of law, empowerment of the people, public security are at stake. The law and order, human rights are terribly affected in almost half of India, people's movements; extremism, terrorism, legal battles, and civil strife are in spate. The police, para-military forces are combating with the people who demand the rights. The quality and the standards of education, health, social and political values have been deteriorated considerably.

One important aspect of the present state of governance is that under the changed circumstances of liberalization, privatization and globalization, the state in India cannot execute many provisions of the constitution of India particularly the chapter III and chapter IV. Therefore, the state in India is gradually withdrawing from original concept of welfare state and democratic socialism. Globalization means the minimal state with regard to public welfare and maximum state to protect the private interests through its coercive operations. It also means less democracy and reduced human rights. The people's sovereignty cannot be protected through their weak state, which cannot represent the public and argue for the public interest, public security and public welfare. Thus, good governance may increase the efficiency and effectiveness of its services but they are not for the common man in the street. It may sometimes trickle down but it has not happened so far. The evidence is the suicidal deaths of the peasants, weavers and the helpless, the retrenchment and voluntary retirement of lakhs of employees and workers in all the sectors leading to unemployment and underemployment everywhere.

Good governance is good and possible in a stable democratic state and society. Instability of the politics has been witnessed for the last 20 years both at the centre and states. While political instability is the order of the day, public administration can not adopt the culture of good governance. There may be citizen's charters, information acts, human rights protection law etc. But the corrupt political master cannot direct and mend the much more corrupt bureaucracy in the face liberalization, where the private interests unleashed their forces to further corrupt the politic-administrative system. Good governance measures if any through e-governance, e-democracy are undertaken, they facilitate some smoothness for the enlightened citizens and the elite but the large sections of people remained as ordinary consumers whose value of the money is not protected or undervalued. To an extent the lower middle class and a section of urban middle class might be happy with the good governance initiatives. Good governance is essential for mass prosperity but the evidence is it better served some vocal sections and economically well-off groups. Good governance has it helped to improve the public distribution system, public health, land reforms, law and order, primary education, human relations, agriculture, the per capital levels? Not much India is in 'slow motion.'[7] It is ruled by 'Kleptocracy'[8] and 'bandit democracy.'[9] Indians want development through freedom. But the agencies/institutions have not been geared up to the speed required by the philosophy of good governance. It appears sometimes, the Judiciary has taken up the job to provide social justice but it ends up momentary. Lok Adalats and the Legal Aid programmes could only make a halt on the system.

Public accountability and transparency is another important aspect of good governance. The Right to Information Act 2005 is expected to do something good in this respect. But the traditional bureaucracy is against the open government.[10]

Summary

Good and humane governance[11] is the most important requirement in India. Good governance implies gearing up the traditional, semi-colonial administrative machinery to provide "a responsive, transparent, clean and people friendly administration". It is linked to changing nature and the role of the state. The current thinking about introduction of good governance measures in the Indian government is only a decade old. Good governance measures like citizen charters, information act, and usage of information technology, e-governance are recently introduced. Their performance cannot be assessed during this short term.

References

1. Kenneth Stowe, "Good Piano Won't Play Bad Music: Administrative Reform and Good Governance", Public Administration, 70(1) 25-34, 1992.
2. Mohit Bhattacharya, Conceptualizing Good Governance, Indian Journal of Public Administration, XLIV (3) 1998.
3. For details, Quan Li and Rafael Reveuny, Economic Globalization and Democracy: An Empirical Analysis, British Journal of Political Science, No. 33, 2003, pp. 29-54.
4. For details Jayanta Kumar Ray, India in Search of Good Governance, K.P. Bagchi & Company, Calcutta, 2001.
5. DMK and AIADMK in Tamil Nadu, left Democratic Front in West Bengal, Kerala and Tripura, TDP in A.P., BJP Government in Gujarat and M.P., BJP and Shiva Sena Government in Maharashtra, RJD in Bihar, BSP, BJP and S.P. governments in UP and alliances governments in some other states and Congress governments in remaining states like A.P., Assam etc.

6. The World Bank, India: Reducing Poverty, Accelerating Development.

7. For details, Mark Tully and Gullian Wright, D, India in Slow Motion, Penguin Books, New Delhi, 2003.

8. *Ibid.*, pp. XIII-XVI and 144-153.

9. Fareed Zakaria, The Future of Freedom: Illiberal Democracy at Home and Abroad, Viking, New Delhi, 2003, pp. 109-11.

10. For Details, Kuldeep Mathur, Good Governance and Pursuit of Transparency in Administration. The Indian Efforts, in Pardeep Sahni and Uma Medury (Eds), Governance for Development, Prentice Hall of India, New Delhi, 2003, pp. 48-56.

11. For details, Rajni Kothari, State Against Democracy: In search of Humane Governance, Ajanta Publication, New Delhi, 1988, p. 14.

13

Human Development and Governance : Challenges in India

Human development may not be possible even by good governance. It is possible only by humane governance[1]. The Lessons of humane governance must be learnt from the peoples movements: Human rights movements, womens movements, environmental protection movements, peasants movements, peace movements, social movements and many other grassroot movements[2]. It is observed that we need to move from "government of humans to humane government", where in civil society orders politics and governance[3] and where human dignity, human values, human rights, democratic values and democratic rights are not only cherished but protected.

The purpose of this paper is to explain the existing pathetic phenomenon of the human development in democratic India under the authoritative bureaucratic governance. While examining the causes for such a kind of pathetic situation[4], an attempt is made here to suggest certain alternative measures which provide democratic opportunities to the people, peoples organizations and institutions particularly at the grassroots level through a newly envisaged third level government at local level, may be termed complete democratic decentralization or gram swaraj. It is "thinking locally and transforming globally" where, people's involvement, participation, cooperation will be predominant. Bureaucracy (traditional) will have less role. By empowering the people, they must be provided with an opportunity to serve themselves through self-governance, which will be good and humane. Development (of people's choice) will take place with the self-efforts of the people and their self-governance. This design may not however, fit in the LPG and the NPM model of governance. At the end, urgent tasks to be taken up are stated for quick human development and some suggestions are made for their successful accomplishment

Bureaucracy, Development and People's Empowerment

Literature on peoples empowerment in the context of public bureaucracy and development is either scanty or mostly negligent. For that matter, there is not much literature on people's empowerment contributed by the western writers[5]. Mostly they did not attempt to think about or to locate the place of peoples empowerment for development through public bureaucracy. Perhaps, it is because they reposited more confidence in the competence of bureaucracy rather the people concerned in getting resolved the peoples problems through their collective action. It may be also due to less faith in the effectiveness of democracy or the political masters to look into the developmental aspects of the people. It is also due to the tendency of the writers to support more the State, government(s), bureaucracy, authoritarianism and anti-people stand semiconsciously adopted due to their earlier ruling class background or support extended to the ruling class.

Public bureaucracy all over the world particularly in the developing countries from the beginning is mostly loyal to the State and to the government of the day. It was an institution created and trained to be perfect to regulate/oppress the society—in the name of maintenance of "Law and Order"—A law created by the ruling class and an order desired by the bureaucratic state and the ruling class. It is the fact to the best of my knowledge and experience of last 40 years as a professor of Public Administration in a developing university of an underdeveloped region[6].

The third world democratic countries when they planned for the development (more economic, less political and nil social) the responsibility for the development was handed over to the then existing (colonial) regulatory bureaucracy. Though it was known to be anti-people, semi-parasitic of the society, it was nominated to act as the agent for the 'development'. The bureaucracy was asked to change and transform from its past orientation to development orientation, and be a 'change' agency. It was made to be an exchange agency, a bridge between the glorious, 'welfare' and 'democratic' state and the 'people', (the politicians, the middle men and the people), scattered millions of the local ordinary people residing in the far off villages.

The place or predicament of public bureaucracy may be observed through out India particularly in the post-independence era and very particularly in Bihar, Uttar Pradesh, Madhya Pradesh, Rajasthan and parts of almost of all the states. Virtually in about 100 districts of India it is police bureaucratic state. In about 60 districts (Tribal India[7]) whether the state or bureaucracy has either not touched them or kept under their grip. Paramilitary, state police, reserve police, specially trained police, revenue, forest, excise and all sorts of regulatory officials usurped the freedom enjoyed by the traditional communities. Public budget is created, revenues collected from the people, raised loans and debts in the name of the people and the state. The expenditure allotted to maintenance of law and order and the welfare services to the poor, was distributed in the form of commissions among the contractors, bureaucrats and the politicians (in the order of merit) and only 10-15% of the budget reached the people for whom it was originally meant for. It has been happening so for the last two decades uniformly throughout India, irrespective of the governments and the parties ruling them[8].

If there are any 'good' public officials (there are some) either they are physically incapacitated, mentally tortured or made them to toe the line of the looters the "kleptocracy"[9], and the "bandit democracy"[10].

One need not deal very exhaustively about the ineffectiveness and the failure of public bureaucracy either in the case of industrial development (public and private sectors) or in the case of social development (welfare services to the poor). It is well recorded history. Somehow in the last 20 years (LPG movement) the rich (industrial class) over powered the public bureaucracy by consoling and convincing their political elite to debureaucratise, deregulate and down-size (at lower levels) the public bureaucracy. It is tamed, cut to its original size in some respects. But at the same time the people, (the poor, the agrarian) who are supposed to be served by the public bureaucracy are still left to the bureaucratic onslaught. The LPG philosophy believes more in delegation and decentralisation but less in peoples empowerment and democratic decentralisation. Now the public bureaucracy is ordered to be liberal towards the elite (political, military, business, administrative) but hold the regimental control over the masses. As such the tamed bureaucracy was permitted to be very shrewd with the general public. It is now authoritative (the police, paramilitary forces, the courts) in nexus with the criminals (some politicians, landlords and underworld). Even school teachers, extension workers, medical and health personnel, are not sympathetic to the people. Illiteracy, illness, and poor sanitation is the result. The evidence is the disgraceful human development index.

Loyal/Neutral/Faithful ?

Governments may come and go but the permanent bureaucracy continues as the State continues to exist. The nature of the State and ideology of the Government may change. According to the dominant theory, bureaucracy is supposed to be neutral, faithful, and loyal to the State. In a parliamentary democratic federal state, the bureaucracy was taught to be neutral to the politics of the Government. However, over a period of time, this concept of neutrality remained doubtful, the extent of loyalty and faithfulness has been questioned. With a great hope, the regulatory revenue bureaucracy ordered to behave as a development bureaucracy. But, indeed, it did not happen so. It is a fact with lot of evidence that bureaucracy seized to be neutral. For some time it was "committed" to the party in the government and played tunes to corrupt politicians. As such much of the bureaucracy (higher, middle, lower and street) has been hand in glove with the criminals and undemocratic politics.

It may be judicial, police, revenue, welfare, commercial or any other services which came into contact with the people and places failed to implement the rule of law and the principle of equality, the "essence" of public administration in a democracy. People started hating the bureaucracy and its master as well. In fact, the government employees as whole has now become an organised interest, a "bureaucratic class"[11]. It is much worse in public undertakings, public corporations and government companies. Therefore, many were denationalised, privatised, disinvested or voluntary retirement applied to the employees and workers of Public sector undertakings or closed down. As a part of the recent LPG administrative reforms (New Public Management) further recruitment is almost stopped and downsized the existing civil service to some extent.

During 2003, more than a lakh of employees were dismissed by Tamil Nadu State Government when they went on a general strike. The employees sought the intervention of the Supreme Court of India which pronounced an historical Judgement stating that the government employees have no right to strike and upheld the dismissal order of the State Government. There was hue and cry all over India against the Supreme Court and the Tamil Nadu State Government, while the Central Government and other State Governments kept quite except the left party government in West Bengal.

It must be interesting to note that even left parties (and Governments) who generally extend their support to the employees could not win back their employees support in their governments. The Writers Office Building in West Bengal is no way different from the Secretariats of any other governments, in their behavioural pattern and commitment to the public service.

It is pertinent to note about the anti-governmental attitude of the bureaucracy which was displayed openly in the elections of 2003 for Rajasthan State Legislature where in the state government employees went on a public compaign not to vote to the Congress party which was in power as the government denied payment of financial benefits, like allowances on par with the Central Government. Congress party was defeated in the elections to the utter dismay of every one and the BJP formed the government and enhanced immediately the retirement age of the State Government employees from 58 to 60 years. While the political parties are trying to score their differences, the employees associations and unions have been negotiating underhand with the political parties for their own benefits and interests.

It also happened in the same way in Tamil Nadu: As stated earlier all those who were dismissed or otherwise, the employees went enblock and voted in the recent parliament elections 2004 against the ruling AIADMK party and the Jayalalitha government which was adamant and the NDA Government at the Centre, which was silent to the Supreme Courts Judgement. They failed to get even a single parliamentary seat, mainly due the animosity of the employees.

In the recent elections 2004 to the Andhra Pradesh state legislature and to the Parliament, the Telugu Desam government was toppled down due to the employees noncooperation and extending open support to the Congress party which was out of power during the last ten years. Chandra Babu Naidu Government in A.P. denied enhancement of D.A. to the retired employees and there was a strong rumour that the retirement age of employees would be reduced to 55 from 58 years, if Telugu Desam party comes into power once again in the elections. A section of the employees of the Telangana region who have been demanding a separate Telangana state also played a dirty role in the polling process as polling personnel. It is alleged, the polling personnel in Telangana region and other places also rigged the polls exercising voting of their choice on behalf of the ordinary illiterate voters who could not properly utilise the electronic voting machines.

Toppling the Telugu Desam Government in A.P. and defeating the AIADMK party in Tamil Nadu enabled the Congress party to get the highest number of seats in Parliament (about 70). This not only enabled the Congress-led parties (Left supported) to defeat the NDA

Government in New Delhi, and TDP Government in A.P., but to regain power by the Congress led coalition Government in New Delhi and in A.P. Behind the debackle of the incumbant Governments, the role of the employees is very much invisible. The Congress party in A.P. promised before the elections to the employees that they will look into their grievances if it is voted to power.

The whole game appears to be played between the political parties and the trade unions of the employees. The latter played their cards very carefully to protect their own interests, such is the dominant position at present occupied by the bureaucracy in different states where the democratic class (political parties) is struggling to gain or retain the political power.

While millions of the employees are struggling to protect their interests, the strongest trade union of IAS/IPS officers who are indeed the eyes and ears of the Government spread all over the country are meddling in the power politics and did not evince much interest either in policy making or in its implementation. They joined hands with the selfish politicians in enjoying the real power and sharing the material loot/booty. Therefore, all this demands the reform of the state and the bureaucratic apparatus, so that people are assured of the benefits meant for them and they get bigger gains[12].

Peoples Movements and Development

People want to live in a developed India[13]. Some Governments and some political leaders in India visualized a developed India by vision 2020. Such visualizers at the Centre and State Governments have been defeated in the recent general elections of 2004. They visualized and planned for a developed India (India Shinning) but not developed people. In many states of India thousands of farmers committed suicide during the last five years. Bureaucracy, particularly the agricultural scientists, extensive personnel of the agriculture department, irrigation and ground water personnel have utterly failed in assisting the poor and small farmers. They helped the agribusiness, who sold unauthorized seeds, dubious pesticides, qualityless fertilizers. The newly developed 'markets' turned to be the farmers enemies by not offering the standard rates to the farmers produce. People in the recent elections voted out the Governments who were anti-farmer and anti-agriculture. The bureaucracy did not lose anything but gained the wrath of the farmers. The farmers at many places have been agitating violently at the market yards and rebelled against the agriculture departmental employees and officers. They abused, attacked and ransacked their offices.

In a democracy whenever it is illiberal, it is but natural to the people whose interests are undermined or not considered by the bureaucracy and the polity, to organise themselves to exercise their right to represent their problems to the concerned authorities. In case, the people and their representatives are not satisfied with the manner and extent of resolving their problems, they may organise strongly and agitate in peaceful and democratic methods and ultimately leading to a sporadic movement involving large number of affected people, mobilising media and intelligentia for their support against the autocratic and undemocratic stand of the administration'[14]. Bureaucracy alone may not be in a position every time to solve such problems. But the problem and its extent and latest issues involved, the question of law/rules may be analysed by the bureaucracy and advise the government (policy makers) in an impartial way. Instead, if bureaucracy misleads the policy makers in the name of security, law, order, national interest etc, it is not only not performing the advisory role properly but, giving wrong advice to the lay politician(s). It is happening like this in most cases. Therefore, the peoples movements, the consumer forums etc are spreading their tentacles to oppose the government (mainly the bureaucracy). Therefore, teachers, doctors, engineers, electricity, revenue, police, bankers, irrigation transport authorities, excise officials, courts, foresters etc are being hated by the common people. Those who come into contact with the people on a daily basis almost lost faith in government authorities and employees. They no longer remained public servants, they are corrupt and harassing people for every small thing. The service motto is not known to them. They believe in authority and demanding bribes for every thing. The amount of corruption in the defense departments is known to every one these days. The national security, education, the public health, the law and order in the civic life, the general welfare is at low ebb. It is all due to the corrupt irresponsible, unsocial, anti-national attitude of selfish bureaucracy and their supporters (the politicians/the under world, criminals). The pervasive cynicism now evident in the system must give way to the people who are ready to participate and cooperate with the administration. Therefore, it is imperative to empower the people[15] (the women, the farmers, the minorities, the downtrodden, the youth). There are many non-governmental organizations (NGO's) delivering service to the people (in education, health etc) without any profit motive. Such NGO's have to be encouraged to play a crucial role in the development. Bureaucracy have to learn lessons from such organisations in serving the masses.

Urgent Tasks for Human Development[16]

In the light of the experience narrated certain urgent tasks[17] have to be undertaken for the maintenance of human development in India:

1. Political Reforms - including electoral reforms - where democracy spreads more widely throughout society. Citizens must be able to exercise their democratic rights with a clear political support. Peoples movements have to be recognized and encouraged as a part of democratic process. Civil society must be strengthened.
2. Greater empowerment of the people (women, minorities, youth, SCs and STs etc) by implementing the 73rd and 74th Amendment Act by devolving full powers envisaged therein and empowering the Panchayats and Municipalities have direct administrative control over their local delivery systems. It enables peoples involvement, participation and cooperation. Strengthening local governments ensures better delivery of public services with more responsiveness and responsibility. This empowerment of local areas emanates the growth of local leadership and enable them to plan[18] for their own areas. Thus, democratic decentralization responds to the growing volume of protests and satisfies to a large extent the local elites who are struggling for political power and participation in governance and development.

3. Inspite of much talk of liberal democracy and liberal economic reforms and training to orient bureaucratic attitudes, not much change occurred in the behavioral pattern of the bureaucracy. Their anti-people, anti-development, corrupt and selfish thinking must be changed by more democratization, enhanced freedom and greater citizen empowerment, and better implementation of the new citizen charters. The corrupt, negative, and lethargic bureaucracy must be whipped without delay. People cannot any more afford such a callous, irresponsible and unaccountable public bureaucracy particularly where it is dealing with human developmental affairs of the people like health, education, employment, irrigation, law and order issues.
4. The elections 2004 in India reveals that people want a welfare state (not the old mai-baap government) with in the LPG policy. It calls for the redefinition of the role of the state. India is rich and the Indians are poor. The riches of India (national resources) have to be distributed equally to all the people, particularly to those poor. It is the development of these with a human face is human development. The vast number of people who live in rural areas on agriculture must be provided adequate productive employment opportunities. It automatically calls for a radical land reforms policy. The policy and the programs have been there for long, only thing is to implement them with all sincerity. The farmers want land, water, power, credit and market. They should have access to the credit cards linked with health and agricultural insurance. Agriculture alone without irrigation and power facilities cannot provide full employment to all. Therefore, off- farm employment opportunities have to be provided for the millions of unskilled hands. All this is a gigantic task which is possible only to a good government (not managed by criminal politicians and corrupt bureaucrats) and good business (not profit motivated and unethical business), which really cares the consumers and unemployed citizen.

5. Good business cannot be visualized in the near future. We want good politicians and good government, which enables to generate wealth and guarantees equitable distribution. The state need to be facilitator, the rule maker as well the game player. It need to be strong to unshackle the "animal spirits" of the free enterprise as well controlling them for the benefit of the vast majority of the people. Politics have to learn the truth from the facts and the reality. The parties in power have to work round the clock as they work during election period. Their leaders, cadre irrespective of the position and ideology have to be with the people by integrating and uniting them. Parties have to create social and economic leaders not *pyravikars* and contractors. Peoples interest and public opinion must prevail.

6. A desired human development is not that easy in Indian stratified society (Hindu). The influence of the caste and traditional culture is predominant. Therefore, deepening and strengthening democracy and replacement of hierarchical interaction with the people by collective interaction is the only alternative for ensuring social and economic justice, through social and economic transformation. This is the duty of the State and politics. The politics of the coalition and alliances along with the civil society organizations must see the 'democracy on the march' which leads to 'common good' and human development[19].

Conclusion

Human development in a country like India is not easy without peoples empowerment and state intervention. Greater responsibility must be entrusted to Local Governments and the political parties must take responsibility of social mobilization. Agricultural production and other small-scale production must be encouraged to provide employment to the rural poor. The state must provide greater human security, help the poor to get united and avoid caste, and communal disharmony. In the absence of an organised civil society, mobilizing economic resources and social forces must be the ultimate responsibility of the state and politics in India. Human development with a human face requires a liberal democratic state, where life is secure with certain guaranteed freedom[20]. Let the people feel free to live in peace if not prosperity and the human development takes place of their own choice.

References

1. For details, Rajni Kothari, *State Against Democracy: In Search of Humane Governance,* Ajanta Publications, New Delhi, 1988, pp. 1-14.
2. For details, Rajendra Singh, *Social Movements, Old and New: A Post Modernistic Critique,* Sage Publications, New Delhi, 2001, pp. 261-298.
3. Rajni Kothari, *Op.Cit,* p. 11.
4. For details, Malay Chaudhuri and Arindam Chaudhuri, *The Great Indian Dream: Restoring Pride to* a *Nation Betrayed,* Mac Millan India, New Delhi, 2003. For facts and figures, See, Mohan K. Mathew, *India: Facts & Figures,* Sterling Publishers, New Delhi, 2001.
5. For details, Michell Dean, Governmentality: Power and Rule in Modern Society, Sage Publication, London, 1999, pp. 67-72.
6. V. Bhaskara Rao, *Public Administration in India,* Ajanta Publications, New Delhi, 1989.
7. Mahapatra, Richard with Prabhanjan Verma, Nidhi Jamwal and Kazimuddin Ahmed, (August 31, 2002), The Second Independence, *"Down to Earth",* pp. 22-36.
8. Congress, Bharatiya Janata Party, CPI(M), DMKs, Telugu Desam Party, Rashtreeya Janata Dal, BSP and SP in U.P., Akali Dal etc.
9. For details, Mark Tully and Gillian Wright, *India in Slow Motion,* Penguin Books, New Delhi, 2003, pp. XIII - XVI, and 144-153.
10. Fareed Zakaria, *The Future of Freedom: Illiberal Democracy at Home & Abroad,* Viking, New Delhi, pp. 109-11.
11. For a detailed discussion, Hartmut Elsenhans, *State, Class and Development,* Radiant Publishers, New Delhi, 1996.
12. Sunita Narain, Time for the Future to Win, *Down to Earth,* June 15, 2004, p. 5.

13. For details, APJ Abdul Kalam with Y.S. Rajan, *India 2020: A Vision for the New Millennium,* New Delhi, Penguin Books, 2002, p.

14. For details, Ved Marwah, Internal Security, Law and Order, in, V.A. Pai Panandiker (Ed), Fifty years of Swaraj, Konark Publishers, New Delhi, 1998, pp. 231-252.

15. Lok Satta (People Power), a Civil Society Organization has been campaigning in Andhra Pradesh, India for the last six years, for the empowerment of Local governance through a Federation for Empowerment of Local Governments.

16. The essential qualitative components for human development are narrated by the Human Development Report of the UNDP (1996) Oxford University Press, New York.

17. For more details, V.A. Pai Panandiker (Ed), Fifty years Swaraj: Highlights and Shadows, Konark Publishers, New Delhi, 1998, pp. 109-116.

18. For Kerala experiment of 'People Campaign for Decentralized Planning' was quoted to be very successful - see for details, Thomas Issac and Richard W. Franke, Local Democracy and Development, New Delhi, Leftword Books, 2003.

19. For details, Peter Self, Rolling Back the Market: Economic Dogma and Political Choice, Macmillan Press, London, 2000.

20. For details, Amartya Sen, Development as Freedom, Oxford University Press, New Delhi, 2000.

14

Democracy and Public Administration in India

Today, many observe that democracy in India is in crisis and note a decline of confidence in public administration. Many factors contributed to the lack of public trust in politics and administration include the growing costs of political competition, the rising role of leaders in decision making, the centralization of governance and the increasing remoteness of politics and administration from the people.

Democracy is a reasonably effective framework for making decisions and delivering public policies. Public administration is very essential to the effective implementation of democratic decisions and all democracies face the challenge of supporting an effective, efficient and fair bureaucracy. In fact the responsibility for making democracy work falls on the bureaucrats as well as politicians.

The purpose of this paper is to assess the existing phenomenon of the democratic India under the authoritative bureaucratic governance. While examining the causes for the kind of pathetic situation,[1] an attempt is made to suggest certain alternative measures which provide democratic opportunities to the people and peoples organizations and institutions particularly at the grassroots level where, people's involvement, participation, cooperation will be predominant. Bureaucracy (traditional) will have less role. By empowering the people, they must be provided with an opportunity to serve themselves through self-governance, which will be good and humane. Development (of peoples choice) will take place with the self-efforts of the people and their self-governance. This design may not however, fit in the LPG and the NPM. At the end urgent tasks to be taken up are stated and some suggestions are made for their successful accomplishment.

Prior to independence, public administration was never 'of' the 'public' nor 'by' the 'public' or 'for' 'public', public administration came into existence in India only with the establishment of the democratic polity under the constitutional directives. Hence, the first and the last duty of public administration in India is to translate the objectives of the constitution. The constitution of India ensured to secure all citizens of India "equality of status and opportunity", and aimed at achieving "socio-economic transformation within the frame work of free society", to ensure socio-economic justice to the masses.

"Public" Administration in India is the product of the constitution framed under the influence and impact of ideals of democracy, welfare state, and socialist planning under the leadership of freedom fighters. But the world scene is now almost changed as the ideals of welfare state, social planning are being given up. The leadership of those freedom fighters who attempted to build a nation of socialist pattern of society, and secular state are now denigrated by the present leaders under the influence and impact of LPG. In fact, now the external factors are shaping much of the destiny of Public Administration in India. Therefore, the state in India after 40 years of its emergence nearly took a 'U' turn to fall inline with the global capitalism. Therefore, it is necessary to reassess the role and functions of Public Administration in India in the contemporary setting of democracy. In the context, the state intervention in economic activity is not justified as the will of politics. Thus, public administration to-day in India is pushed out of economic activity of commanding heights by a political decision of New Economic Policy, 1991. The rainbow coalition governments at the Centre, rudderless regional political party governments in different States are pursuing their 'own' brands of public administration.

During the last sixty years, in general, public administration in India, responded only when it was pressurized through organized agitation, movements and revolt. For, democratization, participation, joint consultation, collective bargaining, egalitarianism are not much palatable to the Indian political and Public Administrative system.[2] The fact of exploitations, economic inequalities, social oppression, and political servitude of people explain the nature of political system and public administration in India.[3]

The Present Scene

India planned for the development (more economic, less political and nil social). The responsibility for the development was handed over to the existing (colonial) regulatory bureaucracy. Though it was known anti-people, semi-parasitic of the society, it was nominated to act as the agent of the 'development'. It was made to be an exchange agency, a bridge between the glorious, 'welfare' and 'democratic' State and the 'people', (politicians, the middle men and the people), scatted millions of the local ordinary people residing in the far off villages.

The place or predicament of public bureaucracy may be observed through out India very particularly in Bihar, Uttar Pradesh, Madhya Pradesh, Rajasthan and parts of almost of all the states. Virtually in more than 100 districts of India it is police bureaucratic state. In about 60 districts (Tribal India) whether the state or bureaucracy has either/not touched them or kept under their grip. Paramilitary, state police, revenue, forest, excise and all sorts of regularly officials usurped the freedom enjoyed by the traditional communities. Public budget is created, revenues collected from the people or raised loans, debts in the name of the people and the state. The expenditure allotted to maintenance of law and order and the welfare services to the poor, was distributed among the contractors, bureaucrats and the politicians (in the order of merit) and only 10-15% of the budget reached the people for whom it was originally meant for. If there are any 'good' public officials they are physically incapacitated, mentally tortured or made them to toe the line of the looters the "kleptocracy",[4] and the "bandit democracy".[5]

One need not deal very exhaustively about the ineffectiveness and the failure of public bureaucracy either in the case of industrial development or social development. It is well recorded history. Somehow in the last 20 years (LPG movement) the rich (industrial class) over powered the public bureaucracy by consoling and convincing their political elite to debureaucratise, deregulate and downsize the public bureaucracy. It is tamed, cut to size in some respects. But at the same time the people, (the poor, the agrarian) who are supposed to be served by the public bureaucracy are still left to the bureaucratic onslaught. The LPG philosophy believes more in delegation and decentralisation but less in peoples empowerment and democratic decentralisation. Now the public bureaucracy is ordered to be liberal towards the elite (political, military, business, administrative) but hold the regimental control over the masses. As such the tamed bureaucracy was permitted to be very shrewd with the general public. It is now authoritative (the police, paramilitary forces, the courts) in nexus with the criminals (some politicians, landlords and underworld).

Under the present perspective, the meaning, the nature, functions, role, and the scope of the state in India is called upon to change. It is imperative for public administration as an instrument of action of the state to change as per the directions of the changing state and its politics. In a federal state like India the sovereignty of the state is vested in the constitution. The protection of the constitution is the duty of the legislature and judiciary, but the executive governments at the centre and the states have been tampering the provisions of the constitution without consulting the legislature and not considering the judicial pronouncements. Public administration as an executive agency has to follow the policies, programmes and activities of the governments at its level.

The present trend confirms the declining role of the state and the aggressive assertion of the market. This leads to the 'decay' of public administration. During 80s and 90s a strong public opinion was mobilized that public administration can no more be agent of economic growth and development. It may be true, that public administration failed to play a welfare and transformative role envisaged by the constitution. But, the fact is, it became ineffective only at the behest of the private interests played against the public interest. Public administration succumbed to the political game. Politics and bureaucracy and their nexus could successfully fail the public policy and its implementation. Corruption has been rampant in every walk of life. People, their representatives (elected), the bureaucracy and everyone was made to believe that public administration in India failed to deliver the goods and services. The objectives of the constitution like welfare state, secularism, cannot be achieved, it was declared, under the direction of the democratic socialism and planning. The constitution also created certain institutions to protect and safeguard some of its essential features, like the independent judiciary, Comptroller and Auditor General, Election Commission, Union/State Public Service Commissions, Finance Commission, SC/ST Commission and Institutes like Vigilance Commission, Central Bureau of Investigation, Lok Ayukthas, autonomous universities, public sector enterprises, nationalized banks, cooperative sector, panchayati raj and many such other institutions had to crumble under the misdirection of the ruling class and the bureaucracy for their self interests. Problems like poverty, unemployment, ill-health, illiteracy, over population insufficient essential infrastructural facilities could not be solved, as the public expenditure went into the pockets of the private interests, with whom the politicians, and the public administrators shared the loot. Under these precarious conditions, instead of mooting reforms in politics and public administration, economic reforms are introduced under the threat of the external/world bodies.

The Future of Politics and Administration

The present status of politics and public administration can be better understood, after realizing the present trends in the world. The ruling ideas in the world have become those of 'free markets' and 'political democracy' representing 'individualism' and 'self-interest'. Powerful business and political interests, are currently in the ascendance in the modern India. Formal democratic institutions and their actions are strongly attached to capitalism than democracy. The domination of the negative liberalism and the individualist tradition dragged towards the corrupt state.

The present and future political system can be mended only by collective democratic action only if the defects are clearly exposed.

For this, for the foreseeable future the Indian nation state need to play a key role in political life, devising a more balanced framework for the market and public services. The state has to rehabilitate its role as provider of public services against the attack upon public administration. The state in general has to reclaim its lost role for protecting social and community values. The word 'public' administration has become almost a dirty word for many under the ruling market system. The state almost lost its democratic trust.

The future of the state in India would be decided, it is observed, by two options: One if it desires to be a positive state, it has to read the pulse of the people carefully and imaginatively adopt the people-oriented policies of development to maintain the social stability and order, contain the social unrest and discontent. This needs not only keeping its own house, i.e., public administration clean and neat, but also regulate effectively the market-centered capitalism permitted by the state. The second option is: If the state is forced by its friends and desires to be a negative, it has to strengthen its coercive apparatus and unleash rein of terror and treat the elementary problems of the people as law and order problems. The symptoms appear to be that the Indian state opted the second option/alternative/choice. Hence, the Indian politics/administration order will move towards authoritarian and semi-fascist model.[6]

It is natural for a such a model of state which depends on its coercive apparatus to change its role, image and style of administration. It will strengthen military, paramilitary and police organs, both at the boarders and in the society. While giving up industry, agriculture, and welfare, it may still talk about relief measures, poverty alleviation, peoples participation, democracy, decentralization, and allocations for the welfare. But in reality as it is not the development agency, it must protect the interests of the market and profit.

The Future: Decentralization

The survival of democracy depends on the nature and scope of the political system, i.e., the state in India. The state, must be positive and resist the onslaught of the market. For the successfulness of its institutions it must seek the cooperation and support of the 'community', and the civil society. The state must delegate much of its functions like schools, public housing, health etc. to partly autonomous local elected governments. Functions and responsibilities on 29 items stipulated by the 73rd and 74th amendments to the constitution must be handed over to the local governments along with financial resources and personnel. Thus, democratic decentralization will not only respond the growing volume of protest but also satisfies to a large extent the local elites who are struggling for political power and participation in governance and development. This empowerment of local areas will encourage the growth of local leadership and enable planning their own areas.

There should be a common interest between the state, governments and the community/civil society organizations for deepening, and strengthening democracy, and promoting the public services, securing peaceful social life, reducing unemployment and preventing violence and crime. The value of democratic decentralization and an active civic spirit achieves regional economic and social development.

Democratic Reforms

Democracy can be made more effective only by a more active, equal and responsible democracy. This is possible through electoral democratic reforms. The job of democracy "begins at the ballot box".

(1) The working of democracy should be spread more widely throughout society.

(2) Serious and sincere electoral reforms for smooth, fair and fearless conduct of elections.

(3) Strong curbs upon political donations, electoral expenditure, the criminalization of politics and use of muscle power.

(4) Regulation of the activities of the recognized political parties by a specific law.

(5) Small cabinets and more legislative deliberations and controls.

(6) Citizens must be able to exercise their democratic rights with

clear political support.

(7) Sincere implementation of the Information Act.

The machinery of government can be made subordinate only by a properly chosen peoples leaders, who can exercise power by themselves as their right and duty. Then only the people can be paramount. Politics and administration must gain control over changes in science and technology. Public Administration must be able to meet the challenges of changing civil society. If it adopts a people-centred vision, where people flourish based on justice, environmental sustainability and political inclusiveness, it will continue and change to the needs of the people.

State as organized political community, market as organized economic community, civil society as organized social community must be interdependent. As the market and civil society in India have not yet organized effectively, the state has a special responsibility through its governance to maintain proper relations and manage the organized communities (political economic and social). The key challenge that has to be met is that the state, the rule of law and governance system actually protect and fulfil the civil and social rights of individuals and all communities alike.[7]

It should be recognized that economic prosperity, social welfare and effective governance are interdependent. The importance of good governance will be magnified when the future ushers in greater change in global economies, technology and global threats to national security. Therefore, there is a need for active and 'stronger' states to manage the interdependencies and interrelationships.

The state has to achieve collaboration and coordination both horizontally and vertically within and among organization and associated institutions.

Challenges

Today, the market model of government in the form of New Public Management (NPM) is threatening to eliminate democracy as a guiding principle in public administration.

The vexing problems of 20th century like poverty, poor quality education, and health, inequalities of gender and wealth, crime and violence, destruction of forest, and other natural resources, and pollution of air and water will continue in 21st century for many decades. The problems persist because people lack information, knowledge and political influence to direct public administrative agencies to solve them.[8]

The people in India started loosing faith in the government. They are regarding politicians as corrupt and bureaucrats as self-serving and inefficient. Today, it is difficult to predict how the globalization and the expansion of the market will affect democracy and public service. India need to adopt "strong" democracy i.e., modern form of participatory democracy by self-governing community of citizens. Public Administration must be a key actor in any effort to rediscover "substantive democracy" because of the complexity of providing public services in the present society. "Substantive democracy involves rekindling a public discourse about the purposes of collective action, accepting the role of citizens and public administration in shaping the future.[9]

The present "phenomenon of economic imperialism" where in the citizens are treated like customers, and consumers separating public administrators from the public policy process, convinces that government is nothing more than a business. This poses threat to democratic governance.

The attempts of introducing NPM hinders "substantive democracy" and limits citizen participation in policy and administration. The NPM reforms fail to understand the basic foundation of public administration in democratic practice, i.e., what people want from government. The ideas of welfare society, citizenship, public interest, social responsibility and dialogue are looked as anachronistic. Whatever may be, there must be connection between public administration is crucial and unavoidable for the social construction of society, for the state under the NPM avoids to address the issues that affect the society such as communalism, poverty etc. through substantive democracy.[10]

Today the citizens are distanced from their public-service

institutions. Therefore, public administrators and academics should play a part in the recovery of a 'substantive democratic' ideal. Democracy cannot be equated with consumer choice. Public administration does play a role in social order. People in public services not only deliver services but also serve as facilitators, interpreters and mediators of public action.

Public administration must not ignore its normative ground in public law. Customer satisfaction, services would not serve as an effective proxy for public interest. There is lot of political pressure on public administrators to adopt the NPM's approach. But the NPM displaces the democratic foundation which is essential to public administrative leadership.[11]

In place of old Public Administration and the New Public Management, Robert and Janet Denhardt in their book suggested, the new public service, for the future to:

- Serve citizens–Not customers,
- Seek the public interest,
- Value citizenship over entrepreneurship,
- Act democratically,
- Recognize that accountability is not simple, and
- Value people - not just productivity.

Now, the normative democratic context of public administration must be reasserted. This context includes achieving a democratic polity.[12] The central element should be a collaborative relationship between citizen and public administration. The citizens have the ability to self-govern. All citizens must be given an opportunity to participate. The emphasis on the collaborative model is to give citizens the knowledge and techniques they need to deal with public policy issues and provide an open and non-threatening forum for deliberation and decision-making. This model is only one way to enhance substantive democracy. It is well developed alternative that could be especially useful and powerful.[13]

"Substantive democracy" emphasizes on social equity and demands changes in the purpose and practice of public administration. It is against the old politics administration dichotomy. Public officials and the elected representatives who interact with citizens can improve the quality of democracy by actively helping people govern themselves. This requires the courage and goodwill to share rather than control knowledge and administrative processes with the people.

In the twenty-first century, there is much for public administration in democracy to do beyond the mandate of perfecting mechanisms for service delivery. Public administration must have to contribute "for achieving a democratic polity, rising to the societal level; confronting the complexity of instruments of collective action and encouraging more effective societal learning".[14]

Urgent Tasks

In the light of the experience narrated certain urgent tasks have to be undertaken for the maintenance of democracy India.

1. Political Reforms - including electoral reforms - where democracy spreads more widely throughout society. Citizens must be able to exercise their democratic rights with a clear political support. Peoples movements have to be recognized and encouraged as a part of democratic process. Civil society must be strengthened.

2. Greater empowerment of the people (women, minorities, youth, SCs and STs etc) by implementing the 73rd and 74th Amendment Act by devolving full powers envisaged there in and empowering the Panchayats and Municipalities have direct administrative control over their local delivery systems. It enables peoples involvement, participation and cooperation. Strengthening local governments ensures better delivery of public services with more responsiveness and responsibility. This empowerment of local areas emanates the growth of local leadership and enable them to plan for their own areas. Thus, democratic decentralization responds to the growing volume of protests and satisfies to a large extent the local

elite's who are struggling for political power and participation in governance and development.

3. Inspite of much talk of liberal democracy and liberal economic reforms and training to orient bureaucratic attitudes, not much change occurred in the behavioral pattern of the bureaucracy. Their anti-people, anti-development, corrupt and selfish thinking must be changed by more democratization, enhanced freedom and greater citizen empowerment. The corrupt, negligent, and lethargic bureaucracy must be whipped without delay. People cannot any more afford such a callous, irresponsible and unaccountable public bureaucracy particularly where it is dealing with human developmental affairs of the people like health, education, irrigation, law and order issues.

4. The elections 2004 in India reveals that people want a welfare state with in the LPG policy, (not the old *mai-baap* government). It calls for the redefinition of the role of the states. India is rich and the Indians are poor. The riches of India (national resources) have to be distributed equally to all the people, particularly to those poor. The vast number of people who live in rural areas on agriculture must be provided adequate productive employment opportunities. It automatically calls for land reforms policy. The policy and the programs have been there for long, only thing is to implement them with all sincerity. The farmers want land, water, power, credit and market. They should have access to the credit cards linked with health and agricultural insurance. Agriculture alone without irrigation and power facilities cannot provide full employment to all. Therefore, off-farm employment opportunities have to be provided for the millions of unskilled hands. All this is a gigantic talks which is possible only to a good government (not managed by criminal politicians and corrupt bureaucrats) and good business (not profit motivated unethical business) which really cares the consumers and unemployed citizen.

5. Good business can't be visualized in the near future. We want good politicians and good government, which (enables to) generates wealth and guarantees equitable distribution. Politics have to learn the truth from the facts and the reality. The parties in power have to work round the clock as they work during election period. Their leaders, cadre irrespective of the position and ideology have to be with the people by uniting them. Parties have to create social and economic leaders not pyravikars and contractors. People interest, public opinion must prevail.

Conclusions

Democracy in a country like India cannot successful without peoples empowerment and state intervention. Greater responsibility must be entrusted to Local Governments and the political parties must take responsibility of social mobilization. The state must provide greater human security, help the poor to get united and avoid caste, and communal disharmony. In the absence of an organized Civil Society, mobilizing economic resources and social forces must be the ultimate responsibility of the state and politics in India. Let the people feel free to live in much peace if not prosperity and the development takes place of their own choice.

The future is uncertain. But the need for change is certain. The goal of strengthening democracy and democratic public administration can be pursued by political mobilization. The future of India can be helped or hindered by the future politics of India. While the LPG politics are dominating the present scene, it should be possible for piecemeal reforms and see the 'democracy on the march' and the 'common good' is protected. Ensuring the quality of democracy and governance would be the major task of India in the coming years.

References

1. For details, Malay Chaudhuri and Arindam Chaudhury, The Great Indian Dream; Restoring Pride to a Nation Betrayed, Macmillan India, New Delhi, 2003.

2. V. Bhaskara Rao, Colonial structure, capitalist policy, socialist slogan, and Hindu State, in Public Administration in India, Ajanta Publications, New Delhi, 1989.
3. Moin Sakir, State and Politics in Contemporary India, Ajanta Publications, New Delhi, 1986.
4. For details, Mark Tully and Gillian Wright, India in Slow Motion, Penguin Books, New Delhi, 2003, pp. XIII - XVI, and 144-153.
5. Farid Zakaria, the Future of Freedom: It Liberal Democracy at Home and Abroad, Viking, New Delhi, 2003, pp. 109-11.
6. G. Haragopal, Public Administration in India: Does it have a future, in Bhaskara Rao V and A.K. Sharma (Eds), Public Administration Quest for Identity, Vikas Publishing House, New Delhi, 1966 and Governance Through Participative Development, in Sahni Pardeep and Uma Madury (eds), Governance for Development, Prentice Hall of India, New Delhi, 2003.
7. Iam Thynne, the State and Governance: Issues and Challenges in Perspective, International Review of Administrative Sciences, Vol. 66, 2000.
8. Richard. C. Box et al, New Public Management and Substantive Democracy, Public Administration Review, Vol. 61, No.5, September/October 2001.
9. *Ibid.*
10. *Ibid.*
11. Larry D. Terry, Administrative Leadership, Neo - Managerialism and the Public Management Movement, Public Administration Review, Vol. 58, No. 3, 1998.
12. Kirlin J. John, the Big Questions of Public Administration in a Democracy, Public Administration Review, Vol. 56, No.5, September/October, 1996.
13. Robert C. Box, *et al, op. cit.*
14. Kirlin J. John, *op. cit.*

15

Re-engineering for Good Governance

Introduction

The first reference about the concept of good governance was made in 1989, in a World Bank report on Sub-Saharan Africa. It defined good governance as a 'public service that is efficient, a judicial system that is reliable and an administration that is accountable to the public'. Falling short of goodness in governance is a very common experience in all nations. Kenneth Stowe, 1992, an experienced British administrator, has set out six characteristics for a better clarification of the meaning of good governance. He has defined the concept as:

1. political freedom, including free speech and a freely elected parliament, assembly or legislature;
2. constitutional and judicial protection for rights of the individual;
3. the maintenance of the rule of law by an independent judiciary;
4. the maintenance of a stable currency, the essential underpinning of economic and social development;
5. development of society as a whole by education and health care; and finally
6. executive accountability to a freely elected legislature.

The World Bank has identified a number of aspects of good governance. One of them is a sound administrative system leading to efficiency and effectiveness in a democratic framework. The emphasis on these in public service is, reorienting public administration towards management philosophy. However, an efficient public service cannot by itself, secure good governance, as also a good government. There cannot be a good governance without a good government and good government is not possible without better civil service.

The focus of "governance" is basically on the process by which authority is exercised in the management of a country's economic and social resources and the capacity of government to design, formulate and implement policies and discharge government functions (Mohit Bhattacharya, 1998). Its concern is for the sound development management and improved performance of public agencies/sector.

For the improvement of public sector performance, public sector engineering is applied through scientific principles so as to benefit the society through public infrastructure and technology provided by government. Public sector engineering, as a phenomenon, has generally been involved in the provision of public goods and utilities like transport, water supply, sewerage, energy, construction of buildings and provision of infrastructural facilities for public services.

The role of public sector engineering has also been significant in the development of public sector management systems. Recently, performance measurement concepts have risen to become a priority. These performance measurement methods are based on Taylor's ideas of scientific management. In improving and measuring performance, the systems engineering framework made a significant contribution for understanding and articulating the analysis of public sector issues.

Public sector engineering has profoundly changed the condition of life of the people. Public sector engineering enables to assess the costs and benefits, and commercial, technical feasibility of activities, along with their social and ecological desirability.

Re-Engineering

Re-engineering is one of the approaches of the administrative reform in Public Administration, besides citizen charters, reinventing government, new public management, decentralization and so forth.

The term 're-engineering' was coined first by Michael Hammer (Hammer, 1990). 'Re-engineering' called upon the managers in the Business Sector to challenge centuries-old notions about work by realising the real power of computers. Hammer observed that many of our job designs, work flows, control mechanisms and organizational structures came of age in a different competitive environment and before the advent of the computer. To meet the challenges of the new decade, i.e., "innovation and speed, service and quality," he suggested that we should "re-engineer" our business: use the power of modern information technology and radically design business processes in order to achieve dramatic improvement in their performance. Re-engineering calls for breaking away from the antiquated processes and advocates evolving imaginative new ways to accomplish work.

Essence of Re-engineering

The essence of re-engineering, according to Hammer, is the notion of discontinuous thinking—of recognising and breaking away from the outdated rules and fundamental assumptions that underlie operations. The rules must he changed not re-arranging them. These old rules and assumptions made the business underperform. Therefore, they must be shed. These rules and assumptions are about technology, people and organizational goals that no longer hold. Quality, innovation and service are more important than cost, growth and control.

One pertinent observation he made was that in present times, a large segment of the population is educated and capable of assuming responsibility, and workers cherish their autonomy and expect to have a say in how the business is run.

Hammer points out that our business processes and structures are outmoded and obsolete; they have not kept pace with the changes in technology, demographics and business objectives. Conventional process structures are fragmented as piecemeal and lacked the integration necessary to maintain quality and service.

Thus, re-engineering looks at the fundamental processes of the business from a "cross-functional" perspective, by assembling a team that represents the functional units involved in the process being re-engineered and all the units that depend on it. Re-engineering should use information technology, not to automate an existing process, but to enable a new process, and yield effective and efficient results.

Principles of Re-engineering

Michael Hammer stated the following as the principles of re-engineering:

1. "Organize around outcomes, not tasks"—This principle makes one person perform all the steps in a process. It is designing a persons' job around an objective or outcome, instead of a single task. It eliminates the assembly-line approach. It compresses responsibility for various steps and assigns it to one person, who oversees the whole process.

2. "Have those who use the output of the process perform the process"—As the computer based data and expertise are more readily available, the individuals who need the results of a process can do it themselves, by the use of computers.

3. "Subsume information-processing work into the real work that produces the information"—While the previous two principles comprise of linear processes, this principle suggests moving work from one person or department to another organization that produces information and also processes it.

4. "Treat geographically dispersed resources as though they were centralized"—By using databases, telecommunication net-works and standardized processed systems to get the benefits of scale and coordination.

5. "Link parallel activities instead of integrating their results"—Communication networks, shared databases, and teleconferencing bring the independent groups together for on going co-ordination.

6. "Put the decision point where the work is performed, and build control into the process"—This compresses the

pyramidal management layers and flattens the organizations. Doers become self-managing and self-controlling; hierarchy and the slowness and bureaucracy associated with it, disappears. This changes the managerial role from being a controller and supervisor to one of supporter and facilitator.

7. "Capture information once and at the source"—Collected information are stored in an online database for all who need it. Bar coding, relational databases, and electronic data interchanging make it easy to collect, store and transmit information.

Hammer pointed out that re-engineering triggers changes of many kinds: job designs, organizational structures, management systems. Everything associated with the process must be refashioned in an integrated way. Re-engineering is a tremendous effort that mandates change in many areas of the organization: career paths, recruitment, training programmes, promotion policies, which have to be revised to support the new process design. Further, for the success of re-engineering, executive leadership with a real vision, is required. Top level managers can only make it possible to get the support of others. If managers have the vision, re-engineering will provide a way.

Reinventing Government and Re-engineering Corporation

The concept of re-engineering the institutional structure emerged out of fascination with new management philosophies (Aun Marie Bissessar, 1998). Re-engineering acquired increased significance in recent years with the publication of works of Osborne and Gaebler and Hammer and Champy in 1992 and 1993 respectively.

Both the works generated a set of propositions for dealing with reforms in the public and private sectors. The idea of re-engineering in the case of private sector is distinguished from the concept of reinventing government by an emphasis on information technology, client, results, and redefinition of the organization's mission. Reinventing government attempts to transfer a part of reformist agenda of the Private Sector to the Public Sector. Thus, issues like competition and the empowerment of citizens by means of customer-oriented approach have become the criteria by which 'good governance' is measured. According to the National Performance Review Team of U.S.A. re-engineering in the Public Sector calls for reforms to forget how agencies were organized, decide what they have to do, design the best structure to do so (Arie Halachmi, 1995). More specifically, the Review Team recommended the adoption of advanced technologies.

Re-engineering, having its origins in U.S. big business, is considered equally applicable to public sector. "Re-engineering is the fundamental rethinking and radical design of business processes to achieve dramatic improvements in critical contemporary measures of performance, such as cost, quality, service and speed". Re-engineering is considered a comprehensive and effective way (or organizations to reduce cycle times, surpass customer expectations, enhance productivity, increase sales and reap higher profits.

However, the concept of re-engineering is yet to be defined precisely. It is felt more worthwhile to analyze the major attributes of the concept rather than define it in precise. The salient attributes of re-engineering are:

1. Developing processes and outcomes. Preference is given to individual performance.
2. Focus on the customer or client with a result-oriented and team-based approach. This requires rigorous measurement of performance and close analysis of change and the rate of change for assessing performance. It is only possible with the total commitment of all the employees and a substantive involvement of top management at all levels.
3. Undertaking systematic searches to bring radical changes for improvements and breakthroughs whenever an incremental approach fails.

However, it has been proved beyond doubt that re-engineering has been more successful in the Private Sector than in the Public Sector. Therefore, reformers are more cautious in their recommendations for re-engineering the Public Sector, confining themselves largely to the reform of selected processes, the introduction of cost-benefit analysis and performance measurement. It is also now being recognized that the two critical obstacles to the re-engineering efforts in public service organizations are structure and culture. Thus, re-engineering of human resource systems in public organization is the most crucial factor. Along with the reorganization of the structure, reorientation of public services and political system are very essential.

Factors of Success and Failure of Re-engineering

Michael Hammer has identified some factors of success in re-engineering, such as the following:

- Combining several jobs into one
- Decision making by workers
- Shifting focus of performance measures from activity to results
- Changing values from protective to productive

Factors which lead to failure in re-engineering according to J.H. Boer (1995) are as follows:

- Trying to fix process instead of changing it
- Not focusing on the business processes
- Ignoring everything except process redesign
- Neglecting people's values and beliefs
- Assigning someone who does not understand the subject to lead it
- Skimping on the resources devoted to re-engineering
- Dragging the project out
- Trying to keep everyone involved happy (Boer, 1995).

Re-engineering requires a change in attitude among all the individuals concerned, such as, trade unionists, employers, paid officials and civil servants. Decision making must be based on participative, democratic and consultative approach, wherein all the stakeholders contribute to the final policies.

Some Implications of Re-engineering

Tony Bovaird and Robert Hughes (1995) list out some of the implications of re-engineering in the following manner:

1. People's role change from controlled to empowered (in work).
2. Workers make decisions (in business processes).
3. Executives change—from scorekeepers to leaders.
4. Advancement criteria change from performance to ability.
5. Focus of performance measures and compensation shifts—from activity to results.
6. Work units change—from functional department to processing teams (often 'case teams') in which several jobs are combined into one.
7. Values change—from protective to productive (employees must deeply believe that they work for their customers, not their bosses).
8. A case manager provides a single point of contact.
9. Organizational structures change—from hierarchical to flat.
10. Hybrid centralized/decentralized operations are prevalent.
11. Steps in process performed in natural order, and work performed where it makes most sense.
12. Checks and controls are reduced and reconciliations are kept to a minimum.
13. From simple tasks to multi-dimensional work.
14. From training to job education (in job preparation) and from performance to ability (in advancement criteria).

Re-engineering in Public Sector

Public Sector engineering is known for its continuous contribution. However, re-engineering, while it is debated and experimented with certain successes and failures in the Private Sector, is not common in the Public Sector. In some small states or local authorities or in some departments, some sort of re-engineering approach had been adopted with little success. But it is evident that debates are being conducted in the form of administrative reform and restructuring. However, the concept of re-engineering, despite its ideal objectives, cannot be totally/fully implemented in Public Sector. For, re-engineering is 'fundamental, radical and dramatic, on all-or-nothing proposition that cannot be carried out in small steps' and re-engineering should be quickly implemented and not be dragged out. Re-engineering seeks breakthroughs, not steady incremental development.

However, the nature of public administration is almost opposite to the concept of re-engineering. The existing culture of public services is characterized by:

1. Culture of 'self-serving individualism', particularly at the top level.
2. Serious dysfunctional processes.
3. Cumbersome centralized system of control and ineffective implementation of agreed policies.
4. Little or no corporate working in the authority and high level of departmentalism.
5. No single strategic thinking on change and community needs.
6. High degree of mutual suspicion and hostility.
7. History of political 'scandals' and 'affairs' which damaged the authority's public image.

Obstacles and Challenges of Re-engineering in the Public Sector

Re-engineering can be successful in the public sector. However, it has more obstacles and risks than the favours it can offer:

1. Re-engineering creates entirely new processes that are facilitated by information technology (IT). As a result, the roles and functions of employees may change, and there may be reduction in pay rolls, downsizing of employees, initiation of cross-functional training, opposition from the union and so forth.

2. Forging consensus among multiple stakeholders of different public organizations for radical changes in the delivery of services and products may be beyond the capacity of many public administrators.

3. Politics may prevail over strict considerations of economy and effectiveness.

4. Politicians may hesitate to approve re-engineering as it displaces too many employees, and causes uproar in the society and resistance from labour, which ultimately leads to withdrawal of political support.

5. Re-engineering requires a substantial investment in training and updating, Information Technology. The costs of re-engineering cannot be borne by the poor governmental agencies.

6. Re-engineering calls for a total breaking away from the past—but government's policy making is incremental and works tor gradual change.

7. Legal constraints and procedural rules and regulations set by Central Staff Agencies, Treasury, Comptroller and Auditor General, Public-Service Commissions, Parliament and Courts. Before any change takes place in governmental structures and processes, government needs to negotiate and consult different agencies. Government is built on the theory of checks and balances, in fact, more checks than balances.

8. Re-engineering demands radical shift towards the decentralization and vesting of more administrative powers in the hands of managers.

9. The culture in the Public Sector is an obstacle and a challenge. Re-engineering upsets the status-quo, the security and demands to accept the new responsibilities. Public managers may not be ready to accept the risks associated with re-engineering.

What To Do

Re-engineering is realistic and even a preferred method of change. Therefore Public Sector may initiate re-engineering in small measures in one division or in one programme.

People in responsible positions who desire re-engineering must initiate and realize the following:

1. Educating the top decision-makers about re-engineering; without their commitment it is not possible.
2. Identifying and assessing the processes that require re-engineering and educating the staff of the organization.
3. Using robust benefit-cost analysis to find out the tangible gains on the investment.
4. Redefining a mission statement based on actual survey of internal and external customers.
5. Finding creative sources of funding and developing human resources base (IT).
6. Benchmarking performance against best in class.
7. Ensuring involvement of all inside and outside the organization about the new work process and providing training for better understanding.
8. Setting clear timetable with measurable milestones to assess progress.
9. Public Sector cannot re-engineer a given process through trial and error (Bovaird and Hughes).

Summing up

In the final analysis of the existing situation of the Public Services, we can assert that re-engineering is possible in the public organizations to a certain extent if the following are provided (Bovaird, 1995). However, to expect such things to get materialized in public administration is very much doubtful, particularly in developing countries.

1. A new and highly respected political leader in the authority with a strong group of political supporters.
2. Chief executives must be vested with the real authority.
3. The political leader and the chief executive must be able to select their team of executive officers and staff.
4. Cultural values of openness, honesty, trust and integrity must be adopted.
5. Positive interactions between politicians, managers and professionals.

References

Arora, Dolly, "Governance As Agenda: The Discursive Shift," *The Indian Journal of Public Administration,* XLIV(3), 385-397, 1998.

Bhattacharya, Mohit, "Conceptualising Good Governance," *The Indian Journal of Public Administration,* XLIV(3), 289-296, 1998.

Bissessar, Aun Marie, "Re-engineering the Public Services of the Commonwealth Caribbean," *International Review of Administrative Sciences,* Vol. 64, 305-326, 1998.

Boer, J.H., "Re-engineering the consultative process between industry, labour and government trade authorities in South Africa," *International Review of Administrative Sciences,* Vol. 61, 344, 1995.

Bovaird, Tony and Robert Hughes, "Re-engineering Public Sector Organizations: A Case Study of radical change in British Local Authority," *International Review of Administrative Sciences,* Vol. 61, 355-372, 1995.

Halachmi, Arie, "Re-engineering and Public Management: Some Issues and Considerations," *International Review of Administrative Sciences,* 62(3), 329-41, 1995.

Hammer, Michael, "Re-engineering Work: Don't Automate, Obliterate," *Harvard Business Review,* 68(4), 104-112, 1990.

Hammer, Michael and James Champy, *Re-engineering The Corporation: A Manifesto for Business Revolution,* Harper Collins, New York, 1993.

Hodge, Graeme A., "Public Sector Engineering," *The International Encyclopedia of Public Policy and Administration,* 1862-63.

Osborne, David and Ted Gaebler, *Reinventing Government: How the Entrepreneurial Spirit is Transforming the Public Sector,* Addison-Wesley, 1992.

Stowe, Kenneth, "Good Piano Won't Play Bad Music: Administrative Reform and Good Governance," *Public Administration,* 70(1), 25-34, 1992.

16

The Second Strike by Central Government Employees : Some Demands*

Strikes and demonstrations have become the order of the day. Perhaps, at no other time the Central and State Governments were more plagued and perturbed by strikes and their consequences in the various stages of social and economic development than the present times have witnessed. Neither is the problem so simple as it appears to be. The conflicting and clashing forces are dynamic in content and elusive in certain other respects. The freedom of choice among the available alternatives is indeed restricted. it is equally difficult to anticipate or locate the equilibrium point. When the divergent social forces are at work, the decision making process inherent in the situation is further circumscribed by concepts or doctrines, which have gained certain social values and approbation, such as, soverignty of the State, the Welfare State, rights of the government employees, rights of the citizens, administrative responsibility and service to public.

The scope of the paper is confined to a brief description of the attempts made by the Government of India from time to time to mitigate the hardship faced by its employees, the situation that led to the second strike by Central Government employees and an examination of some of the issues involved.

The first[1] and second strikes were not the outcome of a sudden and uncalculated outburst of protests or demonstrations on the part

* Co-authored with Prof. P.A. James.

of the employees. Both the strikes had long and continuous history. The main reasons for the strikes appear to be certain undecided issues continuing to remain unsettled. This is not to say that the Government on its part was a silent spectator to the growing unrest that was brewing among the different sections of the dissatisfied employees. The Government has appointed a number of commissions to investigate and report on the unsettled issues with a view to solve the problems facing the Government and the employees.

But the irony of the situation is that for one reason or the other there is so much of vacillation in accepting or rejecting the recommendations of any particular commission that due to efflux of time, the benefits that are likely to accrue to the employees as a result of recommendations have in substance been substantially modified. Further, the fluctuating prices and the economic factors[2] largely beyond human manipulation and control have further complicated the already distressing situation. Before we proceed to discuss the second strike, the steps taken by the Government to meet situation right from 1946 are states below :

A Central Pay Commission was appointed by Government of India in 1946 under the Chairmanship of the Honourable Sir Srinivasa Varadachariar.[3] The Government accepted the Varadachariar Commission's recommendations in May, 1947.[4] At that stage, the Government announced its decision that Dearness Allowance (hereafter known as D.A.) to the full extent recommended by the First Pay Commission was out of question as that could lead to deficit in Government budget and intensify inflationary pressures. However, Government ordered *ad hoc* payments of Rs. 10 and later a further increase of Rs. 250. The Final result was that recommendations of the First Pay Commission in regard to D.A. were not given effect to.[5]

As an interim measure a D.A. Committee was appointed by the Government of India under Chairmanship of Sri N.V. Gadgil in the year 1952. As recommended by the Committee with effect from April 1, 1953, 50 per cent of the D.A. payable to employees whose pay did not exceed Rs. 750 was treated as pay for purpose of retirement benefits and for certain other allowances.

To avert a threatened strike by the employees, the Second Pay Commission was appointed[6] by the Government of India in the year 1957 under the Chairmanship of Justice B. Jagannadhadas. The recommendations of the Commission were accepted and implemented by the Government.[7] The employees were dissatisfied with the recommendations[8] because they thought they were less liberal than those of the First Pay Commission.[9] The Government granted increase in D.A. of Rs. 5 and Rs. 10 per month for employees drawing a pay of less than Rs. 300. But the employees continued their demand for review and arbitration. Due to Chinese aggression, the demand was not pursued. The employees revived their demand for arbitration in June, 1963. The Government sanctioned *ad hoc* additional payment of D.A. with effect from July 1, 1963. Further revision of D.A. was effected from February 1, 1964. But certain associations of Government employees, represented about the inadequacy of increase in D.A. which prompted the Government to appoint[10] Mr. S.K. Das as a One Man Independent Body to enquire into the question of D.A. in August, 1964.

The employees did not agree to the rates of D.A. granted by the Government from 1-3-1965 to 1-12-1965 and they wanted the matter be settled by arbitration. It was at this stage the Government of India appointed[11] the Dearness Allowance Commission under the Chairmanship of Shri Gajendragadkar in July, 1966.

Immediately after the first general strike the Central Government found it very necessary to establish a joint negotiating machinery on the same pattern as Whitely Councils in Great Britain. The Joint Consultative Machinery was introduced in October, 1966 and was accepted by the Organisations of the Central Government employees.

The underlying object of the scheme was to promote harmonious relations and to secure the "Greatest measure of cooperation between Government in its capacity as employer and the general body of its employees in matters of common concern". Clause 16 of the scheme provided for compulsory arbitration in matters of (*a*) Pay and Allowances; (*b*) Weekly hours of work; and (*c*) Leave of a class or group of employees.

It is alleged that the avowed promotion of harmonious relations and attempts to secure the greatest measure of cooperation were not realised in practice as the Official side is said to have stated that issues of need based minimum wage and merger of Dearness Allowance into pay, were non-arbitrable.[12] The Government's contention in this regard was, it was reported, that the issues raised were not confined to a particular class or grade of employees as to merit compulsory arbitration.

The Second Strike

It may not be surprising that in spite of the efforts made by the Government there was large scale disappointment among the employees. The disappointment is partly due to the perfunctory manner in which the Government dealt with the situation, and partly due to the large number of employees who are the recipients. The perfunctory approach will be evident from the following. First, during the First Pay Commission stage the Government appears to have evaded the question by explaining away, mentioning the probable deficit in Government budget and the inflationary pressures.

(That it was not a correct answer is evident from the fact that even now there is inflation). Secondly, the Government restored, to *ad hoc* solution for long term problems which could be solved only by planned long term measures. Thirdly, merger of D.A. with basic pay though it may confer retirement and other benefits is not likely to provide immediate relief as would be otherwise available by an increase in the basic pay. Fourthly, although Joint Consultative Machinery has been introduced with a view to finally resolve the deadlock through arbitration, should consultations fail, the whole process has in effect been nullified and the object of the scheme defeated by bringing into the force subtle and hair splitting distinctions. Fifthly, the terms of reference of the Commissions appointed at a later date like the Das Body and the D.A. Commission which were asked to examine the adequacy or otherwise of the compensation in relation to D.A. were restrictive in scope. Only the D.A. Commission has been asked to lay down the principles that should be followed in future. But for this exception, the measures taken by the Government appear to be short term palliatives than long term cures.

The main demands made out by the employees which formed the basic for the second strike were :

(*i*) Merger of Dearness allowance with the basic pay;

(*ii*) Need Based Minimum Wage;

(*iii*) Full Neutralisation of rise in prices; and

(*iv*) Withdrawal of Government's proposal to retire employees at 50 years of age, who are ineffective or whose integrity is in doubt.

The Central Government employees were of the opinion that these issues on which the two parties to the dispute have been at variance and could not be settled by negotiations, be referred to an Arbitration Board as contemplated and provided in the Scheme of the Joint Consultative Machinery. The Government did not accept the demand for the payment of need based minimum wage, saying that it would be considered by the National Commission on Labour, a high powered body set up by the Government of India on December 24, 1966 under the Chairmanship of Shri P.B. Gajendragadkar. The report of the Commission is expected to be submitted by the end of March, 1969.

The Government was also not prepared to commit itself for full neutralisation and payment of the allowance could not be referred to arbitration. While it is difficult to state as to what prompted the Government to take such a stand, it may not be too much to assume that the financial considerations and the attendant burden there of must have compelled them to do so.

Talks between the Union Home Minister and Central Government Employees' leaders failed by September 12, 1968. At this meeting the leaders of employees Organisations offered to wait till the Report of the National Commission on Labour, provided the Government was willing to treat the recommendations of National Commission on Labour as an award. The suggestion was turned down.

Under these circumstances the organisations of Central Government Employees resolved to organise a token strike for one day on 19-9-1968 as a protest against the attitude of the Government.

Since it is not possible to examine in this paper all the demands made out by the employees, the analysis that follows is confined, to two important (in our view) issues, namely (1) Dearness Allowance and (2) Need based minimum wage, which require careful consideration, and merit appropriate action on the part of the Government.

Dearness Allowance

Two views were expressed regarding the question of the payment of the D.A. to the employees. One view is that D.A. should protect the real wages or salaries paid to the employees on this basis, no category of the employees, however, high paid should be excluded from the purview of D.A.[13] The other view is that the essential object in payment of D.A. is to mitigate the hardship of the employees in the lower pay ranges.

The First Pay Commission brought out two important principles governing payment of D.A. *viz.* (*a*) the adjustments to be made in the pay must be automatic and (*b*) a fluctuation of twenty points in cost of living index calling for a revision.

The Second Pay Commission's recommendations are mixed in character. They were progressive in so far as the Commission recommended a revision of D.A. for a fluctuation of a ten points over a period of twelve months, and constitution of Whittley type of Machinery for negotiation and settlement of disputes. But its other recommendation, *viz.* that revision need not be automatic is considered to be a very retrograde step. It is undoubtedly negative in character and perhaps the root cause for all misunderstanding and suspicion entertained by the employees. The arguments advanced by the Second Pay Commission against an automatic revision were :

(*i*) Long term character of Government employment;

(*ii*) The undesirable practice of the remuneration of the Government servants changing frequently;

(*iii*) That employees must be willing to take consequence of small or short term rise in prices as a counterpart of the security of their emoluments, which are not changed to their disadvantage; and (*iv*) That price trends for a shorter period may not provide a reliable basis for adjustment.

But many associations of the employees have criticised the D.A. formula of Second Pay Commission as unrealistic in theory and unfair in practice. Their contention was that[14]

(*i*) The time factor was long that it prevented a correct reflection of the price movement from month to month;

(*ii*) The number factor of ten points was so large that the employees lost much of the compensation; and

(*iii*) The commulative effect of the two factors was so restrictive that the employees had to suffer a heavy denunciation in their real income.

The Das Body was of the view that the D.A. formula did not ensure just compensation due to employees and they were deprived of the benefit over a long period of time and pointed out the need for revising the formula. It suggested that hardship could be avoided in one of the following three ways, by reducing.

(*i*) The time factor to six months, while retaining ten points;

(*ii*) The number of points to five, while retaining the time factors of twelve months; or

(*iii*) Both the factors—time to six months and points to five (2).

Further, the Das Body suggested that some modification of the formula would be necessary so long as prices do not stabilise and a *via-media* has to be found with flexibility which would admit of special treatment in an abnormal situation.

The Gajendragadkar Commission recommended that compensation to the employees for the future rise in prices should be given in the form of additional D.A., as no alternative form of assistance was considered feasible and practicable. The Commission fielt that it was unfair to leave the question of revision of D.A. to the discretion of the Government and wanted the revision to be automatic on proof of the fact that a twelve months average of ten points has been registered.[15] The Commission fixed the danger mark at two hundred and forty five points and before that point is reached they wanted the Government to take positive action in controlling the prices. Irrespective of price stability they desired a general revision of pay structure of employees at the end of two years.[16]

An important aspect regarding the revision of the D.A. is whether the revision should be automatic or not. Though this may appear as a simple proposition, the crux of the problem lies here in the sense, that failure to effect automatic revision and at proper time has led to widespread dissatisfaction and frustration in the employees inducing in them, a strike mood. Automatic revision has the following advantages.

(*i*) The formula in vogue will be made effective;

(*ii*) The employees can get immediate relief;

(*iii*) The erosion in the real wages of employees can be protected to some extent; and

(*iv*) Strikes can be avoided.

As suggested by the Das Body there is need to modify the D.A. formula. The ends of justice would be met by reducing the points to five and keeping the period as twelve months. But this may not be practicable and it is not recommended in view of excessive burden it may entail the Government. Therefore, at this stage it would be appropriate to think in terms of alternative solutions than merely trying to extend the D.A. formula which does not provide much elbow room for needed adjustments.

Need Based Minimum Wage

The Living Wage concept was recommended by the First Pay Commission. The Commission emphasised on two important aspects of the issue. First, that Government which proposed minimum wage legislation to private industry must be ready to give the benefit of the principle to its own employees.[17] Secondly, as a corrollory of the social policy, the lowest rate of remuneration ought not to be less than the living wage.[18]

The concept of need based minimum wage for the worker was evolved at the 15th Indian Labour Conference which met in July,

1957. The conference, Tripartite in character, was represented by the Central Government, the State Governments and the employers and employees.

It was unanimously accepted that minimum wage was "need based" and should ensure the minimum human needs of the Industrial worker. The following norms[19] were accepted as a guide for all wage fixing authorities, including minimum wage committees, wage boards, adjudicators, etc., in calculating the need based minimum wage:

(*i*) "The standard of working class family should be taken to consist of 3 consumption units for one earner, the earnings of women, children and adolescents should be disregarded;

(*ii*) Minimum food requirements should be calculated on the basis of a net intake of 2700 calories as recommended by Dr. Akroyd, for an average Indian adult of moderate activity;

(*iii*) Clothing requirements should be estimated at a per capita consumption of 18 yards per annum which would give for the average of worker's family of four, a total of 72 yards;

(*iv*) In respect of housing the norm should be the minimum rent charged by Government in any area for houses provided under Subsidised Industrial Housing Scheme for the Low-Income Groups; and

(*v*) Fuel, lighting and other 'miscellaneous' items of expenditure should constitute 20% of the total minimum wage."

Since the Government of India was represented at the Tripartite Indian Labour Conference, many were under the false impression that recommendations of the Conference would also be applicable, in identical matters, to Government employees. To a clarification sought by the Second Pay Commission on this issue, the Government replied categorically that "Government have at no time committed themselves to take executive action to enforce the recommendation."[20]

The Second Pay Commission examined the problem in a wider context of the social, economic and financial problems facing the country. The Commission was of the view that it should be the Government's endeavour, atleast to maintain the real value of wages and salaries of the lowest grades of their employees, but it is pertinent to note that they did not support the view that such a thing should be done irrespective of the situation in which the prices rise or of the broader national requirements.

Depending upon the context in and the background against which it is viewed, need based minimum wage has been visualised and understood differently. First, from the point of the view of the employees, it is nothing but a minimum, based on needs. Secondly, the commissions concerned with this question, being fully aware of the financial implications, desired that the government should move in the direction of giving effect to the principle of minimum wage. Thirdly, as far as the Prime Minister is concerned, she stated[22], that however laudable and desirable may be the principle it would be premature to implement it at this stage.

Under the existing economic conditions, the need based minimum wage is not immediately within the reach of even the lowest paid employees as indicated by the following Table.[23]

Minimum Need Based Wages As per Dietary Norms Recommended by the National Nutrition Advisory Committee (East India)

Item	*oz.*	*Grams*	*Price per kg.*	*Cost per unit*
1. Cereals	17.50	496	0.90	0.4464
2. Pulses	3.00	85	1.25	0.1062
3. Sugar & Gur	1.75	49	1.40	0.0686
4. Milk & Milk products	3.00	85	1.25	0.1062
5. Fish, Meat and Eggs.	2.00	57	4.00	0.2280
6. Oil and Gee	1.00	28	5.00	0.1400
7. Vegetables	9.00	225	1.00	0.2550
Total for one unit				1.3504
for one day :				× 90
For three units for 30 days :				121.53
Expenditure on clothing :				12.00
House rent :				12.50
Miscellaneous at 20 per cent :				36.50
				182.53

The calculation reveal that there is an unbridgable gap[24], between the minimum wage aspired at and the actual wages paid to the employees. So long as this gap continues to exist, it would appear the employees would continue to press for their demands.

The desirability of paying the need based minimum wage is never disputed as a basic requirement of sound personnel administration.[25] However, under the existing social order the following comments may be in order :

(*a*) It is difficult to fix and pay need based minimum wage to employees in all sectors throughout the country. Insistence on payment of minimum wage in other sectors leads to legal complications and proprietary relations;

(*b*) Fixation of need based minimum wage requires periodic revision and re-examination of certain factors which in turn leads to complications. If by any chance need based minimum wage standard is reached with reference to a particular level, there is no hope that the demands will cease at that level; and

(*c*) It is necessary to recall at this stage, that the question of reaching the need based minimum wage is inextricably linked up with industrial development and all-round economic growth and not merely registering infinitesimal increases in agricultural production.

From the above it is clear, that it is somewhat difficult to harmonise the different approaches to the need based minimum wage that present wide gaps, both in social and economic content. This partly explains the difficulty in arriving at an agreeable solution. Under the existing circumstances it would be a Herculian task for the Government to convince the suffering and agitated employees about the practical and difficult to meet economic propositions involved in reaching a need based minimum wage level, specially when they are obsessed with what they term their "minimum demands". It would appear that the probability of avoiding future strikes depends on a workable compromise that can be struck between two extreme views held by the contending parties, the minimum demands from the point of view of employees and social justice and economic betterment of all sections of the people, the view held by the Government.

In the ultimate analysis, there appears to be no alternative except to take effective steps for the objective realisation of payment of need-based minimum wage. But since such a course may not be possible in foreseeable future, a scientific and periodical revision of the pay scales, protecting the erosion would seem to be a practicable solution.

Conclusion

The D.A. Commission fixed the danger mark at two hundred and forty five points. Before the mark is reached, two possible alternatives may be tried. First, there should be rationalisation of the pay scales by a thorough revision as already indicated. Secondly, revision should not only reduce the number of any ranges but there should be an attempt to raise the basic pay of each pay range. In fixing a higher basic pay than the existing for any particular range, the following considerations may be kept in view :

(*a*) The Concept of Welfare State;

(*b*) The desirability of paying need based minimum wage;

(*c*) The rise of prices implicit in a developing economy;

(*d*) The proposal to do away with the Dearness Allowance as a measure of introducing rationalisation in pay structure.

Viewed from another context, the social unrest (Strikes in Government and Private Sector) may be ascribed to the lack of social amenities and want of minimum civic comforts. One way to meet the requirement is to strengthen the provision and administration of social services at three levels of Government *viz*, Central, State and Local.

The Central and State Governments instead of paying D.A. which in the past was also indirectly responsible for the rise of prices may subvent the money for subsidised social amenities which may include supply of food grains, provision of medical aid, educational facilities for the children of employees and housing accommodation at cheap rent etc. The Second Pay Commission opined that such a thing was tried and proved a failure.[26] We disagree with the opinion and hold the failure could be attributed to the limited scale on which it was tried, the inadequate publicity it was given and the unfavourable conditions under which it was implemented. (It may be re-called, at that time the prices of the consumer articles did not soar so high and the employees were not pinched so badly). The Second Pay Commission raised another objection againist the introduction of such a scheme, namely that the Government would be charged with the criticism of favourably treating its own employees. As a Welfare State programme, if, an integrated social service scheme is to be drawn the criticism benefits of the scheme can also be extended to the public in general.

If the various causes leading to the troubled situation are analysed, one would not fail to identify that behind all these lies the basic economic problem of stabilisation of prices, whether it be a question of revision of D.A. need-based minimum wage or full neutralisation. The irony of the situation simply is this. The commissions and Committees that have gone into this question have safely assumed in working out a formula that prices will stabilise at certain point, but unfortunately it did not happen.

Economists believe that certain factors like monetary policy pursued and economy of the country as such have very much to do with price stabilisation. But these two factors are so elusive, it is not always possible to control or guide the economic activity into set and desired patterns. Further, there appears to be no reasonable hope of any stabilisation in the foreseeabe future. For, in an agricultural economy, characteristic of an under-developed country like India, there would be inflationary pressures due to rise in prices resulting also from increase in wages and payment of additional D.A.

Unless price stabilisation can be achieved over a reasonable period of time it looks as though there is no workable solution to this vexed question of enhanced D.A. and payment of Need Based Minimum Wage. It appears as though the imminent threat of strike still continues and the Government will have to face it in future unless there is a marked improvement in over-all production.

References

1. The first General Strike by Central Government employees took place in July, 1960.
2. Some have emphasised the commitments under what is often called as Defence Plus Development on a plane which necessarily involves a very large measure of deficit financing: others have emphasised the slow rate of growth in the matter of agricultural output, coupled with the rapid rate at which population increase in our country; still others have emphasised the factors arising out of defective distribution including hoarding at all stages from production to consumption and deliberate withholding of supplies to the market for the purpose of profiteering by wholesale and retail traders and host of middleman in between. Some have emphasised the disparity between 'in put' and 'output', the magnitude of the investment in its relation to the resulting production of goods. Some again have cemphasised the monetary policy of Government including credit facilities which have enabled producers and traders to hold back agricultural produce from the market, the part played by "unaccounted for money" in that respect, and rising taxation etc. Some have commented on agricultural prices which they say are not "producer-oriented". Report of the One-Man Independent Body to inquire into the question of Dearness Allowance payable to Central Government employees, Ministry of Finance, Government of India, New Delhi, 1965, p. 14, (Hereafter called as the Das Body).
3. Also known of First Pay Commission.
4. Commission of Enquiry on Emoluments and Conditions of Serivce of Central Government employees, Ministry of Finance, Government of India, New Delhi, 1959, p. 89 (Hereafter referred to as the Second Pay Commission).
5. Report of the D.A. Commission on the question of Grant of D.A. to Central Government Employees in future Ministry of Finance, New Delhi, 1967, p. 10 (Hereafter referred to as the D.A. Commission).
6. The purpose of appointment was to :
   "(*i*) Examine the principles which should govern the structure of emoluments and conditions of service of the Central Government Employees.
   (*ii*) Consider and recommended what changes in the structure of emoluments and condition of service of the different classes of Central Government employees are desirable and feasible.

(*iii*) Recommend in particular, the extent to which benefit to Central Government employees can be given in the shape of amenities and facilities;" Second Pay Commission *op. cit.*, p. 3.

7. D.A. Commission, *op. cit.*, p. 14.
8. Briefly stated, the recommendations were :

    (*i*) Minimum wage of Rs. 80/- per month;

    (*ii*) Merger of Dearness Allowance with basic pay;

    (*iii*) The principle of linking wages with prices;

    (*iv*) The guarantee of 50% of neutralisation; and

    (*v*) A Whitley Type Machinery representing the whole body of Central Government Employees should be set up for settlement of disputes. As a necessary complement to a Joint Machinery for negotiation, there should be provision for compulsory arbitration.

9. Das Body, *op. cit.*, p. 3.
10. The body was appointed :

    "to examine and report whether in the matter of Dearnes Allowance payable to Central Government employees compensation already sanctioned by them from time to time in the various pay ranges in adequate and to recommend what changes if any are necessary there in", *ibid.*, p. 1.

11. The object of the Commission was to :

    consider "the question of adequacy of the rates of D.A. granted as from 1st December 1965 to Central Government employees drawing below Rs. 400 per month" ...... "the examination of the principles which should govern the grant of D.A. to the employees in future" D.A. Commission, *op. cit.*, p. 1.

12. See V.B. Mahadeshwar, "Government and J.C.M.", Labour World, New Delhi—5 September, 1968, p. 13.
13. D.A. Commission, *op. cit.*, p. 16.
14. The Das Body, *op. cit.*, p. 40.
15. D.A. Commission, *op. cit.*, p. 36.
16. *Ibid.*, p. 40.
17. First Pay Commission, *op. cit.*, p. 29.
18. *Ibid.*
19. Tripartite Conclusions, 1942-962, Government of India, Ministry of Labour and Employment, New Delhi, 1962, p. 49.

20. Second Pay Commission, *op. cit.*, p. 63.
21. Second Pay Commission, *op. cit.*, p. 94.
22. Indian Express, Vijayawada, dated 18-9-1967.

    "The concept of need based minimum wage is accepted as an unexceptionable social objective. But it will not be just to consider it in isolation exclusively for the employees of the Central Government ignoring the Central Body of Industrial, Agricultural and other workers. The issue in the wider context is already before the National Commission on Labour."
23. Audit, All-India Non-gazetted Audit and Accounts Association, New Delhi-5, July-Aug. 1968, p. 29.

    Note :

    (*i*) The above calculations were submitted by All-India Trade Union Congress before the Engineering Wage Board and were calculated at price level prevailing in second half of 1964—All India Consumer Price Index at 160.

    (*ii*) At All India Consumer Price Index 200 the need based minimum wage works out to Rs. 230.
24. The present minimum wage (Pay + D.A.) of the Central Government employees is Rs. 135/- at 205 points. The minimum wage at 205 points works out to be Rs. 233 (approx). Hence the gap would be Rs. 233-135 = Rs. 98.
25. Cf. Stahl. O.G., Public Personnel Administration, Harper and Brother, New York, 1956, p. 216.
26. Second Pay Commission, *op. cit.*, p. 98.

17

Police Strikes in India

Agitations and strikes by the civil servants and industrial workers in India have been quite common. For the first time, however, policemen in almost all the States started a series of agitations and threatened direct action for redressal of their grievances during 1979. This is the result of failure of the Central and State Governments to identify and tackle the problems of the police several years after Independence. No attempt to change the police system introduced by the British to suit the colonial purposes has ever been made. The only major step that was taken by the Janata Government at the Centre has been to appoint a National Police Commission. But even if the recommendations of the Police Commission are implemented, it is doubtful that the problems of the policemen will be solved without a radical change in the entire approach to police administration.

The main responsibility of the police is to maintain law and order, and protect democracy by strict enforcement of law. In a developing country like ours, implementation of welfare and development activities and social changes cannot be possible if people lack security and have no faith in the law enforcement agencies. A demoralised or diffident police force cannot act as a change agent, or a bulwark of law and order, especially after it has become a tool in the hands of the politicians, or when it interferes and involves in politics. Likewise, when the police personnel management is not in sound health, efficiency and discipline of the force cannot be guaranteed, its superb performance in times of national calamities notwithstanding.

---

* Co-authored with T. Narasimha Rao.

To maintain an effective police force suited to the changing times changes have to be made in the methods of recruitment, facilities of training, prospects of promotion, suitable working hours and conditions, adequate pay scales and provision of amenities and welfare services, particularly at the lower levels. This paper aims at studying the causes of the problems of the police, the genuineness of their demands, and tries to explain the stand of the Central and the State Governments in this regard.

A significant feature of the police agitations has been that they have not been confined only to the level of constabulary but have also brought into their pale Assistant Sub-Inspectors and Sub-Inspectors. A large number of middle range police officers in the districts have openly sympathised with the agitators. Dissatisfaction of the police force thus expressed has been nation-wide. It spread from Punjab, where the agitation first erupted, to Haryana, Delhi, Tripura, Madhya Pradesh, Rajasthan, Orissa, Andhra Pradesh, Gujarat and Kashmir.[1] The agitators demand *(a)* right to form association, *(b)* right to representation, *(c)* increase in salary and allowances, *(d)* reduction of working hours, (e) abolition of 'orderly system', *(f)* cordiality of relations between the superior and subordinate officers, *(g)* adequate promotional avenues, and *(h)* better medical and housing facilities.

To achieve these demands, policemen in different states adopted a variety of methods ranging from peaceful *Dharnas* and processions, demonstrations, resort to violence, insulting of the superior officers, and to the raising of slogans against the politicians.

To appreciate the wild outburst of their anger[2] and suppressed discontent one has only to look at the course of agitations in different states, and the stand taken by the Central and State Governments *vis-a-vis* these demands.

Course of the Agitation and the Government's Stand

The agitation first began at Patiala in the Panjab on 8 May 1979 when about 200 policemen in uniform took out a procession demanding recognition of their newly-formed association, the Punjab Police Union. Their agitation lasted for 8 days. During these days the policemen observed *Dharna,* took out procession demonstrations, raised slogans against the politicians, and nearly 350 of them courted arrest. Army and the Border Security Forces (BSF) were called in to take over armouries in the affected areas.

Punjab Government, in response, raised the salary of a constable from Rs. 427 to 527.50 per month, and of a head constable from Rs. 499.75 to 559.50 with retrospective effect from 1 January 1978 along with an increase in the house rent, and kit and medical allowances. Constables were also to get an extra month's pay per year for being on duty on gazetted holidays, hitherto un-paid. All this involved an additional annual expenditure of Rupees 30,000,000.

The agitation then spread to Madhya Pradesh where it went on for about 10 days. Disgruntled policemen took out processions in almost all the Divisional Headquarters of the state. They organised 'gate meetings' in support of their 20-point charter of demands submitted to the Government. These meetings took the place of rallies, processions and demonstrations. The Government announced a number of benefits to the police constables: such as one month's additional pay to constables, 14 days casual leave *in-lieu* of 89 holidays and off-days in a year; Rs. 10 per month as laundry allowance to constables and head constables; and monthly travelling allowance of Rs. 25 to a constable and of Rs. 30 to a head constable.

The Government had also decided to raise their 'built in group insurance' from Rs. 12,000 to Rs. 25,000 in the case of constables, head constables and Sub-Inspectors, and Rs. 50.000 in the case of Deputy Superintendents of Police. Further, a Pay Commission was appointed to enquire into the pay structure of the state employees, including the policemen, and a high level committee was set up to deal with the problems of police on a priority basis. The Chief Minister, however, rejected the right of policemen to form a union.

In Bombay also, a charter of 20 demands was submitted to the Chief Minister on behalf of the Maharashtra Police. In Rajasthan, the situation took a crucial turn with the State Government's insistence on immediate withdrawal of the agitation. The Government made it clear that it would consider the policemen's demands only after the withdrawal of the agitation. On the strength of a special ordinance, orders were issued for the arrest of 29 constables for participating in the strike. Despite this, the agitation continued for about 12 days.

In Orissa, policemen served an ultimatum to the Government that if their demands were not conceded on or before the 4th of June (1979), they would go on strike. They marched in a procession and presented a memorandum to the Chief Minister. They presented bangles to the Deputy Commissioner and the Additional Commissioner of Police for their inability to solve the problems of the policemen. The Orissa Government announced concessions to over 26,000 non-gazetted policemen involving an additional annual expenditure of nearly Rs. 20,000,000. Thus, a number of the constabulary received additional benefits ranging between Rs. 34 and Rs. 41 per month. An additional sum of Rs. 2,500,000 was also provided for housing, and the Government decided to take up the housing-programme involving an expenditure of about Rs. 10,000,000 during the next 12 years.

The Government also decided to constitute a State-level committee under the chairmanship of the Chief Secretary, with the Home Secretary, the Inspector-General of Police and the President of the State Police Association as members, to take a broad view of the problems of policemen and their efficiency and welfare.

The Government of Orissa expressed its inability, however, to implement all the recommendations of the National Police Commission as it would break the financial backbone of as poor a state as itself (Orissa) unless, of course, the Central Government took full responsibility for bearing the additional burden on this account. The Government saw that the implementation of the recommendations of the police commission would easily entail an expenditure of Rs. 110,000,000 annually, and Rs. 550,000,000 in the next five years.

In Gujarat, police agitation took an unexpected turn. The Government there had to deploy Army and the Border Security Force for patrolling the city of Ahmedabad. Many policemen abstained from duty for about 6 days. Their wives and children marched in procession in protest against the firing by Army personnel on police agitators near Dheli Kev, about 15 kms from Ahmedabad, in which five policemen were injured.

The Gujarat Government came to an agreement after negotiations with the representatives of the police unions. The agreement ensured benefits to 45,000 policemen with an additional financial burden of more than Rs. 40,000,000 per annum on the state exchequer. The agreement provided that all constables and head constables be paid Rs. 60 per month, and the Inspectors and Sub-Inspectors be paid Rs. 75 per month as special compensatory allowance. Casual leave was increased from 15 to 20 days a year, and the washing allowance was enhanced from Rs. 4 to 10 per month. The Government also agreed to recognise the policemen's association and assured not to victimise those who had participated in the agitation.

The Assam Government, anticipating an agitation, on its own announced a number of concessions to the police force. It increased the rate of maintenance allowance to border personnel, enhanced ration allowance for constables and rifle allowance to *havildars* (head constables) of armed police. Besides, the Government decided to pay a pension equal to the pay to those police personnel who die while on duty on the border.

In Andhra Pradesh, the Police Subordinate Officers Association submitted a charter of 23 demands, with the threat of 'direct action' if their grievances were not redressed. The State Government announced a number of benefits to the policemen involving an additional annual expenditure of Rs. 50,000,000 to the state. 'Orderly system' was to be abolished; where orderlies were abolished, an allowance of Rs. 125 per orderly to a maximum of Rs. 250 per month was sanctioned. The Government also decided to grant an additional earned leave of 15 days per year with a provision to encash the same as a compensation for working overtime. Further, the Government increased the rates of conveyance allowance, the uniform allowance was doubled, and the washing allowance was enhanced from Rs. 40 year to Rs. 10 per month. Dietary allowances also doubled the existing rates, subject to a minimum of Rs. 5 per day. To improve the promotional opportunities of the Armed Reserve and Andhra Pradesh Special Police, the Government decided to upgrade all posts of Lance-Naiks and Naiks to that of Head Constables over a period of two years. It also raised the house rent allowance of Sub-Inspectors; Inspectors were made eligible to rent-free quarters. Construction of 163 houses was also decided to be taken up, and a sum of Rs. 8,000,000 was earmarked for this purpose; the Government proposed to spend a total of Rs. 122,500,000 allotted by the Seventh Finance Commission for Housing purposes in the next Five years. An organisation known as the "Andhra Pradesh Police Non-gazetted Officers' Association" was formed on 12 June 1979, which the Government recognised immediately.

The Government of Kerala announced special allowance of Rs. 66 per month to policemen upto the rank of ASI, and upgraded 1,250 posts of constables to those of head constables with effect from 1 June 1979. The new concessions, were expected to cost the exchequer Rs. 16,600,000 a year. The right to form an association was granted by the Government, and staff councils were also decided to be set up.

Clearly then, the Government of India and practically all the State Governments were thus compelled for the first time to give some serious thought to the policemen's grievances.

The Union Minister for Home Affairs convened a conference of all the Chief Ministers of the states on 6 June 1979; the meeting was being convened after a lapse of good deal of time the Government had not reacted quickly enough to a pressing problem. However, the Conference agreed in principle on *(a)* payment of higher pay to the police, *(b)* payment of special allowance to the constables, *(c)* abolition of 'orderly system', and *(d)* recognition of Policemen's Associations.

Almost all the State Governments enhanced the pay and allowances of the police. Some Governments granted the right to form associations and recognised police unions, and decided to abolish the 'orderly system'. Although the policemen called off their agitation in the wake of these expedient measures, the State Governments would be wrong in thinking that they have solved all the problems of the police. There is need for a search of long-term solutions to police demands.

The Demands

(i) Right to form Associations/Unions : The right of association is central to any concept of constitutional democracy[4] and Article 19 (l)c of the Constitution of India guarantees this right. It is natural that millions employed by government thus unite and resort to concerted action, for unionism is an acknowledged method of protecting the service conditions of the employees.

Prior to 1920 the government in India was, in general, opposed to the organizations of the Government employees, and accordingly prohibited submission of collective memoranda or petitions. Policemen started organising themselves after 1920s, although governments did not accord recognition to such associations and unions. The government tried to maintain the distinction between the civil and police employees associations. The same is true even today, recent or previous agitations notwithstanding.

The main cause at the root of the trouble is that the police personnel for long have been denied the right to form associations for representing their grievances. It was their demand for a platform for airing their problems that led to the police strike in Delhi in 1967, the 'revolt' of the Provincial Armed Constabulary in Uttar Pradesh in May 1973, and the present outburst in Punjab and other states. Taking advantage of the agitation in Punjab, the Andhra Pradesh Police Subordinate Officers' Association pressed the Government to concede their 13-year long demand for recognition of their Association. The Gujarat Policemen also joined the stir demanding recognition of their union. The Policemen's demand to form associations is, however, not equally strong in all the states.

Associations of policemen have of course been formed at different points of time[5], the earliest dating back to 1920. But just one of these, the Bihar Policemen's Association, has been a recognised body; all others are in existence today despite the Police

Force (Restriction of Rights) Act, 1966. Though the Act bans the formation of associations by the police, no punitive action has been taken against the unrecognised ones simply because they were not particularly active, and hardly ever caused any trouble to the Government. But the Central Government has now shown a positive attitude in permitting the policemen to form themselves into associations albeit with restricted freedom.[6] However, some of the State Governments seem not to be prepared yet to permit the policemen to form associations or unions. The recognition accorded by some state Governments is only an exception to the rule.

Experience of the past 60 years in this country has been that political parties and their leaders took active part and played a key role in the destiny of the civii service unionism. Consequently, civil service unionism in India today has been divided on party lines.[7] If police personnel also have been granted the right to organise, there is no guarantee that political parties would not enter them and politicise. Responsible people in Government allege that even now some political parties are behind the recent police agitations. This is not to say that the police should not have the right to organise, but merely to caution about the impending danger of political involvement. Therefore, necessary steps should be initiated to protect the real spirit of unionism in police, which may aim at the timely redressal of their grievances.

(ii) Right to Representation: There is no proper machinery at present to redress the grievances of police personnel ; they represent their grievances in *Durbars* and 'orderly rooms'[8] of their higher officers in the force. The existing system is 'inchaotic and chaotic and paternalistic in its form and functioning'.[9] There are only informal avenues for representing, and are of minor importance.

In the wake of the rash of strikes, the Government of India decided to immediately set up joint consultative machinery at different levels in the form of staff councils to provide a forum for identifying policemen's grievances and to consider them across the table.

Significantly, although the Government of India had established a scheme for Joint Consultative Machinery (JCM) and Compulsory

Arbitration in October 1966 for Central Government employees, the scheme excluded police personnel from its coverage.[10] The Government has now decided to set up Joint Consultative Machinery[11] for police, still, in the light of the past experience of the working of the JCM for Civil employees, merely setting up a machinery is not enough; what is required is a positive attitude and faith among the politicians and the bureaucrats in bilaterlism in service matters. As long as these are lacking in practice, strikes and agitations by the affected classes of employees are bound to recur frequently.

Most of the state governments did not establish these institutions (JCM) even in face of strikes every year. Some state governments set up staff committees, but they did not function effectively. As a result, the present position in India is that there is no positive evidence among the politicians and bureaucrats to accept bilateralism and settle disputes peacefully through negotiations with the civil service unions/associations. One cannot expect a miracle to change the attitude of the decision-makers at the top level of administration, with the result that instead of solving the problems, the situation gets aggravated. What is ultimately needed is democratic culture among politicians and top civil servants for resolving conflicts by negotiations and/or arbitration. That the recommendations of National Police Commission to establish DPSCs and SPSCs should be implemented immediately and fully in their real spirit in all the states and at the Centre, is therefore clearly indicated.

(iii) Pay and Allowances: Despite the recommendations of the three Central Pay Commissions and a number of State Pay Commissions, India has not been able to evolve a rational pay structure, nor a national wage policy for its employees. Consequently, the principle of equal pay for equal work has not been accepted and the differences have been maintained in pay and allowances between the central, the state and the local government employees on the one hand and between the civil, the army and the police force on the other. The pay structure evolved in the colonial days which allows a great deal of scope for corruption has continued all the years with *ad hoc* adjustments and temporary measures. The recent police agitations

have been directly consequent upon indequate payment of salaries to the constables. They demand that they should be paid on par with the other public services and their travelling, laundry and rationing and other allowances be enhanced. They were not only paid lowly in some states than the lowest paid category peon[12], but also less than their counterparts in police itself the CRP (Central Reserve Police), the BSF (Border Security Force), and others.

(iv) Working Conditions: The nature of police work is such that a policeman is on duty all the 24 hours of the day, but ordinarily works 12 to 13 hours a day in comparison to 8 hours for the government employees and the Industrial workers who also have a weekly day-off. Apart from the long, arduous hours of work, policemen are also denied holidays and normal leave enjoyed by other services in the government. Therefore, they demand parity in matters of working hours, leave and holidays with the other government employees. Working conditions in police stations are also not conducive to efficient functioning of the force.

More than 80% of the police force consists of constables with low educational qualifications. A large majority of them retire without even one promotion in their entire career. This has been considered a serious demotivating factor that affects the quality of duty performance at constable level. To avoid this stagnation, more promotional opportunities have to be provided in future by recruiting constables with minimum qualification of matriculation and giving promotion within 8 to 10 years after proper training. For this purpose, the hierarchy at the police station level may need restructuring by increasing the personnel at the intermediate level between the Sub-Inspector and the constable.

The force at lower levels is denied proper accommodation, medical and health facilities too. Inspite of separate housing boards for the police and the grants by the seventh Finance Commission to the State Governments the problem is still very acute.[13] Some state governments have failed to utilise the funds provided for this purpose.

(v) Superior-Subordinate Relations : Miserable working conditions apart, another reason for the discontent and frustration

among the police ranks is the almost inhuman treatment they get from their superior officers. The language used towards them is abusive and most of the constables work as 'orderlies' at the residence of the officers, which is often, no better than working as domestic help. They work as cooks, drivers to the private vehicles, maintain the house, gardens, help the wives and children of the officers in their daily activities forgetting that they themselves have wives and children at home. In the colonial days this slavish treatment might have had to be tolerated by the illiterate policemen. But those recruited in the recent years are definitely better educated, and come from a very different social background. They are thus prone to react to the abuse and insult so frequently hurled at them by their superior officers. Hence the demand for the abolition of the 'orderly system.' Even though the Central and some State Governments have decided to abolish the 'orderly system', this has to be implemented strictly in actual practice.

A police constable who is not treated as a human being in a his organisation cannot be expected to maintain proper relations with the public. Therefore the police officers should acquire a new work culture to treat the policemen as human beings and communicate with them in a decent language. This human recognition will not only boost up the morale of the ranks but also lead to cordial relations between superior and subordinate officers, and ultimately, between the police and the public.

Conclusions

The grievances of the policemen are genuine, and they can be redressed to a large extent if the recommendations of the National Police Commission are implemented in the Sixth Five-Year Plan. But it would be very difficult for the Central and State Governments to implement them in view of the huge sums of money—as much as Rs. 3,500,000,000—required. The country may not be able to afford to spend such an amount even in the near future. Therefore, in order to safeguard democracy and maintain a minimum of law and order in the present conditions the only alternative seems to be to introduce democractic element in the police administration, and to grant autonomy in its day-to-day administration. To achieve this goal

Government should accept bilateralism in redressing the grievances and explain to the police representatives on the negotiation table the existing financial difficulties facing the country.

It is high time that the Indian political parties evolve their staff relations policies, and stick to them when they come to power. Politicians in and out of the Government should learn to restrain themselves not to interfere in the administration of law. Bureaucracy should acquire democratic work culture and maintain cordial human relations with their subordinates.

In future, in order to solve such important national problems, it should be possible for the Central and State Governments to adopt an integrated and uniform national approach. The problem should not be left to the individual State Governments. Maintenance of law and order and disciplined police force should be viewed as an all-India problem.

References

1. In Assam, Bengal and Kerala also the police peacefully represented their grievances.
2. Maheshwari, S.R., 'Outburst of Long Suppressed Anger', *The Hindu,* (Madras) 6 June, 1979, p. 8.
4. David, Fellman : *The Constitutional Right of Association* (University of Chicago Press), p. 104.
5. The oldest staff association of the police personnel in India was the West Bengal Police Association, 1921 (recognised in 1923, but the recognition was later withdrawn). The Bihar Police Association, 1925 (recognised); the Bihar Police Association, 1946, the Calcutta Police Association 1947, the Police Non-Gazetted Karmachari Sangh, 1964, the Andhra Pradesh Non-Gazetted Officer's Association 1966, and the Non-Gazetted Police Karmachari Parishad U.P., 1969. However, these bodies are no substitute for a machinery of a general nature addressing itself to the task of redressing the grievances. These bodies may, occasionally, prepare a memorandum to be submitted to a pay commission or an administrative reforms committee, and may even call on the ministers concerned and plead on purely service matters. See, for details, Maheswari, S.R., 'Unionism in the Police', *Indian Journal of Public Administration,* Vol. XXIV, No. 1, Jan-March, 1978.

6. (*a*) Membership is restricted to serving policemen.

   (*b*) No out-sider, whether a Government servant or not, is entitled to membership or function as an office-bearer connected with it in advisory or any other capacity.

   (*c*) Members have no right to strike, withhold their services or otherwise delay performance of their duties in any manner.

   (*d*) The association shall not resort to any coercive method or agitation for obtaining redressal of grievances.

   (*e*) The association shall be absolutely non-political in character and shall not be connected, directly or indirectly, with political activity of any kind. The guidelines should be incorporated in the articles of the association. The restrictions are not something laid down newly or only for policemen. They have been there, and have applied to civil service associations since 1921.

7. Bhaskara Rao, V: *Employer-Employees Relations* (Delhi, Concept Publishing) 1978, pp. 208-209.
8. For detail see Maheswari, S.R., *op. cit,* pp. 73-74.
9. *Ibid.*, p. 85.
10. *Scheme for Joint Consultative Machinery and Compulsory Arbitration for Central Government Employees,* Department of Personnel, Cabinet Secretariat, Government of India, 8 Sep 1971, Annexure-I, p. 3.
11. One of the main recommendations of the National Police Commission for settling disputes was the establishment of District Police Staff Councils and State Police Councils.
12. Interestingly enough, their monthly pay is less than the monthly expenditure spent on the police dog.
13. See for details "The Police: Over worked, under paid, demoralised but militant", *India Today*, Vol. IV, No. 12, pp. 46-47.

18

Discipline in Public Service

Every organisation frames its Laws, Rules and Regulations governing the conduct of its employees in carrying out its objectives. Through this code of conduct discipline among employees is promoted and maintained. Discipline is very essential for any group action or organisational activity. The code of behaviour is a part of the organisational behaviour. The code is supposed to be mutually beneficial to the employer and the employee. Organisation expects the employee(s) reasonably behave in conformity with the rules and regulations of the code of discipline.

Discipline is the force that prompts an employee to observe the rules, regulations and procedures which are deemed to be necessary to the attainment of objectives. Discipline also exercises restraint or the enforcement of penalties for the violation of the rules and regulations. Discipline is a training which rectifies, modifies, strengthens and improves individual behaviour as desired by the organisation/government. It is adherence to established norms and regulations. Discipline is essentially an attitude of the mind, a product of culture and environment and requires alongwith legislative sanction, persuasion on a moral plane.

The code of conduct prescribed to the public employees is based on the authoritarian theory of the State (The king can do no wrong and the Sovereign theory of the State). The civil service is treated on par with soldiers and sailars. The State expects from the servants unquestionable Loyalty and obedience in every aspect of their life and family. The conditions of service are unilaterally laid down by the State in the interest of the state security, public order and national interest.

For each Service/Class/Category of employees, separate conduct rules and disciplinary procedures are laid down. These rules are to maintain the following:

(1) Integrity in the Service,

(2) Discipline in the Service,

(3) Neutrality in politics in the Service.

Integrity of the Public Servants

1. As a part of administrative ethics and morale every employee should maintain at all times absolute integrity and devotion to duty.
2. Employment of near relatives in firms enjoying Government patronage is forbidden. (No Teacher is permitted to be the examiner if any 'relative' is involved or appearing the examination. One cannot be examiner if he is engaged in private tuitions)
3. Acceptance of gifts is forbidden - even by the members of the family - acceptance of contributions or raising of any fund or associating with such activities is forbidden.
4. Private trade, employment, investment, lending and borrowing are forbidden in certain cases.

Rules for Securing Neutrality in Politics

1. Public Servants should serve the Government, not the party.
2. No association with any party or party affairs.
3. Members of the family are forbidden from subscribing assist or aid to parties.
4. Forbidden from taking part in elections.
5. Prohibited from press, broadcast and publications.

Characteristics of Discipline

1. It is a determinitive and positive willingness which prompts individuals and groups to carryout the instructions and abide by the rules of conduct and the standards of work.

2. It is a negative approach which restraints from undertaking some activities.
3. It is a punitive or a big stick approach which imposes penalty and punishment if rules are disobeyed.

Aims and Objects of Discipline

1. To obtain a willing acceptance of the rules and regulations and procedures of organisation.
2. To impart an element of certainty.
3. To develop spirit of tolerance and desire to make adjustments.
4. To give and seek direction and responsibility.
5. To create an atmosphere of respect for the human personality and human relations.
6. To increase the working efficiency and morale.

Forms and Types of Discipline

1. **Positive or Self-imposed discipline** rewards, appreciation, constructive support, reinforcement of actions, incentives, promotions, application of principles of positive motivation. It leads to: Team spirit, mutual respect, respect for rules and procedures, respect for supervisors, self-expression, willingness to co-operate etc.
2. **Enforced or Negative Discipline**

   (*a*) It is to scare, keep in line, check undesirable behaviour.

   (*b*) It is punitive/corrective, autocratic.

   (*c*) Use of techniques like reprimands, fines, lay-outs, demotions or transfers.
3. **Progressive Discipline**

   Five steps: oral reprimand, written reprimand, second written warning, temporary suspension, and dismissal.

Causes of Indiscipline

Discipline is the result of a training of body and mind. The rules of discipline should not violate the rights of the individual:

1. Non-placement of the right persons in the right job.
2. Undesirable behaviour of Supervisors/Seniors.
3. Faulty evaluation of persons.
4. Lack of upward communication.
5. Weak, flexible, incompetent and distrustful of subordinates nature of leadership.
6. Defective supervision.
7. Improper rules/regulations.
8. 'Divide and rule' policy of the management.
9. Low level of education and training.
0. Personal problems.
11. Bad working conditions.
12. Discrimination.

Civil Services (classification, control and appeal rules) CCA Rules;

To inquire into 'misconduct or misbehaviour'

Two stages:

1. Procedural
2. Constitutional safeguards guaranteed

12 stages in the Departmental proceedings

1. Preparation of charge sheet
2. Ending with the imposition of penalty.
   (*a*) Minor penalties: censusing, withholding increments,
   (*b*) Major punishments: downgrading, compulsory retirement, dismissal
3. There are many loopholes in the procedures

Constitutional provisionss

1. Article 311
2. Article 311(2) 42 Amendment Act 1976

   "Except after inquiry in which he has been informed of the charges against him and given a reasonable opportunity of being heard in respect of those charges"

Over-security inservice to a civil servant is a spur to misconduct,

(*a*) difficulty in getting evidence

(*b*) collegial unity among officers

(*c*) corrupt politicians

(*d*) protracted inquiries discourage the superiors to initiate action.

(*e*) 'Softness' towards subordinates

(*f*) lack of work-culture.

19

Trade Unionism Among Public Sector Bank Employees : A Survey

The public sector in India has only a standing of three decades. Some of the organisations like the nationalized banks, are of recent origin. However, trade unions in these organisations have been powerful enough to exert pressure on their management and the Government. The central concern of this survey is to study the degree of awareness and consciousness of trade unionism among Bank employees of public sector. There is no single comprehensive study covering all the aspects of public sector trade unionism at various levels, particularly at grassroots level.

The study attempts to present the views and opinions of the members and office-bearers of the unions elicited at branch level on various aspects of the unionism. An intimate knowledge of the awareness and consciousness of the employees from the grassroots trade unionism on different aspects, based on empirical research helps to understand the various issues of unionism.

The study endeavoured to secure information on the following topics:

> Need for Trade Unions, Membership of the Unions, Activities of the Unions, Aims and Objectives of Unions, Rights of Employees, Trade Union Leadership, Knowledge of Labour Legislation, Methods of Grievances Reddressal and Workers, Participation in Management.

Methodology and the Sample of the Study

The degree of awareness and consciousness of trade unionism among the public sector bank employees was studied by collecting information on the above mentioned topics through a questionnaire to a random sample. Apart from the personal particulars of the respondents, the questionnaire included 12 main questions; the questions covered ten topics referred to above and dealt with each topic. There were 312 employees in all the 22 branches of various nationalised banks located at Warangal.[1] The study covers only 240 supervisory and clerical staff. The questionnaire was administered in person to 178 bank employees (72%) to seek answers from them about various aspects of trade unionism.

Educational, Age and Service Background of the Respondents

About 69% of the respondents were graduates, 9% of them post-graduates and the remaining 22% were under-graduates. About 72% of the respondents were young below the age of 32 years and 92% were below the age of 40 years. The mean age of the respondents was 33 years. About 43% of the respondents were having only five years service, and three-fourths of them come under ten years of service group. The service mean of the respondents was 7 years.

The Findings of the Survey

Trade Union membership in the branches of nationalised banks at Warangal was not only very high (93%) but the members were also well informed. Majority of the members were young. A large percentage (85%) of them were aware of the union activities at branch level, and more than one-fourth about the state and All-India level activities. However, nearly 69% of them never read any union journals, or Information provided by the unions. At the same time not more than 56% attended their branch union meetings regularly. This shows that they were aware of the activities, but less conscious about them.

There was a widespread conviction among the employees about the absolute necessity of the trade unions. In their opinion trade unions were necessary to create better understanding between the management and the staff (79%) while protecting the employees' interests (63%), 24% of them felt trade unions were not meant for assisting the management or developing the institution of their work or to serve the community. But 37% felt that trade unions are necessary to achieve the socialist society.

Trade Union Objectives

That the trade unions should fight for the rights and grievances of the employees as their main aims and objectives was supported by a very large section (82%) of the employees. But only 73% favoured it as the ultimate aim of the unions. This reveals that trade unions in India irrespective of the sector to which they belonged remained undeveloped and wanted only to protect and fight for the grievances of the employees. Some change is also evident in the out look of the employees, because more than half of them (57%) felt that improvement of the quality of public administration in the interest of the nation should be also one of the objectives of the trade unions. About 34% of them wanted trade unions to adopt workers' participation in the nanagement as one of the ultimate objectives.

The views of the employees' would have been well received had larger percentage of them chosen to protect the merit system, (18%) serve the society, act as the agents of social change (31%), and achieve socialist society as the ultimate objectives of their unions. The trade unions at the national level and their leaders should work to change the opinions of their members at the branch level by educating them and also inculcating in them the spirit of service to the community and enable them to act as the agents of social change as no union can achieve its objectives unless the members at grass roots believe in them.

Public employees have been fighting to achieve certain rights on par with the ordinary citizen. More than 85% of the respondents felt that they should have the civil rights like the freedom of speech and expression. They were not interested in political rights viz., membership of a political party (24%) or participation in elections (28%). Although the employees did not like to settle their problems by resorting to strikes. Yet they preferred the right to strike as a weapon in their armour (53%).

Trade Union Leadership

Trade union leadership at branch level occupies a very important position as it is responsible for the enrolment of members and implementation of awards and agreements. They maintain contacts between the national leaders and the rank and file members. The strength of the national leadership depends upon the effectiveness of local leadership particularly in the crisis situation like strikes. Trade unions at the branch level are small in size, strength and activities. Therefore, leadership at this level should pay great attention to effectively organise, build up and sustain interest among the rank and file members. All this largely depends upon the awareness and consciousness of leaders on various aspects of unionism like the type of leadership, the time spared for the union work, the knowledge of industrial relations and commitment to certain objectives.

The study reveals that the members did not evince keen interest to participate in the branch union leadership. The leadership at this level was monopolised by one-third of the members of the unions, but not concentrated (for more years) in a few hands.

The branch level union leadership was largely committed to achieve three objectives; to create better understanding between the management and the staff (92%), to promote solidarity among the employees (81%) and to fight for the rights and grievances of the employees (75%) . Increasing the efficiency of public administration was only the fourth objective in their opinion (59%). The leadership was more committed to above objectives than the rank and file employees. Only 35% of the leadership was committed to achieve socialist society, to act as agents of social change and to serve the community.

The knowledge of the leaders at the branch union level was poor in regard to the industrial relations laws and rules. Only 1/3rd of them read the trade union law. The office bearers in the banks were interested only in regarding the bi-partite agreements. The leadership at the branch union level was not involved in the industrial relations. This could be the cause for their disinterestedness to study the industrial relation laws and rules.

A large section of the leaders (87%) preferred to settle their grievances through Joint consultation and negotiation. But more than half of them (58%) also opted for the collective bargaining. They did not have any knowledge about the methods of impasse settlements. They did not want to go on strike for settling their problems. Instead they expressed faith (35%) in participative management as one of the methods to get their grievances redressed.

A vast majority (90%) of the public sactor bank employees in this study preferred serving employees (insiders) as their leaders. They were not aware whether the full time leadership or part-time leadership would provide more service to them. However, they tended more towards the full time leadership (22%).

Industrial Relations

The employees preferred (79%) to settle their grievances through Joint consultation with the management. Although the public sector in India is plagued by sporadic strikes on various issues at different places very negligible percentage (12%) of the sample opted to solve their problems by resorting to strikes. Further, their faith in participative management (28%) as one of the methods to resolve industrial conflicts indeed, is a welcome sign of industrial peace. However, there is much to be done on the part of the management and the trade unions at higher levels to sustain and increase faith among the employees in the concept of participative management.

The employees at the unit level did not possess much knowledge about the industrial relations laws and rules. This unawareness may be due to the absence of any regular industrial relations agency at the branch level. At present, the union-management relations are maintained only at the national or headquarters level. Therefore, there is a case for the decentralisation of union-management relations to the branch level, whereever there are reasonable number of employees to discuss the local or office problems. Such a step would enhance the consciousness of industrial relations laws and rules in the employees at the branch level.

Workers' Participation in Management

Although, the scheme of workers' participation in management was not in vogue at the branch level, about 75% of the respondents were aware of the concept of the workers' participation in management. However, they did not know much about the forms of participation. But about half of them preferred Joint decision making in all the matters of the management and inclusion of worker director in the Board of Directors of the enterprise (59%) only one-third desired participation at all levels shop/floor of management. It is interesting to note that there was not much of difference of opinion between the office bearers and the rank and file employees over the forms of workers' participation in management.

The employees' faith in the capacity of their representatives was so commendable that a large section (82%) believed that their representatives can participate in the general managerial activities, particularly in the personnel management (78%) and production management (45%).

They also believed (91%) that workers participation would lead to better understanding between the management and staff and solve labour problems (71%) in a more effective manner. It is pertinent to note that those who did not have faith in their representatives capacity to participate in the management (17%) also believed (58%) solution to the labour problems through workers' participation in management. Therefore, for the employees to have faith in the philosophy of workers' participation in management and also in the capacity of their representatives to participate in the managerial activities, it is necessary to implement the scheme of workers' participation in management in all the matters and at all levels of management.

Conclusions

Trade unions are absolutely necessary to create better understanding between the management and the staff. Members were aware only of the branch union activities.

They believed that trade unions should mainly fight for the rights and grievances of the employees.

They wanted the civil rights and the right to strike but not interested in political rights.

Branch level union leadership was monopolised by few and nembers did not evince interest in leadership. The leaders' knowledge in industrial relations was poor. They preferred to settle their problems through joint consultation and negotiation. The respondents of the sample preferred serving employees as their leaders.

The ordinary members and the leaders of the unions did not know much about the forms of participation in management. But they believed that their representatives have the capacity to participate in management, particularly in personnel management. They expressed faith that workers' participation in management leads to better understanding between the management and hormonious staff relations.

References

1. The study was conducted in 1977 at Warangal. Warangal is the second largest city in Telangana region of Andhra Pradesh next only to the capital. According to 1971 census, it has a population of 2,07,520. It is the headquarters of the Warangal district and many of the Regional Offices are located here.
2. It was deliberately avoided administering the questionnaire to the subordinate staff like peons, watchmen and drivers. For it was assumed that they might not understand the questionnaire as they were not educated enough to answer it. In view of this, 72 employees belonging to this category were not involved in this study.

20

Role of Bank Employees' Unions in Development

The Government of India, in 1969, nationalised 14 major Indian banks as a political and economic measure. The objectives of the bank nationalisation are to provide deposit and credit facilities in the rural and semi-urban areas for the development of agriculture, small scale industries and retail trades which contribute over three-fifths of the national income.

It is beyond doubt that no organisation can achieve it objectives completely without the full support and cooperation of the employees to its policies and programmes. Therefore, the Banking Industry needs a clear and effective policy of staff relations to win the unstinted cooperation of its employees in order to achieve the objectives. Such cooperation is possible only by encouraging the Trade Unions to participate in the management for which the unions have been demanding. It is not enough to include a trade union representative as a worker director in the Central Policy making level, but the participation must be full in its spirit at the Branch level, in every aspect of the management. For this purpose, the unions should demand for joint administration and Joint decision-making in all matters. To achieve this demand they should strengthen their unions with strong and matured leadership and informed membership.

The trade unions should organise strongly to direct their members to work efficiently so that the industry gains more profits and reaches a better position to pay fairly to its employees. This can be achieved by the active participation in the management, cooperation within the employees and with the management and avoiding industrial warfare, and settling the disputes in peaceful and regular manner.

Hitherto, the trade unions have been fighting for their rights and demands against a private employer. But in the wake of nationalisation the employees and their unions have to change their traditional role from fighting against the management to participate in the management. They should feel that it is their own property and identify with the goals of the management and the Banking Industry. In this regard, the trade unions are required to pay a new role of learning the art and science of management and reach to the level of dealing with the managerial problems such as planning, finance, proper use of raw material, efficient production, marketing and personnel selection. The Trade Unions should get themselves equipped if they want effective participation at all levels of the management.

Inspite of the considerable development, banking industry has not been able to project their good image in the minds of the public as a service organisation. For, most of the banks had to confront with labour unrest in the recent past. This was considered the major set- back to the goodwill of the banking industry.

Any developing country like India whose economy is passing through a critical stage, banking Industry can ill afford to have any disruption in the working. Therefore the necessity of the harmonious relations between the management and the staff need not be over emphasised. Then only the customers can be expected to receive more courteous, speedier and cheaper service.

Although, banks are nationalised, traditional bureaucratic management and the same monopoly grip on the banks is continuing and they resist laying down social objectives. Poor workers, peasants, small business men are not financed much. It is the time for the bank employees to think about this social objective of the banks and endeavour to achieve the same. Therefore, they should play a great role as 'change agents' for social and economic change of the country.

Bank employees and their unions have a duel role to play in this context. First, as a trade union, to fight for the improvement of service conditions of the staff and secondly, as a representative of the working class to strive for the achievement of the social objectives of the banks, i.e., to serve the poor.

The banks and their employees are now slowly going into the rural areas to provide the banking facilities to the rural poor. It is in this context the bank employees have a role to play in educating the ultimate rural masses, in assisting the economically weaker sections and changing their life course for the prosperity, pulling them away from the clutches of the traditional money lenders. The bank employees as 'change agents' should explain by the borrowers about various credit facilities and schemes and assist them in getting the loans.

If the bank employees serve their cause properly, the image of India would certainly change in a decade or two and achieve a change in the social order. For this purpose they have to play both the political and economic roles.

To achieve this great social objective the employees and their unions have greater social responsibility than the management. For the managerial class by and large belong to the higher middle class and in one form or the other reached to that status may not evince keen interest to serve the interests of the poor and the down trodden. But the unions which are organised to serve the interests of the proletariat or the working class should fight for progressive measures in serving their community in general. In this regard, the bank employees' unions have a higher role to play than the management in the realisation of the goals of the banking industry.

In the past, bank employees unions along with other trade unions fought successfully not only for improvement in their service conditions and pay and allowances but could bring down the prices of certain essential commodities which helped the community at large. Likewise, they should fight with their managements, for giving loans to the needy at reasonable interests so that the investments in agriculture, small scale industries would produce more food and goods. For this purpose the employees should work with responsibility and efficiently so that in the long run their efficient working would provide more employment and more production in all sections.

Thus, the bank employees as 'knowledge workers' should realise that their trade union movement has the responsibility far beyond the realm of industrial relations or simple economic issues. Their ultimate aim should be the achievement of the socialism and socialist state. Therefore, the bank employees and their unions while fighting for their own demands should play an effective economic role in shaping the national economy of the country for the benefit of the working class.

Finally, if the school teachers educate the illiterate people, the bank employees financially assist the poor, the medical staff serve the ailing, electricity board employees provide unhampered power supply for the agriculture, Panchayati Raj staff (village development officer and his staff) assist the agriculturist, the Panchayat provides proper political leadership, there is no reason why the village in India should not prosper in social, economic and political fields in a near future.

21

The Second Strike by Central Government Employees: Some Issues*

Perhaps, at no other time the normal life of the citizens is so much disturbed and dislocated by violence, agitations and strikes than the present times have witnessed. Strikes in industrial sector are understandable, and are even permitted. But due to various reasons, the agitational approach has percolated to the public enterprises and the government employees[1] are resorting to strikes for settlement of disputes. This is not to cast aspertions on government employees that they are easily provoked and are resorting to strikes on frivolous issues. There appears to be a sense of complacency and vacillation on the part of the government in unduly delaying decisions on vital issues and acting only when large scale violence is resorted to. Political scientists have described the present-day governments as governments understanding the language of agitations and violence, usually stepping into action after the fact of violence which could otherwise be avoided.

By a collusion of circumstances and conspiracy of events, strikes did occur inspite of the civil service conduct rules prohibiting employees from participating in strikes and even in the face of an emergency legislation seeking to prevent such indulgence. Therefore, more important than the question, whether strikes should be banned, there are other problems and issues which are to be appreciated by all those who are interested in the prosperity of the Nation, general welfare and public peace. Hence, an attempt is made in this paper to study the following issues:

---

* Co-authored with Dr. P.A. James.

(*a*) The duty of the government to bargain and the necessity of employees' unions for the purpose.

(*b*) The employees' duty to maintain the structure of the State, law and order.

(*c*) The danger of the politicisation of government employees.

(*d*) The right of the government employees to go on strike to press their demands.

In order to study the above, an attempt has also been made to analyse the events preceding, during and after the strike to show the lapses in judgement and action on both the sides. Further, by way of a projection, the long-term implications of government policy of dealing with the employees keeping in view the intractable problems of inflation and living wage have been dealt with.

Having stated the scope of the paper, the issues may now be examined in some detail.

Government's Duty to Bargain and Necessity of Employees' Union

Since a government does not operate in vaccum, the policies and operations of a government are very much conditioned by the climate to which it is subjected. The climate itself, in a large measure, will be the result of a matrix mileu composed of individual aspirations, fundamental rights, social ethic, moral responsibility, rule of law, public interest, efficiency of administration and considerations of economy. The complexity of the composition does not absolve any government to abdicate its responsibility to follow its own free path. It would be too difficult for any government to adopt dictatorial means in any vital matter affecting a large number of its employees. It is a matter of common experience that though such measures may be a short-term success, they cannot be long-term solutions. A democratic government must inevitably adopt democratic means in solving problems. Further, in a country like ours where there is written constitution with a positive commitment to Welfare State and settlement of disputes by peaceful means there is no reason why in general, government should be adopt the method of bargaining. An approach to bargaining ought not to be interpreted as a surrender of sovereignty of the State but can be treated as part and process of the very sovereignty, because the ultimate purpose is of the welfare of the citizens, whom the State has to govern. Moreover, inability and failure to bargain will only lead to industrial unrest leading to general unrest - an unhappy proposition not desired by the government or by the employees. Therefore, collossal loss, in terms of man hours would be prevented if government comes forward to settle disputes by negotiation. It need not be over-emphasised that this is a part of good personnel policy and maintenance of human relations, so very essential for effective management.

So much has been said about the definite advantages that accrue from unionisation of employees, it will suffice to state them briefly. They are:

(*a*) "The union makes it possible for employees to express their point of view to legislative branch and management as a whole.[2]

(*b*) "The convenience ... a union provides when management honestly wants to secure the real opinions of employees as a group rather than to rely wholly on the faulty distillation of opinion that slowly filters through the supervisory line."[3]

(*c*) "It provides a feeling of identification with the securing of certain personnel objectives, that is not present when the solution to personnel policies - even when they are highly acceptable - is handed to workers by management. Employees want to do something for themselves, no matter how enlightened an organisation's personnel administration."[4]

(*d*) "Employees' organisation provides an outlet for natural social aspirations of employees."[5]

The objectives of employee organisations usually are :

(*a*) Promotion of solidarity among the workers;

(*b*) Protection of the merit system;

(*c*) Improvement of status and material welfare of employees, and

(*d*) Improvement of the quality of public administration.[6]

In this context, it may be useful to note the existing legal position regarding the right of government servants to be numbers of an association. Rule 4(B), The Central Civil Service (Conduct) Rules, 1955 (hereinafter called 1955 Rules) prohibited a Government servant from joining or continuing to be a member of any association of government servants which has not been recognised or whose recognition was withdrawn by the government. The Supreme Court held that Rule 4(B) contravened Article 19(1) (C) of the Constitution and was, therefore, unconstitutional and void.

Rule 6 of the Central Civil Service (Conduct) Rules, 1964, (hereinafter called 1964 Rules) prohibits a government servant from joining or continuing to be a member of an association, the objectives or activities of which are prejudicial to the interests and sovereignty and integrity of India or public order or morality.

Sovereignty and integrity of India are accepted propositions and, therefore, activities which may undermine the concept can be prohibited but "public order" appears to be an ambiguous phrase and may include variety of situations which are not defined or easily definable. Similarly, Government servants are prohibited from indulging in criticism of government by making any public utterence or any statement of facts or opinion, if it has the effect of an adverse criticism on any current or recent policy or action of the Central or State Government.

However, an exception is made to bonafide expression of views by office-bearers of trade unions of government servants, for the purpose of safeguarding the conditions of service or for securing improvements thereof.[7]

It appears, unionism among government employees in India has been directed, in particular to achieve items (*a*) and (*c*) and to some extent item (*d*) cited above. The unions would have merited some praise had they taken steps to achieve something in the direction of item (*b*) and also more of item (*d*).

Employees Responsibilities

Just as we have emphasised that government should not hesitate to bargain, it must be emphasised that the employees have a special duty to maintain the structure of the State, law and order. Sometimes it is pointed out by the employees and the unions that there is a difference between the State as a sovereign and the State as an employer. Those who argue on these lines should not ignore that there is a special status or a double-status applicable to the employees as citizens and as employees. If administration has to be maintained in tact, employees cannot isolate themselves and talk against the State. Should this happen many governments would find themselves in peril in times of emergencies, without the unstincted loyalty and support of its own employees.

In addition to the responsibility of maintaining the structure of the State by behaving in a constitutional manner, the employees have an additional duty like any other citizens to help preserve law and order. This can take two forms. First, an employee cannot afford to ignore the Conduct Rules, breach of which would always lead to disciplinary action. It is a different matter popular governments committed to democratic ideals had not taken serious view of such violation of rules, which normally should have resulted in punishment. Such lenient attitude on the part of the government has also led to false impression that the Conduct Rules are inneffective. Secondly, Government, especially when the situation gets out of control in the interest of public peace has to maintain law and order. In all such cases, they have not hesitated to take action against their erring employees under the various provisions of the law of the land. Finally, a fact not to be lost sight of is that in a parliamentary form of democracy, rule of law is supreme and both as an employee and citizen, he has to abide by it.

Politicisation

Political neutrality of government employees is a fairly well accepted principle of personnel administration. But, in practice, due to various factors such as democratic decentralisation, growth and development of Trade Union movement, agitations, increased role of political parties, the principle is getting eroded. While the extent of damage caused by erosion is not assessed, the factors affecting erosion also appear to be un-assorted, jumbled and confused. However, the different factors that appear to be responsible for some amount of politicisation, are now discussed.

The growth and development of Trade Union Movement, it is felt, is inextricably linked with the development and inter-play of political forces and political parties. The same may not be exactly true in case of goverment employees' unions. Neverthaless, there is a feeling that the unions, for one reason of other, also make use of the Trade Union leaders for consultation, guidance and advice. While direct evidence cannot be adduced, one cannot deny the attraction and friendship between the leaders of unions in private and government sectors. From the point of view of political parties themselves, they may be interested in supporting the movements because of he similarity in the objectives, causes, approaches and the identity of interest. But they may not be able to organise solidarity action due to lack of development of real fraternity or solidarity among the masses.

One plausible explanation given as to why the political parties and leaders of other Trade Unions get themselves interested in strikes by government employees is their alleged interest to put spokes in the wheels of the government. Some analysts have gone to the extent of saying that ulterior intent of the leaders is to witness a fall of the government by aggrevating the situation during the strike.[9] The proponents of this view believe that the leaders and political parties are not so much interested in the welfare of the employees which they vouchsafe as in their own selfish ends.

As opposed to this, the employees, however, are interested in gaining the sympathy and support of the political parties for purposes of propaganda and educating the vast number of dis-interested persons for the betterment of their economic position and condition of work.

The important issues arise from this pseudo politicisation. The first has reference to the industrial and semi-industrial workers in government Departments such as the Railways, the Post & Telegraphs and the Defence Department and other Public Enterprises. Since majority of them are not involved in decision making process and their duties are of a routine nature, some believe, that politicisation in this quarter is not harmful, although during strikes, work in different sections and offices may be completely paralysed. In other words, the danger is one of cessation of work with resulting loss, minus the danger of political interference or political subterfuge.

The second issue - the real and the complicated one, pertains to the anonimity to be observed by the government employees of higher and other cadres. The existing norms of public administration demand that administration should move on, irrespective of the party in power and the manipulation, maneouvres and approaches made by other political parties. The employees must serve the public but must not dabble with politics. They can certainly demonstrate for service rights, to better their conditions of work but must not trend grounds that legitimately or functionally belong to the practising politicians.

Right to Strike

Sterling D. Spero vehimently argued as to why government employees should have the right to strike. Briefly stated, the reasons[10] are :

(*a*) Mere denial of the right to strike will not of itself prevent strikes if the employees believe their grievances so great as to assume risks;

(*b*) The danger of complicating otherwise simple problems of industrial relations as major problems, calling for drastic discipline and use of repressive methods;

(*c*) The alternative to the vastly enhanced power of expanding government is a free labour movement;

(*d*) The main danger from the strike appears to be the direct challenge to the sovereignty of the government than the consequences that stem from the resulting cessation of work.

H. Eliot Kaplan, categorically states that public employees have no right to strike. The reasons advanced by Kaplan are :[11]

(*a*) The employees cannot disrupt the public services without people's consent since they are paramount.

(*b*) Government employees need not go on strike, since they have opportunities to educate the public. If people do not get their view point, they can crystallise public sentiment. If the existing methods are slow, they certainly can agitate for change of methods to meet their problems.

(*c*) A super agency will not be in a position to solve strike threats or problems and only the people have to find a solution through their representatives i.e. the legislators.

Under the provisions of Industrial Disputes Act, 1947[12] subject to certain conditions, the employees of public utility services[13] have the right to strike.

Under the 1964 Rules,[14] no government servent shall engage himself or participate in any demonstration[15] or resort to or in any way abet any form of strike, in connection with any matter pertaining to his service or the service of any other government servant.

The crucial issue in all those discussions is whether government employees have the right to strike. Before we proceed to discuss the right to strike, it becomes necessary to distinguish demonstration from strike, because the consequences that flow from the two and how they affect fundamental rights are different.

In Kameswara Pradad and others vs. the State of Bihar, the Supreme Court observed that demonstration is "a visible manifestation of the feelings or sentiments of an individual or a group. It is thus a communication of one's ideas to others to whom it is intended to be conveyed." The Supreme Court also held that 4 A of the Bihar Government Servants Conduct Rules, 1956, in the form in which it stood prohibiting "any form of demonstration was violative of the employees rights under Article 19(*a*) and (*b*) of the Constitution.[15] A similar view was reiterated by the Supreme Court allowing the right to demonstrate in O.K. Ghosh vs. E.X. Joseph.[17]

Regarding the right to strike, there seems to be agreement in the Judgements delivered by the High Courts and the Supreme Court.

The Bombay High Court was of the view that the right to strike was not a collective expression of the views but was a joint or collective action and by its very nature was fraught with possibilities of leading to violence. Further, that if the Constitution makers wished to confer this right to go on strike on the citizen, they would have expressly so provided. The Supreme Court in the Bihar Case observed that right to strike was not a fundamental right.[18]

The 1964 Rules which have cancelled the 1955 Rules, seem to have affected the rights to demonstrate and strike in the following manners.

So far as the right to demonstrate is concerned, the government is armed with more powers than before to prohibit, though not completely, demonstrations. In other words, the government's present definition of demonstration is much wider in scope and perimeter embracing many anticipated forms of threats and protests, correspondingly restricting the effective area of demonstration by the employees. To this extent the new provision seems to run partly counter to the already existing decisions of the Supreme Court. So far, it appears, the prohibition under the latest provisions has not been challenged. The stand the judiciary will take will only be clear when a leading case arises in future.

As regards strike, the old prohibition continues under the new provisions and the Supreme Court Judgement that there is no fundamental right to strike, still holds good. Thus, in effect, there seems to be a discernible addition to government's expanding power and a corresponding reduction in the liberties of the employees.

The Events and the Leadership

Like the first strike,[19] the second strike also had long history. While discontent was brewing among employees, the government was not a silent spectator to the problems facing the employees. It appointed a number of commissions and committees to investigate and report on the problems. Viewed from one context, the second strike became imminent because of the very large number of dissatisfied employees, the ad-hoc and short-term solutions pursued by the government and failure of the Joint Consultative Machinery to provide workable solutions to certain problems.

The employees' themselves felt that the disputes that could not be settled by negotiations be referred to an arbitration board, but the government did not accept that the major issue, need-based minimum wage,[20] be referred to arbitration, as it was already refered to National Commission on Labour.

The employees served requisite statutory notices for a token strike on 19th September 1968. Talks between the Home Minister and the Employees' Leaders failed and no agreement was reached even till 12th September 1968. But the leaders of the employees' organisations agreed to wait till the Report of National Commission on Labour, if the Government was willing to accept the report as an award. The government turned down the suggestion.

The Government of India promulgated the Essential Services Maintenance Ordinance, 1968 declaring the strike illegal. A press release was issued in the name of the Prime Minister explaining the governments's stand[21] in regard to the demands raised by the employees' on September 18, 1968. The employees went on strike from the mid-night of September 19, 1968 for twenty-four hours.

The nature of punishment awarded for participating in strike and the persons affected are shown in Table 1.

Table 1

Persons Affected

Sl. No.	*Nature of punishment*	*No. of employees involved*
1.	Arrested	10,000
2.	Suspended	7.000
3.	Dismissed	4,000
4.	Persons dead in firing	10

Source: "The Indian Express," October 18, 1968, Vijayawada.

Resort to firing by a democratic government in tackling a strike situation is generally described as excessive, undemocratic and at times assessed as unprovoked. Whatever may be the truth in such an allegation, apart from a serious law and order situation, if there be one, such firing in case of one day token strike, appears to be unnecessary.

The Table below presents the loss in some of the important departments of the government.

Table 2

Loss at a Glance

Sl. No.	*Department*	*Subject matter*	*Financial loss (Rs.)*
1.	Railways	5,000 goods trains involving the handling of about 5,50,000 tonnes of food-grains were affected. Passengers inconvenienced – 6.2 million; trains halted – 5,700	2.5 crores
2.	Post and Telegraphs	Dislocating 1.5 crores of letters 1,20,000 telegrams 3,00,000 trunk calls and sale of postal orders worth	Rs. 7 lakhs
3.	Defence	Loss in production	1 crore

Source: "The Indian Express," September 18, 1968 Vijayawada.

As is always the case in the strike by the Central government employees, the Departments badly hit were Railways, Post and Telegraphs and Defence. From the above, one can reasonably infer the followings:

First: The public would be put to lot of inconvenience. Second: The loss in the case of each Department comes to crores of rupees. Third: If strike were to continue for a number of days there would be complete break down in communications disrupting the normal life of the citizens. Apart from all other considerations, there is a strong compulsion as to why the government and the employees should arrive at a workable compromise and avert the strike to necessarily avoid this large-scale public inconvenience and huge financial loss of the order of crores.

Unions have been recognised by the government presuming they would not violate the conditions of recognition. The government has acted suitably to de-recognise the unions once in the opinion of the government, there has been violation of the Conduct Rules or rules of recognition, although it is contended by some that the employees should not go on strike is not one of the conditions of recognition. Legally, there may be no objection to such a course of action, but from the point of view of the employees, they consider such a step as purely vindctive. Moreover, it may be mentioned that some of the actions taken by the government appear to be short-term vindctive measures than long-term peaceful solutions. Therefore, there is all the more compelling need to solve the problem in a practical way. The government, after the strike, has taken two important decisions in order to provide some relief to the employees, though not entirely influenced by the strike. First, it announced increase in Dearness Allowance ranging from Rs. 6 to 11 to all those employees drawing upto Rs. 500 involving an expenditure of about Rs. 30 crores with retrospective effect from September 1, 1968. It is reported that the employees were eligible for the increase in August itself as per the rise in the cost of living index. If this were the case, the pertinent question arises as to why the government failed to announce the increase even by September especially when the employees were agitating for certain demands. Second, the Government has announced merger of 66% of D.A. with basic pay from December 1, 1968. This is expected to cost the exchequer Rs. 17.5 crores immediately and an extra of Rs. 1.4 crores every year for at least a decade or two.

The decision it is felt was possible because certain unions have been de-recognised and it appears that on the staff side nearly all the members representing 26 unions have attended the meeting of the Joint Consultative Machinery. But, irrespective of the de-recognition and an agreement being reached in the Joint Consultative Machinery, the Government could have announced a similar decision prior to the strike even if it were not acceptable to the staff.

Doubtless, if the above two decisions were to be announced prior to the strike, the response to the strike call, the regiour and impact of the strike itself, would have been very much lessened.

There appears to be failure of judgement on either side, government and employees, which in a way may be attributed to the short-comings in leadership on both the sides. Error of judgement on the part of the government may be attributed to the following factors :

(*a*) It appears, all possible preventive measures to avert the strike were not taken by the government.

(*b*) Strike did materialise despite the passage of the ordinance.

(*c*) What was sought to be withheld by government was later given to the employees by parts.

(*d*) The Joint Consultative Machinery neither functioned properly nor was able to deal with the cases in a wider perspective.

(*e*) Although different commissions were appointed by the government, there has been undue delay in the Government accepting and implementing either partly or wholly the recommendations of the Commissions.

Failure of judgement ascribable to the employees is based on :

(*a*) Their participation in the strike in the face of the ordinance.

(*b*) Their utter disregard for the resultant public inconvenience.

(*c*) Their participation in strike, despite their knowledge of the violation of the Conduct Rules and of the repressive methods that would be let loose by the government.

The Need Based Minimum Wage

Before the long-term implications of government's policy are discussed, it is necessary to mention the problems of Need Based Minimum Wage and inflation, as Need Based Minimum Wage forms an important demand of the employees and inflation continues to worry the citizens and the government in an equal degree. There is no dispute whatsoever as to the desirability of paying the Need Based Minimum Wage. But the difficulty is one of harmonising the different approaches to the problem which present wide enough gaps both in social and economic content. Further, the problem must be solved in a larger perspective keeping in view all the other allied problems.[22]

It may be true that Need Based Minimum Wage is being paid in certain industries now. But to extend it to all other industries and to pay it to all the employees is a different question: This is linked up with proprietory relations and fiscal policy. Moreover, like the vexed the question of determining the quantum of Dearness Allowance payable and adequate compensation, even if payment of Need Based Minimum Wage is agreed to, it becomes illusory because at a point of time, the need evades definition. Further, the rate of industrial development and over-all production, apart from the sporadic increases in agricultural production recorded, do not seem to warrant payment of Need Based Minimum Wage at this juncture. While critics of this line of argument may dispense with this as "theoretical economics," one doubts whether there is enough of evidence to support the Need Based Minimum Wage considerations of "practical economics."

Payment of Need Based Minimum Wage and additional Dearness Allowance is linked up via a vicious circle with inflationary pressures. It is observed that there is a rise in prices followed by every increase in emoluments of government employees, the rise leading to further inflation. Thus, some believe that periodic rise in salary or Dearness Allowance is no solution to mitigate hardship faced by the employees.

Conclusion

The following observations may be in order, indicating the long-term implications of the government's policy that is now being pursued:

(*a*) Since the government is committed to Welfare State policy, it should address itself to the question of providing more social amenities to the employees such as housing, medical facilities, educational benefits to the children of the employees, food grains on subsidy and concessional transport. This naturally requires a revised policy on Dearness Allowance issue and may prevent the employees pressing hard their demand for Need Based Minimum Wage.

(*b*) It would be appropriate for the government to appoint a Pay Commission and also to refix the pay scales of all employees providing a higher basic for the pay scales, as that may provide some immediate relief to the employees.

(*c*) So far, government has not taken adequate steps to institute an appropriate negotiating machinery. But, now the government intends to establish "permanent and statutory" consultative machinery, which would provide for arbitration, the award of which would be binding on both the government and the employees. It is too early to comment anything about it at this stage.

(*d*) The government proposes to statutorily prohibit strikes. Recourse to such a measure, it must be admitted, will not be palatable to the employees. Moreover, there is no guarantee that by such a prohibition, the government would be solving the problems leading to strike adequately. The cut or the inclusion must be made where the rancour exists. It would be dangerous in the first instance to diagnoise wrongly and perhaps still more dangerous to suggest unsuitable and inadequate remedy.

(*e*) It appears that the government is not in a position to offer Need Based Minimum Wage. Therefore, it is clear that the employees will continue to be dissatisfied as they have already made Need Based Minimum Wage one of their, so to say, pressing demands. Failure to satisfactorily solve the demand for Need Based Minimum Wage itself may be a potent cause for a future strike.

References

1. Government employee includes every person appointed to a civil service or post (including the civilian in Defence service) in connection with the affairs of the Union, but does not include the following two categories:

Categories I: (*i*) A railway servant as defined in section 3 of the Indian Railways Act, 1890 (9 of 1890);

(*ii*) A person holding a post in the Railway Board and is subject to the Railway Services (Conduct) Rules;

(*iii*) a person holding any post under the administrative control of the Railway Board or a member of the Financial Commissioner of Railways;

(*iv*) a member of an All India Service; and

(*v*) a holder of any post in respect of which the President has, by a general or special order, directed that these rules shall not apply.

Category II: An employee who draws a pay of less than Rs. 500/- and holds a non-gazetted post in the following establishments:

(*i*) ports, docks, wharves or jetties;

(*ii*) defence installations except training establishments;

(*iii*) public works establishments, in so far as they relate to work-charged staff;

(*iv*) irrigation and electric power establishments;

(*v*) mines as defined in clause (i) of section 2 of the Mines Act, 1952 (35 of 1952);

(*vi*) factories as defined in clause (m) of section 2 of Factories Act, 1948 (63 of 1948); and

(*vii*) field units of the Central Tractor Organisation employing workmen governed by labour laws. (See Rule 1, The Central Civil Services (Conduct) Rules, 1964.

2. Stahl, O.G., Public Personnel Administration, Harper & Brothers, New York, 1956, p. 276.
3. *Ibid.*
4. *Ibid.*, p. 277.
5. *Ibid.*
6. Cf. Stahl; O.G., *op. cit.*, p. 286.
7. Rule 9(1), 1964 Rules.
8. Proviso to Rule 9(1), 1964 Rules.
9. In our view this appears to be far fetched. But it may be difficult to reject the analysis outright, since it must be having some basis.

10. Rowat, D.C., Basic Issues in Public Administration, Macmillan, New York, 1961, pp. 257-261.

11. Cf. Rowat, D.C., *op. cit.,* pp. 252-255.

12. Section 22(1), Industrial Disputes Act, 1947.

13. For details see Section 2(n), *Ibid.*

14. Rule 7(1) and (11).

15. Participation in demonstration is prohibited if it is prejudicial to (*a*) interests of sovereignty and integrity of India. (*b*) the security of State. (*c*) friendly relations with Foreign States. (*d*) Public order. (*e*) decency or morality or which involves contempt of court, defamation or incitement to an offence.

16. A.I.R. 1962, S.C. 1166.

17. *Ibid.,* 1963, S.C. 812.

18. A.I.R. 1962, S.C. 1166.

19. The first General Strike by Central Government Employees took place in 1960.

20. The other important demands of the employees were:

    (*a*) Merger of Dearness Allowance with basic pay;

    (*b*) Full neutralisation of rise in prices;

    (*c*) Withdrawal of the proposal to retire employees who are ineffective or whose integrity is in doubt.

21. "Government has not ruled out any of these demands :

The factual position in regard to the four issues is as follows :

(1) Merger of Dearness Allowance with basic pay	—	Government have said in clear terms that this issue can be negotiated and could also be referred to arbitration.
(2) Full neutralisation of rise in prices	—	It is already before the Joint Consultative Machinery.
(3) Withdrawal of the proposal to retire employees who are ineffective or whose inte-	—	Government have already discussed this issue with represen-

grity is in doubt		tatives of the employees; and the matter is being re-examined in the light of the views expressed by them.
(4) Need-based minimum wage :	—	The concept is accepted as an unexceptionable social objective. But, it will not be just to consider it in isolation exclusively for the employees of the Central Government, ignoring the general body of industrial, agricultural and other workers. The issue in the wider context is already before the National Commission on Labour."
		(See "The Indian Express," September 18, 1968, Vijayawada).

22. See Prime Minister's Statement, Supra, p. 14.

INDEX

S

T